CW00363317

Sacred Swords

وَأَعِدُّواْ لَهُم مَّا ٱسْتَطَعْتُم مِّن قُوَّةٍ وَمِن رِّبَاطِ ٱلْخَيْلِ

تُرْهِبُونَ بِهِۦ عَدُوَّ ٱللَّهِ وَعَدُوَّكُمْ وَءَاخَرِينَ مِن دُونِهِمْ لَا تَعْلَمُونَهُمُ ٱللَّهُ

يَعْلَمُهُمْ وَمَا تُنفِقُواْ مِن شَىْءٍ فِى سَبِيلِ ٱللَّهِ يُوَفَّ إِلَيْكُمْ وَأَنتُمْ

لَا تُظْلَمُونَ ﴿٦٠﴾

Against them make ready your strength to the utmost of your power,
including steeds of war, to strike terror into the enemy of God and your
enemies, and others besides, whom you may not know, but whom God
knows. Whatever you shall spend in the cause of God, shall be repaid unto
you, and you shall not be treated unjustly.

Quran: Sura 8, Aya 60

يَٰٓأَيُّهَا ٱلَّذِينَ ءَامَنُواْ خُذُواْ حِذْرَكُمْ فَٱنفِرُواْ ثُبَاتٍ أَوِ

ٱنفِرُواْ جَمِيعًا ﴿٧١﴾

O believers, take your precautions; then move forward in companies, or
move forward all together.

Quran: Sura 4, Aya 71

Sacred Swords

Jihad in the Holy Land
1097–1291

James Waterson

FOREWORD BY TERRY JONES

FRONTLINE BOOKS, LONDON

For B&T&37

FRONTLINE BOOKS, LONDON

Sacred Swords: Jihad in the Holy Land 1097–1291

This edition published in 2010 by Frontline Books, an imprint of
Pen & Sword Books Limited, 47 Church Street, Barnsley, S. Yorkshire, S70 2AS
www.frontline-books.com

ISBN: 978-1-84832-580-7

For more information on our books, please visit
www.frontline-books.com,
email info@frontline-books.com
or write to us at the above address.

Typeset by JCS Publishing Services Ltd, www.jcs-publishing.co.uk
Maps created by Alex Swanston, Pen and Sword Mapping Department
Printed in Great Britain by CPI Antony Rowe

Contents

Illustrations

Maps

Plates

The plates are positioned between pages 110 and 111

The Church of the Holy Sepulchre in Jerusalem

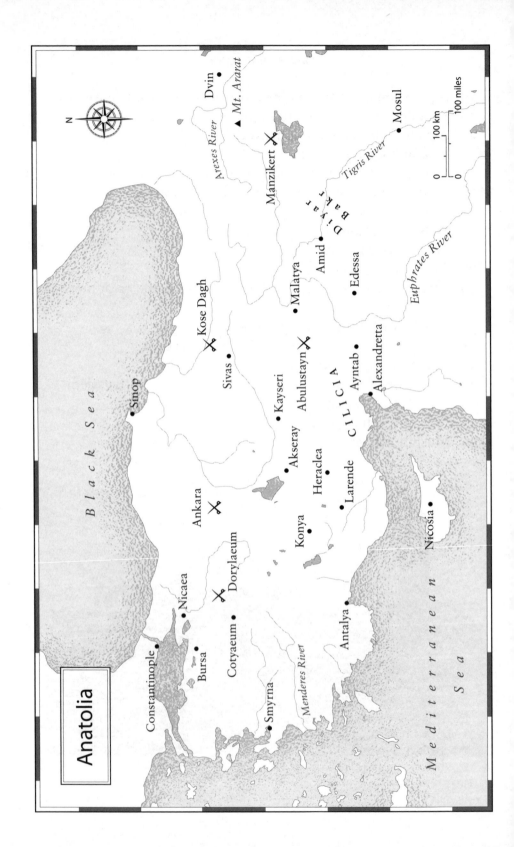

Anatolia

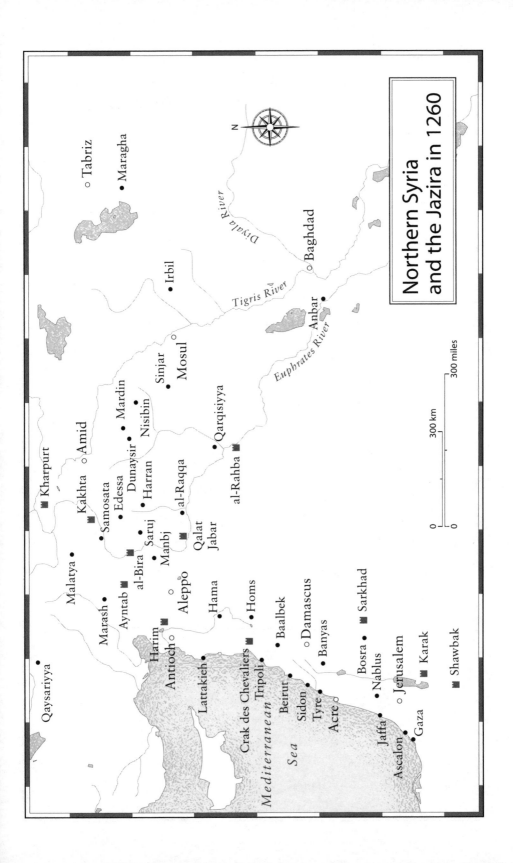

Northern Syria
and the Jazira in 1260

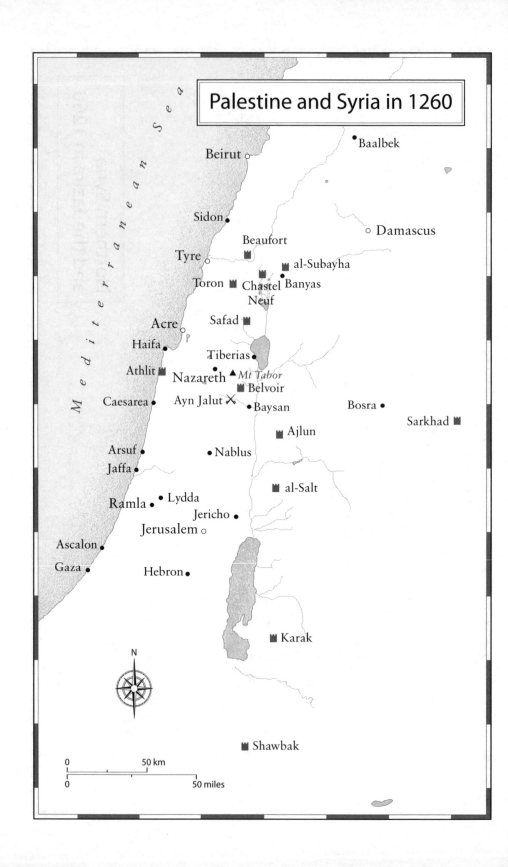

Palestine and Syria in 1260

Mediterranean Sea

•Baalbek

Beirut ○

Sidon •

○ Damascus

Beaufort

Tyre ○

al-Subayha

Toron   Chastel   Banyas
         Neuf

Safad

Acre ○

Haifa •

Tiberias •

Athlit

Nazareth •   ▲ Mt Tabor

Belvoir

Caesarea •   Ayn Jalut ✕

• Baysan

Bosra •

Sarkhad

Ajlun

Arsuf •

• Nablus

Jaffa •

al-Salt

Ramla •   • Lydda

Jericho •

Jerusalem ○

Ascalon •

Gaza •

Hebron •

Karak

N

Shawbak

0   50 km
0   50 miles

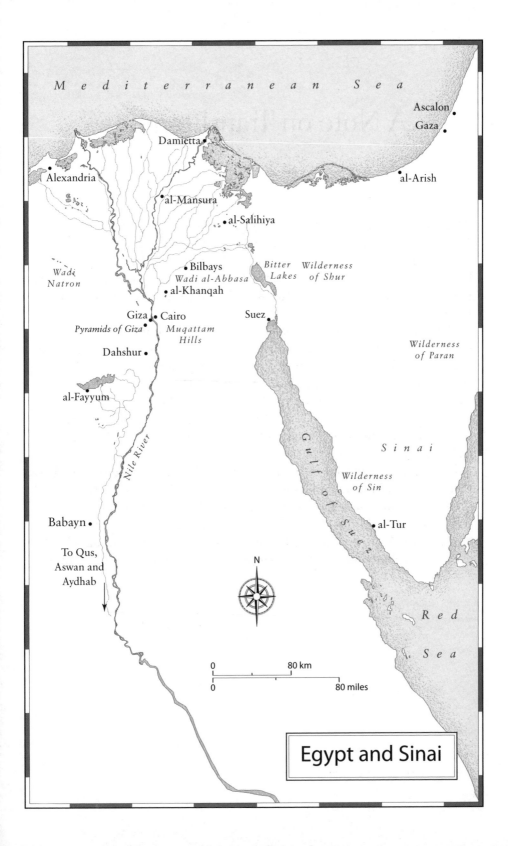

Mediterranean Sea

Ascalon
Gaza
Damietta
Alexandria
al-Arish
al-Mansura
al-Salihiya
Bitter *Wilderness*
Lakes *of Shur*
Bilbays
Wadi al-Abbasa
Wadi al-Khanqah
Natron
Giza Cairo Suez *Wilderness*
Pyramids of Giza *Muqattam* *of Paran*
Hills
Dahshur
Sinai
al-Fayyum *Wilderness*
of Sin
Nile River *Gulf of Suez*
al-Tur
Babayn
To Qus,
Aswan and
Aydhab
N
Red
Sea

0   80 km
0   80 miles

Egypt and Sinai

A Note on Transliteration

There are many, many ways of rendering Persian, Arabic, Turkish and Mongolian into English. I have generally opted for the most commonly used 'short' forms of names rather then the more scholarly forms, simply because the vast swathe of names that the reader encounters whilst reading any history of the medieval Middle East means that any familiar faces are welcome.

For city and country names I have used the nomenclature of the period. The Crusader cities are given their Frankish names rather than the Arabic, as this is how they are most commonly denoted in other texts that the reader might be led to review. Persia has been preferred over Iran simply because the medieval entity of Persia covered a larger geographical area than modern Iran does. Similarly, medieval Syria was far larger than the modern state of the same name and embraced all of Lebanon and modern Israel.

Of course, the events of the medieval Middle East were recorded by contemporary Islamic writers in the Arabic calendar, which is based on a lunar cycle and dated from the *Hijra* – the Prophet Muhammad's flight from Mecca to Medina. I have, however, used the Christian calendar and all dates are Anno Domini as I want the reader to be able to parallel the events described with what was happening in Europe at the same time.

Acknowledgements

My thanks go out once again to friends and mentors who have encouraged me during the writing of this book, and of those that came before it. A special mention needs to go to Dr David Morgan for his continued kindnesses and to Robert Irwin for planting the seeds of this particular volume in my mind as we floated gently, well and truly up the creek, on one of Dubai's waterways last spring.

Of course I will be indebted to the end of my days to Terry Jones for finding the time, amongst the myriad of other things that he always seems to be either in the process of creating, seeing to completion or dreaming up, to produce a foreword that truly fulfils what good history is all about and proves Benedetto Croce's dictum completely. 'Every historical judgement gives to all history the character of contemporary history, because however remote in time events thus recounted may seem to be, history in reality refers to present needs and present situations wherein those events vibrate.'*

I would like to thank my editor Deborah Hercun for her *pazienza* and I also have to apologise to my dear wife Michele for repeatedly dragging her around some of the dustier parts of the Middle East, and also for having said, some two years ago, 'This is the last book', when it wasn't.

---

* In Croce, B., *La Storia Come Pensiero e Come Azione*, Naples: Bibliopolis, 1938/2002, p. 42.

Foreword

In 1995 my friend and collaborator, Alan Ereira, suggested we make a series for BBC TV about the Crusades. My initial response was lukewarm as I didn't think I had any interest in religious wars that happened such a long time ago that they were scarcely relevant today. However, when I discovered that the aim was to tell the story from the Arab point of view, I was hooked. I was captivated by the idea of exploring a culture that I knew little about, and by the idea of presenting the story of those aggressed against rather than heroic tales of the aggressors.

Now, in the twenty-first century, when the Western military-industrial complex has selected Islam to replace Communism, the story has even more resonance, and there is even more need to understand the Muslim world. That is why this book by James Waterson is important. Although it is covering events that happened almost a thousand years ago, the lessons to be learnt from the West's aggression against Islam during the eleventh to thirteenth centuries are as vital today as they were then.

Shortly before the First Gulf War in 1990–1, I bought a copy of an in-house magazine for the arms industry called (if I remember rightly) *Weapons Today*. The editorial told how the arms industry had been in the doldrums since perestroika and the collapse of Communism. However, it continued, we now have Saddam Hussein as an enemy, and in the future the defence industry could look to Islam replacing Communism to ensure that its order books were kept full.

At the time it seemed a truly absurd statement, but not now – not in this new century. The so-called 'War on Terror' has become the lifeline of the arms industry, and commentators don't mention the neat coincidence of Islamic fundamentalism filling the gap left by Communism. Nor do they mention how this convenient substitution must have brought great relief to the arms industry, which, I assume, has been secretly beavering away since 1990 to stoke up further conflagration between the West and Islam.

In the same way that the arms industry today needs an enemy –
no matter who – the Church in the Middle Ages needed to divert the
violent, militaristic culture of knighthood away from the destruction of
Christendom, and the events in the Holy Land provided them with the
perfect excuse.

Of course there are differences between then and now. In the eleventh
century the pope could appeal to religious fervour and indignation
amongst Christians regarding events that were happening far away in
the Holy Land, whereas nowadays the Western governments have to rely
on creating a climate of fear themselves.

Nonetheless there are still similarities. Now, as a thousand years ago,
the first rule is to make it look as if Islam is the aggressor. So instead of
the monster caliph, al-Hakim, who destroyed the Church of the Holy
Sepulchre in 1009, we have (or had) Saddam Hussein. In both cases, an
enemy we love to hate. Similarly, the panic generated by 9/11 gave the
US government carte blanche to invade Iraq – just as in 1071 the disaster
at Manzikert induced panic in Byzantium and, as James Waterson puts it,
'started the chain of events that sent Urban II to the pulpit in Clermont
in 1095'.

In the Middle Ages, the Church stereotyped Muslims as 'idolaters',
which clearly shows how much they knew (or rather didn't know) about
their enemy. Then, as now, we need to understand each other better.
Sacred Swords, whether intentionally or not, does just that. It illuminates
the Islamic world of the eleventh to thirteenth centuries, along with its
attempts to defend itself against Mongols from the east and Christians
from the west. It tells a story that is primarily focused on military and
political campaigns, but it also contains a wealth of detail that brings to
life the Muslim world of those times.

James Waterson, for example, points out that the Saljuq Empire was
based on family enterprises, but that the sons of the father very often
had different mothers and hence a lot of the civil war of those times was
the result of 'pushy mothers' ambitions' for their sons. Another detail
that tickled me was that, after the defeat of the Crusaders by the Turks at
Dorylaeum, it became fashionable for German knights to pretend that
they had Turks in their family tree!

He paints a sympathetic picture of the great Turkish leader Nur al-
Din and pays tribute to his sense of justice, but at the same time records
how he allowed Baldwin III of Jerusalem to send help to Antioch, which
was then being threatened by one of Nur al-Din's fellow sultans. Nur al-

Din regarded Antioch as his family's business and didn't want any other sultan muscling in on it.

James Waterson also gives an insightful account of 'the confused political landscape' of the 1170s and Saladin's achievement in trying to bring unity to the Muslim world.

Perhaps the most relevant message is how the Christian attack on Islam forced the Muslims to create an increasingly efficient military machine, until by the time of Baybars, in the thirteenth century, the state had become, in effect, the Mamluk army – the only army, what's more, that was capable of turning back the Mongols.

Terry Jones

Preface

Most histories tackle the Crusades from a Western perspective and there are many difficulties attached to approaching the period from the Muslim point of view. 'One would search Muslim historical writings in vain for a composite, specific history of the wars against the Franks,'* and the 'Frankish problem' must be viewed as only one element in the wider world of Syrian, Iraqi and even Persian politics with which Muslim leaders had to deal. The other problem is that the recorders of this history were chiefly religious writers who wrote from the position that history unfolds according to the will of Allah. They tend, therefore, to ascribe jihad to almost any action against the Franks by Muslim leaders and to define the Frankish threat in simple terms of its infidelity rather than the complex of religious fervour, commercial interests, rivalries and personal ambitions that it in fact was. This said, they are no worse than their Latin contemporaries who, when trying to achieve an understanding of their Muslim enemies, merely created fantastic constructions that have little to recommend them.

With all the above taken into account, it is still, however, a worthwhile activity to address the period from the *Dar al-Islam*'s perspective and to focus on the individuals that created the Islamic response to the Crusades, as we can discover a lot about the action that occurred, much more about the motivations of these characters, and bring a little more illumination to our understanding of the contest for the Holy Land.

---

* Gabrieli, F., *Arab Historians of the Crusades*, translated by E. Costello, Berkeley: University of California Press, 1969, Introduction.

~ 1 ~

An Exhausted Distracted Land
Syria is Invaded by the *Franj*

You will find that the most implacable of men in their enmity to the faithful Muslims are the Jews and the Pagans, and that the nearest in affection to them are those who say:
  'We are Christians.'
  That is because there are priests and monks among them, and because they are free from pride.

Quran: Sura 5, v. 82

Many Crusade histories begin their narratives with a description of the Byzantine army suffering a crushing defeat at the hands of a Muslim-Turkish army at Manzikert in 1071, and how this led to a call for assistance to the pope and kings of Europe – who somewhat belatedly responded with an *expeditio* to the Holy Land. However, in our narrative, whilst we will certainly be looking at this battle, we need to change our focus from west to east and assume the viewpoint of the Muslims who were on the receiving end of western Christendom's response to Byzantium's distress. This will allow us to understand the initial response of the soldiers and princes of Syria to the arrival of the pilgrim armies in the Levant at the end of the eleventh century.

What is evident from a review of the near-contemporary Muslim sources is that no connection was made between Manzikert and the First Crusade, nor did the Muslims have any understanding that the Crusaders had Jerusalem as their objective. This is not surprising, given that the Crusaders were only one of the many threats to the civilisation of Islam at this time. It is therefore impossible to see how the princes of Islam could have created a cogent strategy to meet the Crusaders, since they completely failed to grasp their opponents' motivations and aims. The goal of defensive warfare is to inflict enough damage or loss on the enemy to make him desist from his objective, and the Muslims, in the early stages of the encounter, did not have this information, or an understanding of just how important Jerusalem was to the Franks, or *Franj* as they are named in the Arabic sources. Islamic princes were educated in the art of war, but the First Crusade did not fit within the ideals of warfare as an eleventh-century Muslim commander would have understood them. Religious wars had forged the Islamic Empire in the seventh and eighth centuries and had built the early Fatimid state in Egypt. However, by the eleventh century, war in the Middle East was a professional endeavour, aimed at securing economic advantage by the acquisition of agrarian resources and trade centres. Preservation of one's forces was a paramount objective and the extermination of one's enemy was unimportant, provided that the goal of the campaign – usually the acquiring of the city that controlled a region – was achieved.

Ibn al-Qalanasi's chronicle of 1096–7 shows what an unexpected event the Franks' arrival in the Levant was.

> In this year there began to arrive a succession of reports that the armies of the Franks had appeared from the direction of the sea of Constantinople with forces not to be reckoned for multitude. As these reports followed one upon the other, and spread from mouth to mouth far and wide, the people grew anxious and disturbed in mind.
>
> During *Shaban* a comet appeared in the West; it continued to rise for a space of about twenty days, and then it disappeared.*

Even Ibn al-Athir, writing in the late twelfth century, with the benefit of both hindsight and an impressive intellect – which managed to create a unified, if somewhat slanted, examination of the Islamic world from Spain to beyond the Persian hinterlands – failed to comprehend fully the motivation of the *Franj*. His words do, though, hint at some understanding of the political fault lines that ran through western European politics and which would be central to the Crusader kingdom's eventual fall:

---

* Ibn al-Qalanasi, *Dhayl Tarikh Dimashq (Damascus Chronicle of the Crusades)*, translated by H. A. R. Gibb, London: Luzac and Company, 1932, pp. 41–3. The Muslim month of *Shaban* equated to July in 1097. Comets, just as in the medieval West, were seen in Islam as harbingers of plagues, wars or other disasters.

In 1097 the *Franj* attacked Syria. This is how it all began: Baldwin, their king, a kinsman of Roger the Frank who had conquered Sicily, assembled a great army and sent word to Roger saying: 'I have assembled a great army and now I am on my way to you, to use your bases for my conquest of the African coast. Thus you and I shall become neighbours.'

Roger called together his companions and consulted them about these proposals. 'This will be a fine thing both for them and for us!' they declared, 'for by this means the lands will be converted to the Faith!'

At this Roger raised one leg and farted loudly and swore that this was of more use than their advice. 'If this army comes here it will need quantities of provisions and fleets of ships to transport it to Africa, as well as reinforcements from my own troops. Then if the Franks succeed in conquering this territory they will take it over and need provisioning from Sicily. This will cost me my annual profit from the harvest. If they fail they will return here and be an embarrassment to me here in my own domain. As well as this the emir of Tunisia will say that I have broken faith with him and violated our treaty, and friendly relations and communications between us will be disrupted. As far as we are concerned, Africa is always there. When we are strong enough, we will take it.'

He summoned Baldwin's messenger and said to him: 'If you have decided to make war on the Muslims your best course will be to free Jerusalem from their rule and thereby win great honour. I am bound by certain promises and treaties of allegiance with the rulers of Africa.' So the Franks made ready and set out to attack Syria.*

Thus the Islamic powers misread the Crusaders' intentions and thereby the path and strategy their enemies would employ, but this is not enough in itself to explain completely their failure to meet the challenge of the First Crusade effectively. The leaders of the Islamic world at this juncture were, after all, men of the sword, and a near-contemporary text shows the degree of development of the art of war in the Middle East. It states clearly the need for reliable intelligence about one's foe: 'If a man regulates any undertaking according to hearsay, he will build upon possibilities; but if he regulates it according to what he sees with his own eyes, he will build upon certainties.'† A summary of the cautious approach to warfare used by Turkish warriors goes: *tadbir* or planning based on a 'real' perception of the enemy rather than 'approximations'

---

* From the *Kamil al-Tawarikh* (or Perfect History), in Gabrieli, pp. 3–4.

† Dekmejian, R., and Thabit, A., 'Machiavelli's Arab Precursor: Ibn Zafar al-Siqilli', *British Journal of Middle Eastern Studies*, November 2000, pp. 125–37.

is used in partnership with *hila* or artifice that will allow the effective utilisation of *quwwa* or force.

The most important factor in the failure of the Islamic response to the First Crusade was not in fact the military per se, but rather the collapse of the polities controlling these forces. The Middle East on the eve of the First Crusade was a region that contained two power blocs, the Fatimid Empire of Egypt and southern Syria and the Saljuq Turkish Empire that controlled Persia, Iraq, eastern Anatolia and northern Syria. Both empires boasted large armies and the trade revenues to support them, but both were in decline. In the case of the Fatimids, a slower collapse was taking place. In the case of the Saljuqs, a shattering of the state had taken place in 1092.

In the early eleventh century, it had looked entirely possible that the Shia Fatimid Empire would move out of Egypt and Syria and on to Baghdad, to conquer the Sunni Abbasid Caliphate. However, the Fatimid caliph al-Hakim then mysteriously disappeared in 1021, and a stalemate ensued between the two sides, with the Fatimids holding Syria but unable to advance in their conquest of Iraq. With the death of al-Hakim, the Fatimid state lost all its dynamism and the heady cocktail of militant Shia Islam and personality cult, based around the *Mahdi*, which had brought the dynasty from the obscurity of the North African deserts to the conquest of Egypt, was rapidly dissipated. Al-Hakim was the epitome of the divinely inspired *Mahdi* and whilst his behaviour has been seen as insanity by many historians, he should in fact be viewed as a leader who truly bridged the divide between worldly and divine rule. Even his more bizarre behaviour – such as giving sealed gift-tokens that, upon presentation to the treasury, would ensure the bearer's instant execution; the joy he derived from cutting hands off secretaries and ministers and then financially rewarding them; forcing Christians to wear oversized crucifixes and Jews to wear bells – whilst unnerving to his close companions, cannot detract from the fact that conversion to the Fatimid Shia cause was extensive in Syria, and even in Iraq, during his reign. The West remembers al-Hakim, via Pope Urban II's call for the liberation of the Holy Land at Clermont in 1095, as the cruel caliph who ordered the destruction of the Church of the Holy Sepulchre in Jerusalem in 1009. However, there was certainly a strong sense of reverence for him in Muslim lands. It seems likely that he was murdered during a desert hunting trip on the instructions of his sister, who probably felt that it was better to strike first before her brother got around to killing her. His body was never discovered and his return is still awaited by the followers of the *duruz* or Druze religion.*

After al-Hakim's death, the Fatimid caliphs became mere figureheads for ambitious senior ministers or *wazirs*, many of whom were in fact Sunnis and all of whom were professional Turkish or Armenian soldiers. The dynasty decayed, but its empire retained economic power through control of the Red Sea and extensive European trade; its army was large and diverse. The importation and use of slave soldiers and mercenaries from the Turkish lands of the Caucasus had begun in the late tenth century and this provided the Fatimid army with much-needed heavy-cavalry archers. The Berber cavalry that the army had been reliant on was not up to the task of taking on the Turks of Syria. The major problem with this military reform was, however, that there were no more charismatic leaders such as al-Hakim to follow. This meant that there was a loss of direct identification with the dynasty for the soldiers of the army and internecine racial infighting often broke out between black African troops and the 'new' Turks. In order to quell the mini-wars between the two factions – wars that frequently came close to destroying large parts of Cairo – the Fatimids had to choose a side; they settled for the Turks. The black African troops remained, but in very reduced circumstances, even being forced to eat dogs just to survive in 1025.†

The Fatimid attempt to conquer all of Islam for the Ismaili Shia creed was effectively over by the first quarter of the eleventh century. The project was then put into reverse by the coming to power in Persia and Iraq of the Saljuq Turks.

Turks had been entering the eastern lands of the Islamic Empire in large numbers from central Asia since the early tenth century. Indeed, the caliphs of Baghdad had been actively importing slave boys from the Turkish lands beyond Persia to train as personal bodyguards from the early ninth century. The caliphs had even, at times, become the helpless puppets of these palace praetorians as well as being the political captives of a Shia dynasty called the Buyids, which had originated in the northern mountains of Persia and had taken Baghdad in 945. However, in the eleventh century the sheer volume of Turkish steppe nomads that began

---

* A concise analysis of the reign of al-Hakim can be found in Kennedy, H., *The Prophet and the Age of the Caliphates: The Islamic Near East from the Sixth to the Eleventh Century*, London: Longman, 1986, pp. 330–7.

† Lev, Y., 'Army, Regime, and Society in Fatimid Egypt, 358–487/968–1094', *International Journal of Middle East Studies*, August 1987, pp. 33–65.

to enter Persia from the east was such that the Arab chroniclers of the time started to differentiate them from the 'early' *Mamluk* or slave-soldier Turks* and the Ghaznavid Turks who had been the effective rulers of eastern Persia. They called these new, more barbarous, arrivals the Turcomen.

The most significant group among the Turcomen were the Ghuzz tribes, and within this division the most important clan to enter Islam at this time was the Saljuqs. It is likely that the Saljuqs were converted from their tribal religions to Sunni Islam by wandering *Sufis* or holy men in the hinterlands of eastern Persia. In 1040, their chief, Toghril Beg, proclaimed himself sultan and under his command a vast Saljuq-Ghuzz army, made up almost entirely of horse archers, defeated the Ghaznavids at the Battle of Dandanqan, just north of Marv. By this one battle the Saljuqs took the whole of eastern Persia.

The Saljuqs consolidated their new conquest and moved on through a series of year-round campaigns. They moved through Azerbaijan and into northern Iraq, but were halted and defeated in mountainous country by Kurds near Mosul. Turning south, they marched on Baghdad and had removed the Buyids and 'liberated' the Sunni caliph by 1055. The caliph accepted the idea of a Saljuq sultan readily enough, and a little bit of skilful political redefining allowed business as usual to continue for the Sunni world. In the new formula for power, constituent authority belonged to the sultan, who designated the caliph, but the validity of the sultan's government required an oath of allegiance to the caliph, and that the caliph appointed the sultan and issued a diploma to that effect. The institutional authority of the caliph rested on the Sunni community, and his functional authority on the *sharia*.† This complex formula was vital to the next stage of the Sunni revival. The Saljuqs attempted to retake the lost lands of Syria from the Fatimids. This required not only military muscle but also an intellectual and theological rearming of Sunnism, and the grand *wazir* of the Saljuq state, Nizam al-Mulk, provided this. A long section of his *Siyasatnama*, or *Book of Government*,‡ is dedicated to the requirement for 'right religion' in order for the state to run smoothly.

---

* For the evolution of the institution of military slavery in early Islam, see Waterson, J., *The Knights of Islam: The Wars of the Mamluks*, London: Greenhill Books, 2007.
† Lambton, A. K. S., 'The Theory of Kingship in the Nasihut al-Muluk of Ghazali', in *Theory and Practice in Medieval Persian Government*, London: Variorum Reprints, 1954.
‡ Darke, H., *The Book of Government or Rules for Kings: The Siyar al-Muluk or Siyasat-nama of Nizam al-Mulk*, London: Routledge, 1960.

To this end he built and patronised the Nizamiyya: a great *madrasa* or Islamic university in Baghdad to challenge the Ismaili Shia al-Azhar *Dar al-Ilm*, or House of Knowledge, in Cairo. It became the model for Sunni *madrasas* that were built in every region that the Saljuqs retook from the Fatimids, as well as in north Persia, where other dissident Shia groups such as the Ismaili Assassins had their strongholds.*

The Saljuq invasions of Syria began in 1063. In 1077, an attempt was made to invade Egypt itself, and by 1079 the Turks had garrisons in both Damascus and Jerusalem and *madrasas* propagating the Sunni creed in Aleppo, Damascus and Mosul. During this push west, almost inadvertently, the Turks met the Byzantines in battle. Sultan Alp Arslan tried his very best to parley with the Byzantine emperor, Romanus Diogenes, and thereby avoid battle. The sultan apologised for the excesses of his Turcomen irregulars, but the emperor was having none of it. He had brought an impressive army into Anatolia and was under political pressure at home to obtain a decisive victory over the Turks. In truth, the Turcomen who had been raiding Byzantine territory, and whose incursions had brought the emperor and his field army into Anatolia, were freeloaders who were barely under the sultan's command at the best of times; when he was unable to give the Byzantines cast-iron assurances of their continued good behaviour, the emperor rashly decided on war. His army was decimated at Manzikert on 19 August 1071 by a 'classic' Turkish assault. The armies met in a valley and, as the Byzantines advanced, the Turks just fell away. Turkish archers rode up and down the Byzantine flanks, showering them with arrows and then fleeing, but there was no force per se for Romanus to engage with. Towards the end of a day of futile pursuit, the emperor decided that he could not move any further from his camp and the army turned back to retrace its steps. At that moment, when the Byzantine army's order was broken and the troops were in the process of changing their grouping for the return journey, the Saljuqs attacked with a charge of mounted archers that broke the Byzantine column into small groups of panicking men. Many of the Greek mercenaries fled the field immediately, as did the Byzantine nobles, who were the emperor's rearguard. The Byzantines were crushed and Romanus was taken prisoner. The panic this defeat

---

* For a comprehensive history of the genesis of the Assassin sect and Nizam al-Mulk's perception of their threat to the state, see Waterson, J., *The Ismaili Assassins: A History of Medieval Murder*, London: Frontline Books, 2008, Chapters Two and Three.

induced in the Byzantines started the chain of events that sent Urban II to the pulpit in Clermont in 1095.

In fact, the Saljuqs were not interested in the conquest of Constantinople.* That would have to wait for another generation of Turks. The Saljuqs still had unfinished business with the Fatimids, and by 1092 only the Syrian coastline remained to be conquered. The Fatimids were able to hold onto the coastal cities due to their naval strength, a situation that would later repeat itself with the Crusaders taking the place of the Fatimids.

Both the expansion and, indeed, the very cohesion of the Saljuq state ended in the 1090s, as its major political leaders were either murdered or died unexpectedly. The year 1092 saw the murder of Nizam al-Mulk by the Assassins, and the death of the sultan, Malikshah, amidst rumors of the caliph's involvement. The sultan's wife, grandson and other senior politicians also all died soon after. The centripetal force of Nizam al-Mulk's government was lost and the Saljuq Empire splintered. This was not surprising: the empire was, like so many other medieval enterprises, a family business, and the death of its head was enough in itself to cause chaos. Turkish tradition worsened the situation, however, as each son was entitled to an equal share of the father's possessions, and so the state was broken up. Also, while these sons all had the same father, each one had a different mother. Civil war based on a pushy mother's ambitions for her son may seem slightly absurd, but in the closing years of the eleventh century it was very much a fact in Iraq and Syria. Powerful military lords, emirs, used their forces to their own advantage and formed unstable allegiances with candidates for the sultanate. In this poisonous atmosphere, regional leaders became mutually suspicious of each other and the unity of the state disappeared.

The Abbasid caliph, al-Muqtadi, also died in 1094, but more important than this was the demise of Sultan Malikshah's brother, Tutush, the ruler of Damascus. When Tutush heard of Malikshah's death, he made a play for the entire Saljuq Empire. He mustered his army and, between 1092 and 1095, conducted bloody campaigns against Aleppo and Antioch that brought Syria's already weak infrastructure to near collapse. He then

---

* An attempt was, however, made by the Norman, Roussel of Balliol, who deserted the emperor just prior to the battle, to set up a Norman state in Galatia in the chaotic aftermath of the battle. It eventually failed but such adventures, and the consistent use of Western mercenary forces in Anatolia by the Byzantines, would have further confused the Muslims over the issue of the First Crusade army's significance and aims.

challenged his young nephew Berkyaruq for the Saljuq throne in 1095. He failed in this larger enterprise: Berkyaruq marched out of Baghdad, and defeated his uncle in the Battle of Dashlu. Tutush was killed in the battle and Syria was left wrecked and rudderless, a vulnerable prey for the Crusaders, who were just on the point of leaving Europe's shores.

Western Persia and Iraq then became the main theatre for the contest between the sons of Malikshah. A civil war between Berkyaruq and his half-brother Muhammad continued until Berkyaruq's death in 1105, by which time the Crusaders had conquered Jerusalem and consolidated their position, without interference from the region's major power. Ibn al-Jawzi wrote that Sultan Berkyaruq, during one of his brief periods in control of Baghdad, and before the fall of Jerusalem, had assembled a force to challenge the *Franj* in Syria but that, 'then this resoluteness fizzled out'.* It is hard to contemplate how this expedition would have been funded, given the absolute exhaustion of the state treasury – brought about by Baghdad having been occupied by different opposing armies some thirty times between 1099 and 1101, as well as by the constant 'buying off' of emirs during the civil wars. Indeed, al-Bundari described later how Sultan Muhammad lacked funds even to provide for his emirs' daily beer allowance.† Ibn al-Athir's verdict on the Saljuq sultanate's isolation from Syrian affairs in this period seems entirely valid, 'the Sultans did not agree amongst themselves and it was for this reason that the *Franj* were able to seize control of the country.'‡

Tutush's campaigns had also left Syria financially and politically shattered, but this really just compounded already existing problems. There had been a 'collapse of the agricultural economies in districts that had once been the granaries of the Abbasid Caliphate' between 950 and 1050,§ and the banditry of Bedouin tribes such as the Banu Kalb and Banu Kilab disrupted commercial life around Aleppo and Damascus,

---

* In Hillenbrand, C., *The Crusades: Islamic Perspectives*, Edinburgh: Edinburgh University Press, 1999, p. 78.
† Lambton, Chapter Eight, p. 255.
‡ Ibn al-Athir in Maalouf, A., *The Crusades through Arab Eyes*, translated by J. Rothschild, London: Al-Saqi Books, 1983, p. 55. Ibn al-Athir was writing long after the events but a contemporary Cassandra-like prophecy was made in 1105 by a certain citizen of Damascus, al-Sulami, who wrote a treatise on Holy War very clearly stating that if the Muslims remained disunited then the *Franj* would take all of the Syrian coastline. See Irwin, R., 'Church of Garbage', *London Review of Books*, 3 February 2000, pp. 38–9.
§ Kennedy, pp. 293–338.

the major centres of Syria. Plague affected both these cities in 1097, and revisited them in 1099 and 1100. All these factors, and the continuance of poor harvests, particularly in northern Syria, contributed to the reluctance of the forces of Aleppo and Damascus to face the Crusaders. A long war against the invaders may not actually have been economically sustainable for either city.*

Perhaps if Damascus and Aleppo had been of a mind to unify in their resistance to the *Franj*, there might have been some hope for an early Syrian-Muslim response to the Crusaders, but the 'patrimonial share out'† of Tutush's possessions upon his death meant that his sons, Ridwan and Duqaq, each obtained a city: Aleppo and Damascus respectively. From the outset of this arrangement there was only animosity and suspicion between the two brothers. In 1096, Ridwan failed twice in his attempts to take Damascus; likewise, in 1097, Duqaq failed to take Aleppo. These failures are not that surprising, given that the forces that each brother had inherited from their father were both grievously depleted by the movement of most of the Turcoman forces, on whom Tutush had relied, back to Iraq, where they could continue to involve themselves in the lucrative business of the Saljuq civil wars.

Gone, at least in Syria, were the days when a sea of men took the field under a Saljuq commander. Alp Arslan, according to Ibn al-Qalanasi, took four hundred thousand men with him into Anatolia in 1071, and, whilst we may doubt the chronicler's figures, there are other witnesses to the fact that it took a month to transport a Saljuq army across the Oxus in 1072. The Syrian cities could not afford to pay such vast armies, and in any case many Turkish troopers and emirs would have left Syria even if triple pay were offered. Each man was paid partly through booty, but the majority of their income came through the *iqta* system. A Saljuq trooper's *iqta* was similar to the fief of a Western knight, in that it paid his salary. The *iqta* was, however, more complex, in that while it could simply be a piece of land like the Western knight's fief, it could also be a 'share' of an industry – such as the spice trade or a textile production centre. Unlike the Western knight, the *iqta* holder was not necessarily resident on the land from which the *iqta* was drawn. Treasury officials managed it

* El-Azhari, T., *The Seljuqs of Syria during the Crusades: 1070–1154*, translated by Winkelhane, Berlin: Schwartz-Verlag, 1997, p. 117.

† Bosworth, C., 'The Political and Dynastic History of the Persian World 1000–1217', in J. Boyle (ed.), *The Cambridge History of Persia. Volume Five: The Saljuq and Mongol Periods*, Cambridge: Cambridge University Press, 1968, p. 111.

for him and collected the rents for him. The *iqta*, in theory, was also not hereditary like a fief, so in some ways it paid for current service rather than a family's history of allegiance to the ruler. The distribution of *iqtas* was therefore a powerful means of ensuring loyalty to the sultan and of rewarding emirs. In the late eleventh century, the problem was that the prosperous Persian *iqtas* of many 'Syrian' Saljuqs were being overrun by the Ghuzz, so they abandoned Syria in order to defend their sources of income in the east.

This would all seem to suggest that all the Crusaders had to do in order to take the Levant from the Muslims was to 'kick in the front door', but this was far from the truth. A number of very tough soldiers and skilled commanders still stood between the *expeditio* and its goal of Jerusalem. We cannot doubt, therefore, that the army of the First Crusade was an effective fighting force and that it was led by some exceptional individuals. Their bravery is attested to by a backhanded compliment from Usama Ibn-Munqidh, a Syrian-Arab warrior who both fought with them and against them in the middle of the twelfth century. He wrote that, 'the Franks possess none of the virtues of men except courage.'* The size of the force has been estimated to have been about seventy-five thousand persons, including non-combatants, at the start of the Crusade. There has been much debate over technological and tactical advantages that the Crusaders may have held over their Muslim adversaries, with historians arguing both for technological determinism in the case of the crossbow, and for tactical superiority in the development of the charge by the *Franj*. In fact the reverse, at least in terms of the land war, was very much the case, and the sole advantage the Crusaders seem to have held over their Muslim foes during the First Crusade was their fanatical drive and courage and an 'all or nothing mentality'† that developed during the venture. It is hard to imagine the Crusaders declaring themselves as 'we happy few, we band of brothers' during the terrible siege of Antioch – of which Peter Tudebode wrote that, 'the anxieties and hardships are more than I can recount',‡ and during the numerous privations that they endured throughout the Crusade – but these experiences brought

---

* Hitti, P. K., *An Arab-Syrian Gentleman and Warrior in the Period of the Crusades: Memoirs of Usama Ibn Munqidh*, Columbia, NY: Columbia University Press, 1929, p. 93.

† France, J., *Victory in the East: A Military History of the First Crusade*, London: Cambridge University Press, 1994, p. 367.

‡ Peters, E., *The First Crusade: The Chronicle of Fulcher of Chartres and Other Source Materials*, second edition, Philadelphia: University of Pennsylvania Press, 1998, p. 202.

an almost unbreakable cohesion to the force. This cohesion was only maintained in the early period of the Latin state but it was central to its birth.* We also cannot overstate the importance of the religious fervour that gripped the Crusaders in dire times. The psychological 'draw' of celestial Jerusalem was powerful and William of Tyre wrote vividly of the powerful effect of the procession of the 'relic of the true cross' on the troops before the Battle of Ramla in 1105.†

The Muslim defenders of the Holy Land stood at the other end of the dichotomy to this Frankish display of unity and passion for their cause. Yet when the People's Crusade‡ – which, despite its somewhat amateur-sounding appellation, was a strong force, containing over five hundred knights and a large body of infantry – met the Turkish forces of the minor sultan Kilij Arslan of Nicaea in the autumn of 1096, it was rapidly annihilated. Two groups of Italian and German knights first got into trouble, by carrying out raids in north Anatolia and then moving on to try and capture Xerigordos, a fortress within the lands of Kilij Arslan. They were quickly surrounded by the sultan and his *askari* (bodyguard), and they soon surrendered after discovering that the fortress had no water supply. Kilij Arslan then followed the Muslim process of war outlined by Ibn Zafir al-Siqilli. He worked first on *hila* (artifice): he dispatched local Anatolian spies to the *Franj* camp to describe how the Italians and Germans had been successful in their venture, and also to report back with information on the force confronting him. The ruse was successful, despite the arrival of an escapee from the debacle at Xerigordos back in the Crusader camp, who cast doubt on the spies' tales. The Crusade then moved out into open country, under Walter Sansavoir, to join in their companions' success. Turkish tactics, as we have seen at the Battle of Manzikert, worked best when engaging an enemy strung out on the march. Usually the enemy had to be drawn into a battle before he was fully organised, by the use of hit-and-run raids and through harassment of his rearguard. However, on 21 October 1096, the People's Crusade offered itself up for a battle that suited Kilij Arslan's forces perfectly. The sultan

---

* Indeed it has been suggested that the First Crusade was unique and unrepeatable in its nature. See Tyerman, C., 'Were there any Crusades in the Twelfth Century?', *English Historical Review*, June 1995, pp. 553–77.

† Edbury, P., and Rowe, J., *William of Tyre, Historian of the Latin East*, Cambridge: Cambridge University Press, 1988, p. 156.

‡ The popular movement created through the preaching of Peter the Hermit, which had marched ahead of the main forces of the First Crusade.

has been much maligned for his later failures against the First Crusade, but his skilful ambush of the People's Crusade, and the overwhelming archery fusillade that his troopers unleashed on it, show that he was more than capable of using his *quwwa* (force) to its full effectiveness, given the right conditions. Albert of Aachen's narrative puts the following speech in the mouth of Kilij Arslan: 'Behold the Franks, against whom we are marching, are at hand. Let us withdraw from the forest and mountains into the open plain, where we may freely engage in battle with them, and they can find no refuge.' Albert then quickly relates how, 'when they had seen the Turks, they began to encourage one another in the name of the Lord. Then Walter Sansavoir fell, pierced by seven arrows which had penetrated his coat of mail.'*

It seems evident then that the Turks started their volleys of arrows at a phenomenal distance from the *Franj* army – the Turks were sighted by the Crusaders and then Walter fell almost immediately, struck by seven arrows – and that these arrows were delivered with a force capable of penetrating the knights' double-link chain mail. The Crusader force rapidly broke up under this onslaught and the Turks pursued the remnants for three miles and besieged them inside an abandoned coastal fortress. The Turks then displayed another important tenet of near-eastern warfare before the arrival of the *Franj* in the Levant – preservation of the force. Turkish warfare emphasised weakening the enemy and degrading his force, rather than attempting to break it quickly, which would likely result in a heavier loss of one's own manpower. Therefore, rather than making continual frontal assaults on the fortress, the Turks used 'shower shooting' to allow a rain of arrows to fall without respite on the heads of the defenders. The few remaining Crusaders were only saved by the arrival of a Byzantine force.

Kilij Arslan had secured an impressive victory in the opening of the 'campaign' but it still seems, despite the sultan's impressive espionage network, based on traders and merchants in Constantinople, that he had little idea of the Franks' intentions. He was therefore ill-informed about the new Frankish army that was arriving, piecemeal, during the spring and summer of 1097 in north Anatolia. He was also distracted by a rival emir, Danishmend, who had besieged the city of Malatya in north-eastern Anatolia. When he heard of the Franks' advance from the Bosporus the sultan was already heavily engaged in his campaign against

---

* See Peters, pp. 146–9.

Danishmend. He sent small detachments to the west, but he could spare very few troops as the siege of Malatya dragged on. Then Kilij Arslan was surprised by news of another siege – that of the *Franj* against his capital, Nicaea.

Reports stated that the enemy was significantly larger than the forces that the sultan had engaged the year before, and that they were accompanied by Byzantine units. Given this new information, the sultan worked hard to negotiate a truce with Danishmend; and even before it was concluded he began to dispatch a considerable amount of his forces to the defence of his capital. If Kilij Arslan thought the arrival of his army in the vicinity of Nicaea would be enough to deter the Franks from their encirclement of the city, he was to be disappointed. The *Gesta Francorum* records how far advanced the siege was:

> We began to attack the city on all sides, and to construct machines of wood, and wooden towers, with which we might be able to destroy towers on the walls. We attacked the city so bravely and so fiercely that we even undermined its wall.

The *Gesta* also gives us an account of Kilij Arslan's abortive attempt to relieve the city:

> The Turks who were in the city, barbarous horde that they were, sent messages to others who had come up to give aid. The message ran in this wise: that they might approach the city boldly and in security and enter through the middle gate, because on that side no one would oppose them or put them to grief. This gate was besieged on that very day – the Sabbath after the Ascension of the Lord – by the Count of Saint Gilles and the Bishop of Puy. The Count, approaching from another side, was protected by divine might, and with his most powerful army gloried in terrestrial strength. And so he found the Turks, coming against us here. Armed on all sides with the sign of the cross, he rushed upon them violently and overcame them. They turned in flight, and most of them were killed. They came back again, reinforced by others, joyful and exulting in assured outcome of battle, and bearing along with them the ropes with which to lead us bound to Khurasan. Coming gladly, moreover, they began to descend from the crest of the mountain a short distance. As many as descended remained there with their heads cut off at the hands of our men . . .*

---

* See the *Gesta Francorum* in Krey, A. C., *The First Crusade: The Accounts of Eyewitnesses and Participants*, Princeton: Princeton University Press, 1921, pp. 101–3.

It seems, from the evidence available, that the sultan rushed into battle because his sultana was within the city's walls, and he also feared that the longer his forces had to contemplate the size of the *Franj* army, the less likely they would be to commit to battle. His army was repulsed by the Franks as they attempted to reach the middle gate, and the *Gesta* narrative also indicates that the Turks came on in waves and then feigned retreat, but could not draw the Franks out into the open field where they might destroy them with an archery fusillade. It seems too that Saint Gilles did not pursue the Turks any great distance, even after his successful assault on them, and this was certainly wise. The terrain also favoured the Franks, as a mobile and dispersed battle – where mounted archery would be able to penetrate the Crusaders' ranks – was unlikely to develop as the lake and folds of the mountains on either side of the approach to the city limited flanking options and protected Saint Gilles and his knights' flanks as they made their charge.

Nicaea now seemed a lost cause and Kilij Arslan retired from the field. The city did not, however, fall easily to the Crusaders and a strong resistance was maintained by the garrison. The city finally 'fell' to Alexius, the Byzantine emperor. Having assisted the Franks to a great degree through victualling of their army, he then outmanoeuvred his own allies by securing Nicaea's surrender to Byzantium alone. Greek troops entered the city unopposed via gates on the Lake Askanius side.

Kilij Arslan had meanwhile retired to lick his wounds. His forces had suffered only light losses during the engagement at Nicaea, but his prestige as a warrior-chief had certainly been damaged. He spent the next few weeks gathering nomadic Turcoman warriors to his standard and negotiating with chiefs like Danishmend to unite against the invaders. It might be a little strong to suggest, as Ibn al-Qalanasi did, that he 'set about collecting forces, raising levies, and carrying out the obligation of Holy War',* but he certainly attracted both nomads and more importantly the *askari* of his brother to his banner.

It is common to call the *askari* of a Turkish prince his 'bodyguard', but this is something of a misnomer. For a minor potentate this was accurate, but for a Saljuq prince the *askari* was more like a large company of heavy cavalry, around which lighter-armed Turcoman irregulars could be deployed. In Crusade histories one often finds the notion that the Turks were lightly armed and could be pushed from the field by the charge

---

* Al-Qalanasi, p. 42.

of mail-clad 'heavy' knights – provided that the Crusaders survived the initial Turkish mounted-archery attack. This is true as far as the Turcomen were concerned, but in terms of a Mamluk *askari* it is far from correct. The *Gesta Francorum* tells us about the *agulari*, Muslim cavalry that rode armoured horses, an unknown phenomenon in the West at this time. These were almost certainly heavily armed troopers of the *askari*. The problem was that, until relatively late in the Crusades, there simply weren't enough of these *askari* Mamluks united long enough under one leader to counter the knights that the Crusaders brought into the theatre.

Kilij Arslan gathered his forces and obviously hoped to use them with much greater utility than he had at Nicaea. His Turcomen, as nomads who hunted from the saddle on a daily basis, were experts at hit-and-run raids. Ibn al-Qalanasi wrote, 'he marched out to the fords, tracks and roads by which the Franks must pass, and showed no mercy to all of them who fell into his hands.'* Harrying the two columns of the *Franj* army as they moved towards their next goal, the city of Antioch, was not, however, going to be enough to halt the Crusaders. Kilij Arslan recognised this and realised that his army, built on temporary alliances and on the ephemeral loyalties of Turcomen, would break up without a decisive engagement and the booty that battle could bring. He therefore decided to meet the Franks with his full force, on ground suitable for an ambush. As the Franks passed through a pass on the road close to the abandoned Byzantine military outpost of Dorylaeum, he made his attack. Fulcher of Chartres wrote that he was horrified by the 'clouds of arrows' fired at the Crusaders by their assailants, and initially it seemed that the onslaught would be enough to break the *Franj*. Bohemond, the leader of this division of the Franks, ordered his infantry to pitch camp when he realised that the Turks were closing, and he attempted to meet them with his cavalry. The mobility and archery skills of his adversaries, however, stymied the Norman, and his cavalry was soon pressed back upon his infantry. The Franks were nicely hemmed in by Kilij Arslan's troopers, but this presented a problem for the Turks – the sultan's troops could not break up the Crusaders' formation into islands of men who could then be surrounded and killed with arrows. As the Franks pressed closer and closer together, they presented a formidable defensive 'wall' of armour, in which the Turks could not find a weakness. Added to this was the fact that Bohemond was a skilled general, who soon saw that the initial disadvantage of not being able to break out of the camp was

---

* Al-Qalanasi, p. 43.

now in fact proving to be a strength. One is reminded of the description of the first great Frankish victory over Muslims at Tours in 732, when, under Charles Martel, 'the nations of the North standing firm as a wall, and impenetrable as a zone of ice, utterly slew the Arabs with the edge of the sword.'* Perhaps Kilij Arslan could have succeeded with his *askari* heavy cavalry where Abd al-Rahman's eighth-century Arab light troopers had failed, but the arrival of the second detachment of Crusaders after five hours put paid to any such hope and its attack on his flank sent him once more defeated from the field.

Kilij Arslan went east; while his policy of burning and spoiling everything that might be useful to the Franks during his retreat may have made the Crusader advance more difficult, he essentially abandoned the approaches to Syria. This was not entirely surprising as the battle had cost him some three thousand men. As Ibn Qalanasi recorded, 'the *Franj* cut the Turkish army to pieces. They killed, pillaged and took many prisoners, who were sold into slavery.'†

With the withdrawal of Kilij Arslan, information on the Crusaders was lost again. Of course, the amount of time that it took such a vast host to travel in the arid conditions of Anatolia and northern Syria meant that, for the Muslim princes of the region, the Crusaders were 'off the radar' for a prolonged period. There was a sighting of the enemy near the village of al-Balana in northern Syria and cavalry were sent to intercept them, only to find no trace of them. Then the *Franj* appeared at Heraclea, whose small garrison rapidly deserted the fortress at their approach. The Crusader force then split again. A small force was sent south through the Cilician Gates in the Taurus Mountains, whilst the army's main body took a longer route through the Anti-Taurus Mountains. Both had Antioch – a former possession of Byzantium, which had fallen to the Turks after Manzikert – as their objective. However, the smaller force had the secondary task of allying with the region's Armenians, who now found themselves free of Turkish overlords and who were looking to establish an independent Armenia.

It is difficult to assess how much the population of Syria, with its complex ethnic and religious mix, hindered an effective Muslim response to the First Crusade. Certainly the small Turkish garrisons of

---

* Creasy, E. S., *Fifteen Decisive Battles of the World: From Marathon to Waterloo*, London: Bentley, 1851, p. 250.
† Al-Qalanasi, p. 44.

many minor cities feared their own subjects – a mix of Arabs, Greeks and Armenians – and the hard-taxing Turks were seen as tyrannical aliens, and this meant that Turkish domination was built on very shaky foundations. The Arabs' disparaging view of the Turks is illustrated by the poet al-Basri's lines of the tenth century:

> I am told: You spend too much time at home, and then I answer:
> It is no longer fun to walk in the streets, for whom do I meet when looking around?
> Monkeys on horseback.*

Kurds had also created independent states inside Turkish lands, and maintaining control of the southern part of Syria was proving equally difficult for the Fatimids, due to opposition from increasing powerful Arab tribal coalitions. The presence of Maronite Christians in the Syrian Mountains, Nusayri Shiites in the north of the country and Druze in the south also effectively impeded communication between the coastal cities and Aleppo and Damascus in the interior. In parts of Syria and Anatolia, Christians formed a majority of the populace, and there is evidence that they provided direct assistance to the Crusaders. The Christians of Artah, the last fortress-town before Antioch, massacred its Turkish garrison upon the approach of the Crusaders; Tarsus fell rapidly after its Turkish garrison made a desultory assault on the Crusaders and then thought better of attempting to defend a city with an Armenian population who really were not that interested in being defended.

The Crusaders reformed as one army before taking the Sirat Farfar or 'Iron Bridge' that crossed the Orontes and then began their investment of Antioch. Antioch epitomised the problems of Turkish lords in Syria. Ibn al-Athir tells us that when its governor, Yaghi Siyan, was informed of the approach of the Franks, 'he feared possible sedition on the part of the Christians of the city.' He therefore decided to expel them. This was achieved in a fairly crafty manner:

> When Yaghi Siyan heard of their approach he was not sure how the Christian people of the city would react, so he made the Muslims go outside the city on their own to dig trenches, and the next day sent the Christians out alone to continue the task. When they were ready to return

---

* In Haarmann, U. W., 'Ideology and History, Identity and Alterity: The Arab Image of the Turk from the Abbasids to Modern Egypt', *International Journal of Middle East Studies*, May 1988, pp. 175–96.

home at the end of the day he refused to allow them. 'Antioch is yours', he said, 'but you will have to leave it with me until I see what happens between us and the Franks.' 'Who will protect our children and our wives?' they said. 'I shall look after them for you.'*

Ibn al-Athir goes on to tell us that if all the Franks who died during the siege of Antioch had survived they would have overrun the lands of Islam, and he states that the governor was of 'unparalleled courage and wisdom'. This overstates the case a little, but the siege very nearly broke the Crusaders, and Yaghi Siyan generally managed the city's defence well.

Antioch was a Byzantine creation – its six fortified gates, 5,000 metres of walls (which were three metres deep at some points) and 360 turrets presented an impressive obstacle to the Crusaders, as did the fact that the walls on one side fell away into a precipitous valley, and a river ran along much of the front section of the walls. Furthermore, its citadel sat almost atop Mount Silpius, which lay within the city's walls, and the garrison, though reduced, still numbered five thousand men. The city was also well supplied with food and had sufficient water sources.

Defensive castle warfare was a well-developed art in the Islamic world at this time – the resistance at Antioch lasted nine months, while Tyre and Tripoli made even more impressive stands against the *Franj*. Much had been learnt during the early Arab campaigns against fortified Byzantine cities: treatises on *naft* (incendiaries), mangonels and defensive weapons were produced, often by *manjaniqiyin* – the engineers who designed and produced siege engines for the Islamic world.† A detailed description of the comprehensive organisation of Tarsus's defences in the tenth century has been left to us,‡ and a later treatise written for Saladin tells us about the *jarkh*, an oversized crossbow that required a windlass to reload it and which fired *nabalah* – heavy arrows. It seems likely that the *jarkh* was an import from Persia and may even have had Chinese influence in its construction.§

---

* Gabrieli, p. 5. Preceding and subsequent quotes also from the same source.
† One siege-engine builder of Baghdad was Ibn Sabir al-Manajaniqi (d.1220). His *nisbah* or taken name is derived from the word *manjaniq*, which is commonly translated as mangonel, but in fact refers to any projectile-throwing device. His treatise, famous in its day and referred to by other writers, is unfortunately lost. See al-Sarraf, S., 'Mamluk Furusiyah Literature', *Mamluk Studies Review*, vol. 8, no. 1, 2004.
‡ Bosworth, C., 'Abu 'Amr 'Uthman al-Tarsusi's Siyar al Thughur and the Last Years of Arab Rule in Tarsus', *Graeco Arabica*, vol. 5, 1993, pp. 183–95.
§ Nicolle, D., 'Medieval Warfare: The Unfriendly Interface', *Journal of Military History*, vol. 63, no. 3, July 1999, pp. 579–99.

The problem for Yaghi Siyan was the lack of an effective field army in the region that could relieve the siege and threaten the besieging *Franj*. In classic castle warfare, as practised with exemplary skill by the Crusaders of Syria in the twelfth century – up until King Guy's loss of the field army at the Battle of Hattin – the defenders of a fortified place aimed simply to hold out until the arrival of the state's field army.* The problem for the Syrian Muslims in the late eleventh century was that no such force existed as long as Damascus and Aleppo stood at loggerheads with each other and with Antioch. The nearest alternative powerbase outside Syria was Mosul: its forces were small and its rulers were heavily involved in the Saljuq civil wars in Iraq.

Following a two-week standoff, during which time the Crusaders realised that they could not hope to invest the entirety of Antioch's walls, the Turks opened the contest for the city with harassing archery fire from the mountains around Antioch. Cavalry squadrons were also dispatched through the Bridge Gate, which faced the Orontes. They were able to raid with relative impunity for a while, because the river protected them during their archery assaults. However, these hit-and-run tactics could not degrade the Franks' manpower to any appreciable degree, as they wisely refused to close with the enemy, but they certainly took their toll on the Crusaders' horses and this would become important later in the struggle. The Turks from the nearby fortress of Harim also ambushed *Franj* foraging parties and the Crusaders became increasingly vulnerable as they went further and further afield to hunt for food for their vast army.

The Franks responded to these challenges with two initiatives. First, they secured a bridge of boats across the Orontes, and Bohemond solved the second problem of Harim through a neat bit of decoy work. He sent a small patrol out to ride through known danger areas and took a larger squadron of cavalry to tail the first at a safe distance. When the first party was set upon they retreated and Bohemond's second body of knights ambushed and slaughtered the Turkish troopers. The threat of Harim was thereby extinguished by mid-November. Antioch was now alone, as its port, Saint Simeon, had already fallen to an enemy fleet. The Franks' ability to maintain a strong naval presence in the eastern Mediterranean, a key feature of the next two centuries of warfare and beyond, began with the fall of Saint Simeon.

---

* See France, pp. 24–6.

Yaghi Siyan was losing the contest, but he did have a stockpile of food and the Franks were running low on supplies. He had also sent his son to Duqaq, the prince of Damascus, and to the other princes of smaller cities in the region in July, and must have hoped that relief was on its way. By December, famine had struck in the Crusader camp and even executions of captured Turks before the walls of Antioch had done little apparent harm to the garrison's morale. They responded with like-for-like executions of Armenian Christians and the regular suspension, via his feet, of the city's patriarch over the walls. Ibn al-Qalanasi tells us about the oversized foraging party that the Franks resorted to at the end of December 1097. He claims that the Franks dispatched some thirty thousand troops to the mountainous district of Jabal al-Summaq, but it was probably closer to four hundred mounted knights with supporting infantry, and was led by Bohemond and Robert of Flanders; this force pillaged the town of al-Bara.

Meanwhile Duqaq of Damascus was heading towards them with a large force en route to Antioch. Early in the morning on New Year's Eve, the Damascenes surprised the Franks' camp; employing two simultaneous flanking manoeuvres, they tried to encircle the Crusaders. Bohemond's generalship and the disciplined mobility of his Normans once again saved the Crusaders. Bohemond had learnt much about his adversaries from contact with Turkish mercenaries during his earlier campaigns against the Byzantines and from his engagements with Kilij Arslan. As he was undoubtedly the most intelligent of the Crusader princes, he would also have taken a deep interest in all the instruction that Emperor Alexius – his former enemy and now (admittedly untrustworthy) ally – had given to the Crusaders about the Turkish method of warfare. The Byzantines had a tradition of meticulous inquiry into the actions of all their foes. For example, the famous *Taktika* of Leo the Wise, tells us of the Muslim foes of his day:

> Saracen armies use camels for baggage, rather than oxen, donkeys or mules, because these animals frighten [attacking] cavalry. They also use cymbals and kettle-drums to scare the enemy's horses; their own horses being accustomed to these. They normally have camels and other baggage animals in the centre of their army, and they attach flags to them. They enjoy war and are accompanied by many 'priests'. They are hot blooded and do not like cold weather. Their infantry is composed of Ethiopians who carry large bows. They are placed ahead of their cavalry while the cavalry prepares to attack. The cavalry also carry the infantry on their cruppers

when the expedition is not close to their own frontier. [The cavalry] are
armed with swords, spears and axes.*

Bohemond had worked out how to counter the Turkish threat and
how to allow the Crusaders to close with their enemy and deliver their
charge. The Turks' attempts at encirclement were thwarted by dividing
the Crusader force into a forward and rearguard unit. The rearguard
effectively plugged gaps around the forward unit, allowing the latter to
organise its cavalry charge behind a screen of heavy infantry. Raymond
of Aguilers described how all this took place on the day in question:

> Bohemond indeed followed at a distance with the rest and guarded the rear
> lines. For the Turks have this custom in fighting: even though they are fewer
> in number, they always strive to encircle their enemy. They attempted to
> do this in this battle also, but by the foresight of Bohemond the wiles of the
> enemy were prevented. When, however, the Turks, and the Arabs, coming
> against the Count of Flanders, saw that the affair was not to be conducted
> at a distance with arrows, but at close quarters with swords, they turned in
> flight. The count followed them for two miles, and in this space he saw the
> bodies of the killed lying like bundles of grain reaped in the fields.†

The tactic was a success, as Robert's charge broke the army of
Damascus, which fled the field, but the Crusader princes were so
hopelessly outnumbered that they promptly deserted their infantry and
loot and fled for Antioch. Strategically the foraging venture had been a
success, in that it had turned Duqaq back to Damascus. Operationally,
however, it constituted a setback for the Franks as they had lost a
detachment of infantry, and this was especially significant as at this time
many knights were acting as infantry due to the earlier Turkish tactic of
killing Crusader steeds. Furthermore, Bohemond and Robert's departure
had encouraged the Turks of Antioch to engage the reduced forces at
their walls. On 29 December Yaghi Siyan had sent out a detachment
from the Bridge Gate that was pursued by a body of Provencal knights

---

* From the *Taktika*, translated by M. Joly de Mazeroi, in Nicolle. There were no Nubians
to contend with in the Turkish forces that the Crusaders had thus far faced, but there
would be in the Fatimid armies they would encounter further south. Muslim armies right
through to the end of the Crusades period employed bandsmen with giant drums and
cymbals to terrify the enemy. The *tabarzin*, a vast axe used by early cavalry, would be re-
introduced by the Mamluks of Egypt in the thirteenth century as part of their formidable
personal armoury.
† Krey, pp. 136–9.

under Raymond of Toulouse until they were out in open country. The Turks then turned and rushed back upon them and pushed them pell-mell onto the Franks' Bridge of Boats, where a crush and panic ensued. The Turks only killed a few knights, but they wrested a banner of the Virgin Mary from the bishop of Le Puy's standard-bearer and delighted in displaying it on the walls of the city upon their return.

The siege ground on over the winter. Ibn al-Qalanasi tells us, 'oil, salt and other necessaries became dear and unprocurable in Antioch,' but then, 'so much was smuggled into the city that they became cheap again.'* Outside the walls, thistles were being boiled and seeds were being scavenged from animal dung by the Franks. At this point Yaghi Siyan must have considered that he might well have already won the encounter. There was heartening news of a massacre of six hundred Crusader 'civilians' who were desperately searching for food away from their army by one of his detachments, as well as desertions from the *Franj*, both by their own people and by the Greek contingent under Alexius's lieutenant, Tacticius. The near betrayal of the city, by the family of a captured Turkish aristocrat, was stymied by Yaghi Siyan's removal of one of the key gate-towers from their care and the Crusaders executed their hostage when their plan failed. Then word came that Ridwan of Aleppo was coming with twelve thousand men to break the siege in early February 1098. The lord of Aleppo came to the aid of Antioch not for high-minded motives, but rather because Frankish foraging raids had begun to impact on his own lands.

Ridwan's army formed two lines of battle, with the Orontes on their right and the foothills of Mount Staurin on their left. This was foolish, as they therefore effectively made the river and mountain barriers to any outflanking manoeuvres they could have conducted against the small number of mounted knights that they faced. However, Ridwan's plan may have been to force the Franks to commit to battle. Like all the Saljuq princes, he was always thinking of possible domestic revolt whenever he was away from his capital, and he wanted to return to Aleppo as soon as possible. He also made the cardinal error of so many commanders in history, and indeed of our own time – he fought not simply to defeat the Crusaders, but rather to preserve his force *and* beat the Franks. As Herodotus would have it, the attack was guaranteed to fail, because it was prosecuted with 'that most dangerous tendency

---

* Al-Qalanasi, p. 48.

in war: a wish to kill but not to die in the process'. The narrow-front battle of limited commitment that Ridwan chose to fight suited the Crusaders perfectly. Bohemond arranged his mounted troops in six lines, with his own knights as the last line. The infantry was given the task of repelling any sorties from Antioch. The Turks closed with the *Franj* much faster than the Saljuq commanders had expected. The *Franj* cavalry may have been hidden in a fold of land and Ridwan's van was engaged by the first line of mounted Franks even before a flight of arrows could be launched. The lightly armed Turcomen that the Crusaders engaged in this early stage of the battle quickly fell away. It was only when the Franks met the *askari* in the rear of the Turkish army that they were halted, at least temporarily. The *Gesta Francorum* tells us of this moment in the battle, when the result was in doubt, as the *askari* loosed their arrows and then came forward to meet the *Franj* with mace, sword and lance:

> The clamour resounded to the sky, showers of weapons darkened the sky. When their troops of greatest valour, who had been in the rear, came up they attacked our forces sharply, so that our men fell back a little.

The battle went to the Franks simply because of inspired leadership – of which Ridwan could claim none – and because the Crusaders held a religious fervour that was totally lacking in the Turks of Aleppo. This is clear even amid the hyperbole of the *Gesta*:

> As the most learned man, Bohemond, saw this, he groaned. Then he commanded his constable . . . 'Go as quickly as you can, like a brave man and remember our illustrious and courageous forefathers of old. Be keen in the service of God and the Holy Sepulchre, and bear in mind that this battle is not carnal but spiritual. Be therefore the bravest athlete of Christ. Go in peace. The Lord be with you everywhere.' And so that man, fortified on all sides with the sign of the Cross, went into the lines of Turks, just as a lion, famished for three or four days, goes forth from his cave raging and thirsting for the blood of beasts and, rushing unexpectedly among herds of sheep, tears them to pieces as they flee hither and thither. So violently did he press upon them that the tips of his renowned standard flew over the heads of the Turks. Moreover, as the other lines saw that the banner of Bohemond was so gloriously borne before them, they went back to the battle again, and with one accord our men attacked the Turks who, amazed, took to flight.*

---

* Krey, pp. 136–9.

The rout didn't end until Harim was burning and the victory was rounded off by executions of prisoners before the walls of Antioch, as a further dire warning against continued resistance.

Despite Ridwan's obvious failures as a commander and the Crusaders' 'all or nothing' mentality, the Turkish defeat still seems surprising, given that their army was so large and that the Franks' supply of horses had been degraded both by Turkish archery and through starvation and disease. However, it must be remembered that the *regular* Saljuq forces available to Ridwan and to his brother Duqaq were few in number. Aleppo and Damascus both held no more than a thousand regular soldiers each, and Nizam al-Mulk's *Book of Government* gives the standing army or bodyguard of the great Saljuq sultan, at the height of his powers, as being just over four thousand men, mostly unmounted. The army would then have been mostly composed of Turcomen with doubtful loyalties to the unpopular Prince Ridwan. Large Turkish-Muslim regular standing armies would not be seen in Syria for another 150 years, whilst the men of the First Crusade had forged a powerful cohesion and familiarity with each other, at least on the battlefield, which allowed them to operate well as an army, rather than as discrete groups of warriors. It has even been suggested that the European charge evolved during the Crusades, because the Crusaders had a unity of purpose that allowed men and horses to move as one. Without such unity the charge is useless, and its shock is dissipated if members of the unit arrive piecemeal.* It would take a revolution in both Islamic government and its military before the same kind of force appeared among the Muslims. However, when it did occur, it was devastating to the Crusader states.

Ibn al-Athir gives us an introduction to the next Muslim encounter with the *Franj* and looks back at the history of Syria in the 1070s to make his point: 'The Fatimids of Egypt were afraid when they saw the Saljuqs extending their empire through Syria as far as Gaza, until they reached the Egyptian border and then [the Saljuqs] invaded Egypt itself. They therefore sent to invite the Franks to invade Syria and so protect Egypt from the [Sunni] Muslims.'†

Ibn al-Athir wrote for the family of the Sunni hero Nur al-Din and viewed history in the light of the Syrian Sunni jihad that had evolved by

---

* France, pp. 34–8.
† Gabrieli, p. 4.

the end of the twelfth century as the major challenge to the Franks. In fact, there is no evidence in the contemporary texts available to us that the Fatimid envoys who appeared in the Crusader camp in February 1098 proposed a division of the Saljuq possessions of Syria between the Crusaders and the Fatimids.* This said, it is feasible that the Fatimids would not have been displeased by the formation of a Latin state in *northern* Syria. Al-Azimi wrote that in 1095–6, 'the Byzantine Emperor wrote to [The Fatimids] informing them of the appearance of the Franks.'† The Fatimids may have tried to utilise this outside force in their strategy to meet the Saljuq threat. They were used to accounting for the presence of a 'third force' in Syria: Byzantine operations in northern Syria had been common in the eleventh century and the Fatimids were often apprised of their aims. The Fatimids also managed to retake Jerusalem and the southern Syrian seaboard from the Saljuqs, while their foes were distracted by infighting and by the Franks.

The most likely scenario is that the Fatimids' taking of Jerusalem in July 1098 was a reaction to the possibility of a Frankish assault on southern Syria, rather than being part of an agreement between Cairo and the Crusaders for a division of the Levant. The idea that the Fatimid assault on Jerusalem was directly related to Frankish success at Antioch is given credence by the treatment of these two events by al-Qalanasi in the *Damascus Chronicle*. In the chronicle, the writer describes the fall of Antioch in June 1098 and then immediately discusses the Fatimid *wazir* al-Afdal's taking of Jerusalem in July:

> He encamped before Jerusalem, where at that time there were two emirs and a large body of Turks, and he sent letters to them demanding that they should surrender Jerusalem to him without warfare or shedding of blood. When they refused his demand, he opened an attack upon the town, and having set up mangonels against it, which effected a breach in the wall, he captured it and received the surrender of the Sanctuary of David. Al-Afdal returned, then, with his *askari* to Egypt.‡

---

* This suggestion was made by Steven Runciman in his otherwise magisterial study, *A History of the Crusades. Volume One: The First Crusade and the Foundation of the Kingdom of Jerusalem*, Cambridge: Cambridge University Press, 1951, p. 139. The idea is untenable given the evidence available and given the fact that the Fatimids imprisoned Frankish envoys sent to Cairo in 1098.

† In Hillenbrand, p. 44.

‡ Al-Qalanasi, p. 45.

It may also have dawned on the Fatimid leadership during their talks with the Crusader princes that the *Franj* were not a Byzantine mercenary army that could be negotiated with. However, evidence of such an understanding of the Franks' motivation and intention is lacking in any existing contemporary Muslim written source. What we can be sure of is that the Crusader–Fatimid negotiations at Antioch were vital to the survival of the Crusader army at a time when it was in a weak condition, having just survived the winter and Ridwan's assault. Churchill famously claimed that, 'to jaw-jaw is always better than to war-war', and the Crusaders gained a valuable breathing space from potential Egyptian aggression at a stage when the Crusade was in danger of collapse. The most important aspect of the Fatimid reoccupation of Jerusalem and reassertion of control in southern Syria was that they did not have time to consolidate their grip on the region before it was wrested from them by the Crusaders in July 1099. Their campaign against the Turks ultimately benefited only the Franks.

Antioch was finally betrayed to the Franks after they paid a defender of one of the city's towers named Ruzbih or Firuz with 'a fortune in money and lands', as Ibn al-Athir would have it, to allow Bohemond's Normans to enter the city at a point near Saint George's Gate. The Normans infiltrated the tower overnight:

> Another gang of them climbed the tower with ropes. At dawn when more than five hundred of them were in the city and the defenders were worn out after the night watch, they sounded their trumpets. Yaghi Siyan woke up and asked what the noise meant. He was told that trumpets had sounded from the citadel and that it must have been taken. In fact the sound came not from the citadel but from the tower. Panic seized Yaghi Siyan and he opened the city gates and fled in terror, with an escort of thirty pages. His army commander arrived but when he discovered on enquiry that Yaghi Siyan had fled, he made his escape by another gate. This was of great help to the *Franj*, for if he had stood firm for an hour they would have been wiped out. They entered the city by the gates and sacked it, slaughtering all the Muslims they found there.*

This scapegoating of Yaghi Siyan and the commander is a little misleading. The Franks had made a diversionary attack on the citadel – this, added to the chaos created by Bohemond's troops raising their standards once inside the walls and screaming out 'Deus Lo Volt!',

---

* Ibn al-Athir in Gabrieli, p. 6.

practically ensured a panicked Muslim response. Armenian Christians inside Antioch had also turned on the Turkish garrison and after killing them had opened more gates for the Crusaders. In the light of this rapid collapse of the situation, Yaghi Siyan's 'desertion' doesn't seem so foolhardy or cowardly. He certainly paid heavily enough for it: his head was presented to the Crusaders by an Armenian some days later. Now only the citadel remained in Turkish hands, under Yaghi Siyan's son, Shams al-Dawla.

Another reason for the Antiochene Turks' collapse on the morning of 3 June 1098 was that they were expecting the imminent arrival of Karbuqa, the Turkish *atabeg** of Mosul, with a relief force. To combat this, Bohemond once again showed a level of acumen surpassing that of his contemporaries, when he arranged for a large part of the army to depart the siege on the afternoon of 2 June, ostensibly to meet the army of Karbuqa, which had been rumored to be arriving soon. Seeing this apparently put the garrison dangerously off its guard.

The Antioch garrison would also have been given a false sense of security by news of the size of the army Karbuqa was bringing with him. He was certainly prepared, unlike Duqaq and Ridwan, to commit an impressive force to the relief of Syria and, more importantly, to remain in the region and perhaps even attempt to annex northern Syria to his lands in the Jazira around Mosul. This would become a trend in the future, with Islamic princes launching both their assaults on the Crusaders and their attempts to carve out a Syrian empire for themselves from Mosul. Unfortunately, to obtain a force large enough to take on the Crusaders, Karbuqa had been forced to form a coalition that saddled him with potential competitors for any territorial gains in Syria. Forces were drawn from Damascus, Homs and Hama, as well as from Mosul.

Scouting parties arrived at Antioch on 5 June and there were immediate skirmishes with Crusader knights around the walls of the city. The main army had already taken the Iron Bridge just north of Antioch and had slaughtered its Crusader garrison. The Muslim army then camped three kilometres from the city and proceeded to try to make contact with the survivors of Antioch's garrison who still held the citadel, and to probe

---

* *Atabeg*, literally 'father-lord', was a guardian in the Turkish world, usually of a child prince. In reality, political power flowed through the *atabeg* and he commonly married the prince's mother to legitimise his rule. *Atabegs* also commonly supplanted the royal line with their own dynasty.

for weaknesses in the city's defences. They then settled on attempting to reduce the Crusader fort guarding the road to Saint Simeon, via which the Crusaders were receiving their supplies. Karbuqa sent a detachment of troops to tackle the garrison, and the converted mosque fell on 9 June. Its garrison retired to Antioch under furious pressure from Karbuqa's men. The capture of the fort allowed Karbuqa to then move to a full siege of the already famine-struck Crusaders. He had obviously received intelligence from the citadel that the Franks were in a severely weakened condition. Both Ibn al-Qalanasi and Ibn al-Athir record how the Franks were 'reduced to eating carrion', how 'the wealthy ate their horses . . . and the poor the leaves from the trees' and that an embassy was sent by the Crusaders to Karbuqa asking for safe conduct through his lands if they abandoned Antioch, to which he replied, 'You will have to fight your way out.'

By reinforcing the citadel and deploying troops on the slopes of Mount Silpius, Karbuqa now made his investment of the city complete. This, along with the danger of a breakout into the city from the citadel, forced the Franks into a direct attack on Karbuqa's camp, hoping to panic the Muslims into retiring from the siege. At first, this daring strike seemed successful, but Karbuqa was quickly able to organise and launch a counter-attack that both swept the *Franj* from his camp and resulted in a panicked stampede among the Crusader infantry back to the city gates, during which many troops were trampled to death. Attempting to build on this success, Karbuqa then launched a double-pronged assault on Antioch. Whilst troops made a sortie from the citadel, the Crusader defenders were also engaged by troops on the southern walls. The breadth of the attack was designed to stretch the Crusaders' reduced manpower. Some idea of the numbers of troops that Karbuqa committed to the fray is given by the Latin chroniclers who report endless waves of Muslim attackers entering the battle over the space of some four days and by the fact that Bohemond was prepared to sacrifice part of the city to fire, in an attempt both to prevent any more Crusader desertions in the face of seemingly overwhelming odds, and to deny the Muslims a wide front on which to attack. The defence was desperate, but it became clear to Karbuqa that attacking only the southern walls would not lead to the city's fall. He therefore pulled back from the assault on 14 June and re-deployed on an even larger section of the walls. However, this gave the Crusaders some respite – by giving them this small reprieve, Karbuqa broke one of the rules of siege warfare that al-Ansari describes as being key to the reduction of fortified places:

When the investment is under way there should be no pause in the discharging of the mangonels against them and there should be no abating of the amount of mangonel fire in any hour of the day or night. To desist in attack against them is among that which cools their fright and strengthens their heart.*

Obviously Karbuqa would not have known that the *Franj* would have their faith reinvigorated by an apparent miracle within the city, or that this would sustain both their resistance and their will to win, whatever the cost. As a non-military man, Ibn al-Athir can equally be excused for not appreciating what Napoleon certainly did: that 'the moral is to the physical as three to one.' His description of the unearthing of the Holy Lance of Longinus does not fully gather what this event meant in terms of the contest for the city, although, albeit cynically, he does suggest that this event was directly related to the Crusaders' decision to offer battle on 28 June:

There was a holy man who had great influence over them, a man of low cunning who proclaimed that the Messiah had a lance buried in [Saint Peter's Church] in Antioch. 'And if you find it you will be victorious and if you fail you will surely die.' Before saying this he had buried a lance in a certain spot and concealed all trace of it. He exhorted them to fast and to repent for three days, and on the fourth day he led them all to the spot with their soldiers and workmen, who dug everywhere and found the lance as he had told them. Whereupon he cried. 'Rejoice! For victory is secure!'†

There was no reason to expect any difficulty securing victory over the Franks. They were outnumbered and virtually without warhorses. However, Karbuqa had his own problems, relating to the composite nature of his force. It was unlikely to hold to an extended siege without desertions by many of the leaders who had brought their troops to his service. Ibn al-Athir also tells us that Karbuqa was a haughty leader who rapidly alienated the other princes. Therefore, it is feasible that Karbuqa wanted the Franks to risk an all-or-nothing battle. This would

---

* Al-Ansari in Scanlon, G., *A Muslim Manual of War*, Cairo: American University at Cairo, 1961.
† In Gabrieli, p. 8. Ibn al-Athir gives his description of the discovery of the holy lance and then moves straight on to the Battle of Antioch in his narrative. He has Karbuqa refusing the Franks safe passage before the 'miracle' of the holy lance. The Western sources place Karbuqa's denial of a negotiated retreat some time after the discovery, which seems odd given the electrifying effect the lance was supposed to have had on the Franks.

explain why Bohemond was given ample time to deploy his now largely infantry-based formations outside the walls of Antioch, and thereby gain the advantage of protection of his right flank by the River Orontes. He was even able to dispatch a detachment of infantry and cavalry to reach the high ground some two miles away to secure his left flank. Each detachment of Crusaders covered the column of the following detachment as it moved into line and linked up with the detachment on its left. Bohemond's planning was masterly, but there is little doubt that Karbuqa restrained his commanders from rushing upon the Franks. As Napoleon said, one should 'never interrupt your enemy when he is making a mistake'.

However, what Karbuqa failed to realise was that his strategy was being taken as cowardice by his allies. He also mistimed his main force's attack, so that it fell upon the Crusaders only after they had repulsed attacks from the Turkish contingents who had been guarding the south and west walls. If he had released his mounted archery as the attacks were being made by the 'wall garrisons' the battle could have been closed in classic Turkish fashion with the enemy destroyed by archery fire from all sides. As it was, Karbuqa's tardily dispatched force met the retreating forces of the gates headlong – this, added to the rapidly failing confidence of many of the emirs in their commander, was enough to cause a rout of the whole army. The fact that Karbuqa's army was never seriously engaged by the Crusaders, and that its flight from the field was precipitous, is evident from the few casualties it suffered and by its abandonment of its women and tents to the enemy. The citadel also fell rapidly to Bohemond's troops.

A crucial element of the Crusader victory at Antioch was the religious fervour that gripped the Crusaders. It would take a little longer for any such passion to be ignited within the Turkish military men of Syria, but the Crusaders were now moving on to meet a new foe, the Fatimids, who would press the Holy War against the invaders with all the strength they had.

~ 2 ~

Stirrings of a Response
Shiite Jihad and Sunni Expeditions

This is war,
And the man who shuns the whirlpool to save his life
shall grind his teeth in penitence.
This is war,
And the infidel's sword is naked in his hand,
Ready to be sheathed again in men's necks and skulls.
This is war,
And he who lies in the tomb at Medina
seems to raise his voice and cry: 'O sons of Hashim!'
*Al-Abiwardi, twelfth-century Iraqi poet**

Muslim resistance effectively collapsed following the Battle of Antioch and the Crusaders' route to Jerusalem was unimpeded. Only logistics and arguments between the Crusade's leaders delayed their advance on the city. Foraging parties went further and further abroad to secure foodstuffs and fodder. Some knights 'deserted' the cause of Jerusalem and went instead to Edessa to seek service with Baldwin of Boulogne. Baldwin had managed to wrest control of Edessa from its Armenian lord during a breakaway expedition from the Crusade in late 1097. His supplying of Armenian horses to the Crusaders before the Battle of Antioch and the three weeks that Karbuqa had wasted in besieging Edessa before moving on to Antioch had been crucial factors in the survival of the Crusade.†

---

* In Gabrieli, p. 12. 'He who lies in the tomb' is the Prophet Muhammad. 'The sons of Hashim' are his unworthy successors, the caliphs of twelfth-century Baghdad.
† Riley-Smith, J., *The Crusades: A Short History*, London: Athlone Press, 1990, p. 27.

A Crusader force also struck out towards Maarrat al-Numan. Its assaults on that city are interesting in a number of ways. First, the *Gesta Francorum* records how Christian Syrians aided the Crusaders during the siege of the city. 'Good will' such as this was soon squandered by the Franks through religious and racial intolerance. A Crusader letter to the pope sums up their perceptions, 'the heretics, Greeks, Armenians, Syrians and Jacobites we have not been able to overcome.'* This inability to integrate with the local Christians would later leave the Crusaders in the same position as the Saljuq Turks were in 1098 – isolated and unpopular rulers with little local support to draw on when they were under pressure.

The second noteworthy point about Maarrat is that a reputation of savagery preceded the Franks after the siege of Maarrat. Whatever occurred at Maarrat – and we are given the choice between Fulcher of Chartres's starved Franks turning to cannibalism or Ralph of Caen's children-devouring fanatics – Muslims from this point until the fall of Jerusalem seem to have genuinely feared the Franks and were reluctant to take them on. Fortified cities such as Homs and Tripoli appeased the Franks with fresh mounts and supplies. Of course there was also a degree of realpolitik in all this. As petty rulers, they could not stand alone against the Franks, and by aiding the Crusader march they effectively pushed them onto the Nahr al-Kalb, or Dog River, which marked the beginning of Fatimid lands. In fact there *was* resistance when the Franks refused to negotiate: as at the coastal city of Arqa, where the Franks' brutality – neatly summed up by a poet of Maarrat, 'I know not whether my native land be a grazing ground for wild beasts or yet my home . . .'† – was actually counterproductive. Clemency might have yielded better results in a region where the Turks were unpopular, even with Syrian Muslims.

The last point about Maarrat is that the first Crusader assault was soundly defeated by a force of isolated Aleppan troops, and that even when the Franks returned with hugely increased numbers, a hastily recruited city militia, who threw beehives upon their attackers as they scaled the walls, held the Franks at bay for some two weeks:

The inhabitants valiantly defended their city. When the Franks realised the fierce determination and devotion of the defenders, they built a wooden

---

* In Fink, H., *Fulcher of Chartres: A History of the Expedition to Jerusalem 1095–1127*, translated by F. Ryan, Tennessee: University of Tennessee Press, 1969, p. 111.
† In Maalouf, p. 37.

tower as high as the city wall and fought from the top of it, but failed to do the Muslims any serious harm. One night a few Muslims were seized with panic and in their demoralised state thought that if they barricaded themselves into one of the town's largest buildings they would be in a better position to defend themselves, so they climbed down from the wall and abandoned the position they were defending. Others saw them and followed their example, leaving another stretch of wall undefended, and gradually as one group followed another, the whole wall was left unprotected and the Franks scaled it with ladders. Their appearance in the city terrified the Muslims, who shut themselves up in their houses. For three days the slaughter never stopped . . .*

At Maarrat, up to a point, the townspeople had resisted the professional soldiers of the Crusade, and a small group of Turkish soldiers had fought alongside Arab townsfolk and peasants. The Arabs of the Levant had not been militarily significant since they had been removed from the state salary roll by Caliph al-Mutasim in the ninth century. Whilst Bedouin were wooed as allies by both Turks and Franks in the early twelfth century, the Arabs of the cities were viewed disparagingly by the Persian and Turkish professional soldiers of the region. These metropolitan Arabs formed the religious intelligentsia, or *ulama*, and provided the government with *qadis*, or religious judges. The most extensive military action they were involved in was the organisation of the *shurta*, or local police.† What would occur over the next few years, in terms of resistance to the Franks and a union between the Sunni *ulama* and Turkish military men, crystallised from the resistance at Maarrat.

The reluctance of the northern Syrian lords to attack them strengthened the Franks' spirits at a point when the Crusade was near collapse through disease. Typhoid fever killed fifteen hundred newly arrived troops and the important leader the bishop of Le Puy. The Fatimids showed an equal unwillingness to engage them. The Franks passed through numerous narrow valleys en route to Jerusalem in which they could have been halted by a small detachment of troops. The failure of the Fatimids to do so or to have a relief army moving to Jerusalem seems inexplicable, given that the *wazir*, al-Afdal, had received a letter from Emperor Alexius stating that the Crusade was no longer under Greek control and now had, as its

---

* Ibn al-Athir in Gabrieli, p. 9.
† 'It is astonishing how soon the Arabs fade out of Muslim history, Arabia itself excepted.' See Tritton, A. S., 'The Tribes of Syria in the Fourteenth and Fifteenth Centuries', *Bulletin of the School of Oriental and African Studies*, vol. 12, 1948, pp. 567–73.

exclusive goal, the capture of Jerusalem. The Fatimid garrison of Ramla, the last military post before Jerusalem, obviously knew what the Franks wanted; they abandoned their posts and fled before the Franks. The Crusaders reached the walls of the Holy City on 7 June.

Al-Afdal may have been confused by the fact that the Crusaders did not attempt to secure the coastal city of Jaffa before striking inland to Jerusalem. It had only the barest of defences and a small garrison, and would later play a key role during the Third Crusade's campaign for Jerusalem. It was impossible to hold Jerusalem without access to, and succour from, the sea, so perhaps al-Afdal felt he could allow the Crusaders to make the mistake of marching on Jerusalem and then simply cut them off in the middle of Palestine – he had reinforced Jerusalem's commander, Iftikhar al-Dawla, with another four hundred cavalry with which to slow the Crusaders' progress.

If this was his strategy then it was simply brushed aside by the courage and proficiency of the Crusaders. Iftikhar, like Yaghi Siyan before him, had prepared for the coming conflict by expelling many of the city's Christians and by spoiling all the local water sources. However, the Crusaders refused to repeat their mistakes at Antioch. Their thirteen hundred knights and twelve thousand men moved quickly to an all-out attack. Both the north and south walls were assaulted as early as 13 June. The Crusaders, in their fervour, did not even concern themselves with building siege towers and engines, and their first unsuccessful attack on the walls was carried out with only one ladder. They regrouped and were heartened by news that a Genoese fleet of only six ships 'took' Jaffa on 17 June by simply harbouring there and watching the port's garrison flee. The cargo and crew of this fleet were brought to the camp and a certain Genoese called William Embracio – whose clan we shall find right at the end of our story intriguing with the Mamluk sultans who brought Outremer to its end – was placed in charge of siege-engine production. A large Fatimid fleet arrived and retook Jaffa soon after.

By the second week of July, the Crusaders were ready with towers and ballistas, and they had filled the city's moat. The Fatimid garrison had been busy too, maintaining an archery assault on any Crusader brave or thirsty enough to approach the one unpoisoned spring beyond the walls, as well as upon any religious processions the Franks dared to attempt around the city's walls. They also secured bales of hay to the walls to lessen the shock of mangonel missiles and moved their own artillery to points where they expected the Franks' rams and towers to be applied.

On 14 July 1099 the attack began and Ibn al-Athir succinctly explains the mechanics of the city's fall. 'They built two towers, one of which, near Zion, the Muslims burnt down, killing everyone inside of it. It had scarcely begun to burn before a messenger arrived to ask for help and to bring the news that the other side of the city had fallen. In fact Jerusalem was taken from the north . . .'* The Crusader assault on the city had been planned as a simultaneous attack on both the north and south walls, but Godfrey of Bouillon, leading the north wall's forces had also outmanoeuvred the Fatimid defenders. Godfrey's tower had been swiftly dismantled during the night of 13 July and moved a kilometre down the walls from its original position. The Fatimids were unable to move enough artillery quickly enough to repulse Godfrey's attack effectively. That Godfrey's stratagem was a stroke of genius is evident from the fact that, two days later, the Fatimids were able to completely raze a tower that Raymond of Toulouse brought into action at the southern Zion Gate. Muslim forces were skilled in the use of *naft*, or 'Greek fire', and al-Tarsusi has left us some hints for its use:

> Melt the tar, add the fats, and then throw in the resin after having melted it separately. Then grind the other ingredients, each one separately, add them to the mixture, put fire under it, and let it cook until all is thoroughly mixed . . . take the pot, which should be earthenware, and a piece of felt. Then throw it with a mangonel against whatever you wish to burn. It will never be extinguished.†

But we need the Crusader Raymond of Aguilers to tell us what it was like to stand in the path of this firestorm:

> As the machines [of war] came close to the walls defenders rained down upon the Christians stones, arrows, flaming wood and straw and threw mallets of wood wrapped with ignited pitch, wax and sulphur, tow and rags on the machine. [This] kindled fires which held back those whom swords, high walls, and deep ditches had not disconcerted.‡

The Fatimid artillery men also managed to set fire to a vast battering ram, but it still destroyed the north-side curtain wall on 14 July. They failed, the next day, to torch Godfrey's tower, despite the use of a

---

* In Gabrieli, p. 11.
† In Hillenbrand, p. 528.
‡ In Raymond d'Aguilers's *Historia Francorum Qui Ceperunt Iherusalem*, translated by J. Hill and L. Hill, Paris: Bibliothèque National de France, 1969, p. 148.

'flamethrower' when the tower was within a sword's length of the inner wall – at this point the tower was too close for the wall-mounted mangonels to fire at it, and the piped and piston-driven fire-sprayer was the city's last artillery defence.

A section of the walls then went up in flame, as the Crusaders also employed fire as a weapon, and the northern wall's defenders panicked. Crusaders, under Godfrey's leadership, deployed from the tower and onto the walls. News of the breach caused a collapse of courage among the defenders of the southern wall too. Apart from a desultory resistance at the Temple Mount and the retiring of Iftikhar and his bodyguard to the Tower of David, from where they were able to negotiate their surrender and safe passage to the port of Ascalon, there was little else to interrupt the Crusaders' sack and slaughter.

Al-Afdal's tardy response to the Crusade's march on Palestine was too late to save Jerusalem. When the Crusaders captured some of his scouts on the coast north of Ascalon they also discovered where al-Afdal was gathering his troops; the Crusaders took the initiative and marched on the Fatimid port. The army that had been sent to eject them from Jerusalem should have been more than adequate: it met them in open country and outnumbered them two to one. There has been a general conception among historians that the Fatimid army was a declining force of ill-disciplined troops during the Crusades period. There is some truth in this, but the Fatimid armies that met the Crusaders in battle at the turn of the eleventh and twelfth century, despite some deficiencies, should have been capable of defeating the *Franj*. It was poor generalship, some lack of fortune, Frankish naval assistance and the fact that the Fatimids were always operating at a distance from their garrisoned lands of Egypt, and in an area consolidated by the Franks, that ultimately brought failure.

The army brought into Syria by al-Afdal was, as was common, ethnically mixed. Fulcher of Chartres described Ethiopians in the Fatimid Jerusalem garrison, but in fact the infantry were commonly Sudanese. A wing of Arab cavalry was deployed alongside heavier Turkish cavalry. Each unit had clearly defined tactical roles. The Fatimid army had been reduced from the hundred thousand men of the 1060s due to Egypt's shrinking fortunes. However, the army of the early twelfth century was, in fact, better for this downsizing: it was more professional and less tribally split, and was well provisioned, at least initially. A treatise by al-Tarsusi, though it was written for Saladin, shows how the Fatimid army was divided into distinct roles:

Place the infantry ahead of the cavalry to make a firm fortress. In front of every foot soldier place a kite-shaped shield or a screen as a protection against those who attack with sword, spear, or arrow. Behind each pair of men place an archer with a crossbow or with heavy bows and arrows. Their role is to drive back the attackers. The cavalry and heavy defensive cavalry to the rear are separated from danger by the archers. Meanwhile the offensive cavalry wait to deliver a charge. Troops are grouped together into units with a prearranged separation between them. These they open up as properly co-ordinated units, thus making a passageway for the cavalry charge. When the cavalry return from their charge, and flow back towards their point of departure, the infantry return to their original places, reassembling like the elements of a building. On the field of battle it is necessary to arrange the ranks gathered into squadrons of soldiers and with the cavalry grouped flag by flag and battalion by battalion. This should be done when it is the enemy's habit to charge in a mass and to rely for impact on separate detachments of their force, as is the case with the evil Frank Crusaders and those neighbours who resemble them. In fact the correct array is the essence of the disposition of battle and this disposition stupifies and embarrasses this sort of enemy because, when they launch their charge against one rank and come near to it, the other units can attack the enemy from both sides and so surround it.*

This all sounds highly effective in theory but battle is always a chancy business and there are no guarantees that the enemy will play his part in one's strategy. Al-Tarsusi suggests that the 'evil Franks' are a foe likely to be defeated by this particular battle plan. In fact, when the Fatimid army met the Crusaders on 12 August, just north of Ascalon, the Fatimids were roundly beaten. It is difficult to reconstruct the battle from the sources but the evidence available indicates that the Fatimid force was stationary and presented the perfect target – a fixed mass of men – for the Crusader charge, which turned their 'fortress' of troops into a chaotic shambles of panicking men. One charge was enough: 'pro solo impetus nostro', was recorded by Latin eyewitnesses. It seems that the Fatimids were caught out by the speed of the Crusaders' move to the charge. After so long fighting together, the Crusader knights would have been able to organise very swiftly behind an equally quickly formed wall of infantry. The Fatimid deployment would have taken far longer to organise and if it was incomplete this would have been another cause for their rapid defeat. Al-Afdal had also failed to set scouts, and the Crusaders' pre-

---

* From Cahen's original translation. See Nicolle.

dawn attack caught him unawares.* Al-Afdal had obvious failings as a general and this first defeat both set a pattern and gave the Crusaders time to consolidate their hold on Palestine and Syria.

The Fatimid army had been badly mauled. As a result of these losses and the fact that so many of the Fatimid troops had been slaughtered in their pell-mell retreat to Ascalon it was two years before the *wazir* would return with his army to attempt once more to push the *Franj* from Palestine. By this time Godfrey, the *advocatus* of the Holy Sepulchre, had died† and been replaced by king Baldwin of Jerusalem, formerly the lord of Edessa; the *Franj* had taken Jaffa, Hebron, Haifa, Arsuf and Caesarea. A major component of the early Latin consolidation was the construction of fortifications. Fortification effectively tackled many of the problems regarding manpower shortage that the Crusaders began to face as many of the knights and sergeants returned home to Europe, having completed their pilgrimage. Baldwin was 'offensive' in his building programme. His fortresses across the River Jordan were specifically designed to control the area around Damascus, threaten the agrarian economies of the Muslim lands and to impede the Egyptian caravan route.

Given the above Crusader expansion, the Fatimid *wazir* was left with little choice but to try to pen them in. His second expedition against them left Egypt in July 1101 under the emir al-Dawla. The army pushed on to Ramla in the hopes of taking and garrisoning it. This would cut Jerusalem off from Jaffa: it could then be besieged and pressured into submitting. That the Fatimid expedition began at Ascalon is no surprise tactically, as it was the last remaining Fatimid port in Palestine, and the fleet would be acting in support of the army during the operation. However, there is a second reason why Ascalon was important. The city held a shrine to the grandson of Muhammad, the Shiite imam Husayn, and the Fatimids most certainly viewed their war with the *Franj* as a holy war blessed by their imams. This has often been overlooked by historians

---

* Asbridge, T., *The First Crusade: A New History*, London: The Free Press, 2004, pp. 324–5.
† All the Muslim sources claim that Godfrey was killed by a Muslim arrow whilst besieging Acre. Western sources state that he died of an illness in Caesarea in June 1100. The change of title from *advocatus* to king was significant: Outremer slipped from the control of the church and became a kingdom with a throne, which would become the source of contest, factions and eventual divisions within the state.

since jihad is not a discrete act in Shiism as it is in Sunnism, but rather a constant doctrinal presence in the religion.

The army reached Ramla in September 1101 and was engaged by the Franks on the 7th of the month. It is likely that the Fatimid army took up the same deployment as it had in 1099. Its Berber cavalry was given free rein and was protected until it took the field by the massed infantry, archers and heavy cavalry. The Crusader force, which was small, divided its 260 knights into six squadrons, which were dispatched from behind a curtain of infantry into the Fatimid army as paired units. This time the Fatimid centre held and Fulcher of Chartres tells us that Baldwin had to ride with his last squadron into the massed ranks of the Muslims in order to break them. According to al-Qalanasi, the Fatimid army's left and right wings broke with the shock of this last charge, but al-Dawla held his centre together and came close to winning the battle through simple attrition. However, he was then killed and the army's resistance collapsed. The main Fatimid army was also let down by indiscipline from its Berber cavalry and by poor battlefield communications. The Berbers had ridden out wide during the early Crusader charges and had surprised the Franks' infantry line. They did extensive damage to the infantry but then left the battle and rode on to Jaffa, probably in search of loot. Their 'desertion' allowed Baldwin to launch his last charge without fear of encirclement, despite the fact that his supporting infantry had been ridden down.

It is possible of course that the Berbers just didn't feel capable of taking on the Crusader knights. They did not have the deadly archery fusillade of the Turks to rely on and they were not as heavily armored as the Franks or *askari* Mamluks. They carried a lance and sword only – it is notable that the Muslims' lances lengthened over the period of the Crusades, as if every Muslim soldier was reluctant to get within reach of the knights' two-handed battle swords. The Berber cavalry's reluctance to continue the fight was also symptomatic of the deep-rooted problems of the Fatimid military complex. There was both a lack of leadership and finance: Egypt had not fully recovered from the famine or *shidda* that had affected it from 1066 to 1073, and the revenues of Syria had now, of course, also been lost along with its *iqtas*. Low army morale and internecine arguments among its commanders over the remaining *iqta* allocations were common.

The Fatimids engaged the Crusaders again in May 1102 at Ramla under al-Afdal's son, Sharaf. They defeated Baldwin's small force but they were unable to dispatch enough of his army to make the victory immediately valuable. They also failed to take Jaffa, which made their victory a very hollow one. Once again, Baldwin had charged at the centre of the Fatimid force, but this time it had held firm and the Crusader charge shattered. Baldwin only survived his force's disintegration by riding from the field and hiding from pursuing Fatimid troops in a reed bed; he was badly burnt when the reeds were set on fire by his pursuers, but then escaped to Arsuf. Ibn al-Athir claims that the Fatimids could have moved on Jerusalem, but in fact marched on Jaffa in the hope of plunder. However, Baldwin still had a good number of troops in Jerusalem and had only committed a small number of the knights available to him to the battle, as he had underestimated the strength of the Fatimid force. Sharaf's decision to move against Jaffa was therefore tactical and not related to plunder, and the commander was unlucky to miss out on his prize due to the Latin infantry's fierce defence of the city. A Frankish fleet also broke through the Fatimid naval blockade of Jaffa and a bloody battle then broke out between the Fatimid army and its own fleet's marines. The Egyptian army managed to carry out a fairly wholesale slaughter of the survivors of the Battle of Ramla, but when Baldwin led fresh forces out from Jaffa and engaged Sharaf once more the Fatimid troops broke under his charge and fled the field. The retreat only ended at Ascalon.

Despite these problems, al-Afdal continued to confront the Franks with all the means at his disposal. He sent letters in 1102 to Damascus requesting the help of its army, 'for Muslim lands and for Muslim folk',[*] and he repeated these appeals in 1105, as he sought to form a united front with his Sunni enemies against the new foe. The new 'alliance' caused the Sunni al-Qalanasi to state that the Egyptian Shiites were engaged in 'Holy War' against the infidel.

Al-Afdal's diplomacy seemed to have paid off in August 1105, when once again he sent forces from Ascalon to Ramla. Saljuq troopers from Damascus came in support of his force and were almost enough to bring about victory. Baldwin had to drive these Turks from his army's rear, before moving forward to engage the Fatimids. He held the field at the end of the day but the victory was inconclusive, if bloody, as the Egyptians managed a well-ordered retirement to their redoubt of Ascalon. Fatimid *khila*, or robes of honour, were given to the leading men of Damascus: during this period the *khila* was a vow of *aman*, or protection, and by this

---

[*] Al-Qalanasi, p. 53.

act the Fatimids were stating that an understanding of mutual defence existed between the two states.

The Fatimids' war against the Crusaders was jihad, but it was unsuccessful on the battlefield. Even when they did gain the initiative, as at Ramla in 1102, any advantage was squandered away through their commanders' ineptitude. Command structures within the army were overly complex. Surviving documents, of which there are many, discuss in detail the various command levels in the army and the regalia attached to these individuals. There were 'emirs of the necklace' and of the 'golden chain'. The parades carried out in Cairo were far more dazzling than the army's display on the field of battle. Decadence seems to have replaced dedicated service and application to the military arts by the officer class. Fatimid raids on Crusader lands did, however, distract the Franks from their reduction of the coastal cities of Palestine and this should not be underestimated. Raiding, in a fragile agrarian economy such as Syria, was as likely to bring an area under control as was the winning of a pitched battle,* or at least make its continued occupation untenable. Combined with al-Afdal's Damascene diplomacy and the efforts of the Fatimid fleet, this was enough to keep at least some of the cities of the coast under Muslim control for the early part of the twelfth century.

This was no mean feat for the Fatimid navy. The coastal cities of Syria did not have their own warships, and the Turks' naval threat had been contained by the Byzantines following Alexius's massive naval rearmament program, which produced three fleets between 1090 and 1105.† The Fatimids had also lost Cyprus and Crete to the Byzantines and Sicily to the Normans before the Crusades period. These bases had held 'screening' naval forces that covered the maritime approaches to Syria and Egypt. Once they were lost, it became increasingly difficult to ensure the safety of the coast and to mount a counter-threat against Byzantine possessions.

The navy of the Almohad Sultanate of North Africa – numbering seven hundred vessels, the largest naval force in the Mediterranean

---

* Later the Mamluks would make it simply impossible for Crusader lords to hold onto territory by the simple expedient of inviting Turcoman tribes to settle in the area and repeatedly raid across it. For the importance of raiding in the Crusades period, see Gillingham, J., 'Richard I and the Science of War in the Middle Ages', in J. Gillingham and J. C. Holt (eds), *War and Government in the Middle Ages: Essays in Honour of J. O. Prestwich*, Woodbridge: Boydell & Brewer, 1984, pp. 78–91.
† Angold, M., *The Byzantine Empire 1025–1204: A Political History*, second edition, London: Longman, 1997, p. 134.

in this period – was never employed in the defence of the Holy Land. Egypt, therefore, fought the naval war single-handedly and still managed to maintain a concerted but onerous campaign until 1124.

After its failure at Jaffa in 1103, the Fatimid fleet scattered along the coast and brought succour to the besieged cities of Tyre and Acre. Acre, however, fell soon after under the combined attack of Raymond of Saint Gilles and Baldwin. The beaching on the Palestinian coast of twenty-five ships in a storm and the capture of their two thousand oarsmen in 1105 was a heavy blow to the navy, but it enjoyed success at Sidon in August 1108 against Baldwin's attempts to take the city. Baldwin had besieged the city in 1107 but the citizens had paid him off. However, the citizens' dinars only bought them a year's grace and Baldwin returned in 1108: he managed to close the harbour with ships as well as besieging the landward walls. He had nearly succeeded in bringing the city to surrender when the Fatimid fleet ran the blockade and brought relief to the city. This, combined with the arrival of Damascene troops – who had been promised thirty thousand dinars, twice the price that Baldwin had obtained – forced the Franks to retire.

The Fatimid fleet's heroics off Sidon, against a sizeable Genoese fleet, required its return to Egypt for repairs, and this meant that it was too late to save Tripoli from a Crusader joint operation involving Baldwin's army and a Genoese fleet in July 1109. The stores and provisioning for the fleet and for the city could not be made ready until the spring harvest, and then a contrary wind kept the fleet from reaching its destination. The fleet was trapped in Beirut's harbour and badly mauled during the city's fall in April 1110; it also failed to sail to Sidon's rescue in December 1110. Ibn al-Qalanasi tells us of Baldwin's final successful operation against Sidon:

> There had arrived in Syria from beyond the sea a fleet of sixty vessels, filled with men and provisions. The fleet was under the command of a king from among the Franks, who desired to visit the Holy City, and to make himself, as he believed, acceptable to God by making war against the Muslims. This king united with Baldwin, King of Jerusalem, and they arrived before Sidon. The city was pressed from sea and land. At this time the Egyptian fleet was detained at Tyre, and could not come to the assistance of the besieged. The Franks constructed a barricade of wood and made it very solid. They made it also proof against fire and against stones. Then they began their attacks. When the inhabitants saw this their courage failed, and they feared that they would have to endure the same fate as the inhabitants

of Beirut. They sent, therefore, the *qadi* of their city and several of their sheikhs as delegates to the Franks, and asked permission of their king to capitulate. The king promised safety for their lives, their possessions, and the troops of the garrison. Everyone was to be free to remain in the city or to depart from it. The king made these agreements under oath. Baldwin returned to Jerusalem, but a short time afterward he returned to Sidon and imposed upon the inhabitants of the city who had remained in their homes a tax of twenty-thousand dinars and thus impoverished them. They used force to extort money from those they knew to be concealing some.*

The Egyptian fleet was effectively defeated in the early part of the twelfth century, much as its land forces were. The reasons for this are not difficult to find. There was a superiority of numbers in the forces available to the Crusaders from the Italian maritime republics. Genoa's support for the Crusaders was almost guaranteed and in the early Crusades period it committed many vessels to the Holy Land. The republic's records indicate that Genoa had aimed to challenge the Venetians' dominance of the northern Mediterranean by the taking of bases in the south. Urban II's sermon was just the opportunity they were looking for. In the first thirteen years of the twelfth century, Genoa sent six armed fleets to Syria, and at times up to sixty galleys were available to the King of Jerusalem to aid his assaults on the coastal cities. The Genoese gained a share of much of the Crusaders' conquests on the Syrian coasts and secured much of Outremer's trade. They were the first of the maritime republics to be granted a city quarter – in Antioch in 1098 – and were also rewarded with churches, warehouses and shares of taxes and customs duties.†

It must be remembered that there was no such thing as naval supremacy per se during the time of the Crusades. Control of the sea meant rather control of the coast and ports. No galleys of this period could stay at sea long enough or had sufficient offshore range to patrol the open sea effectively or effect a true naval blockade and thereby claim 'ownership' over the eastern Mediterranean. Also, the Mediterranean has a strong current that runs from west to east, along the African shore, which, along with prevailing winds largely from the north, would have made its eastern shores a constant danger to vessels of this period – none

---

* In Gabrieli, pp. 27–8.
† Byrne, E. H., 'Genoese Trade with Syria in the Twelfth Century', *American Historical Review*, January 1920, pp. 191–219.

of which could tack into the wind. Under oar-power these ships could only make an average speed of about two knots (two nautical miles per hour) and the large crews of galleys had to be fed and supplied with water.* Therefore if land forces controlled the ports or islands, then their fleets could effectively control the crucial offshore waters.

The Crusaders began their campaign against Antioch by the reduction of Saint Simeon; they were supplied via Byzantine-controlled Cyprus and worked hard at taking the Muslim coastal cities of Syria. This was a wise policy and it paid them dividends, both in terms of supplies and largely neutralising the effectiveness of the Fatimid fleet. Also the Muslim-held cities of the coast could be dominated from the sea by the Genoese once Jaffa was established as a Crusader port. This explains why Sharaf turned away from Jerusalem in 1102, and attempted to take Jaffa. The ports were the key to Italian dominance of the coastal waterways.

The ships of the Italian maritime republics were superior to the Muslim vessels of the early twelfth century and they could be produced faster as new shipbuilding technology, which built the ship from a frame of ribs and spars, had been developed in Italy. Egyptian ships continued to be built by the more laborious planking method – the depleted resources of Egypt, as well as a lack of raw materials, precluded any chance of the Fatimids winning a naval arms race.† It also appears that, during this period, the Italians were better sailors than the Muslims. The Fatimids never developed a separate ministry for the upkeep of the fleet and, perhaps more importantly, for training captains. The fleet came under the *diwan al-jihad*, or department of war, and it was only when Saladin came to power in Egypt that a *diwan al-ustal*, or department of the navy, was created. Without an active admiralty, the navy lacked leadership and an *esprit de corps*. Contemporary Muslim writers consistently excuse the navy's tardy arrival at the scene of fallen Muslim cities, but there is a detectable undercurrent in the chronicles that the Fatimid navy was lacking in courage. Low morale, low pay and the fact that rowers for the galleys were press-ganged and not volunteers were all likely causes. Generally the Fatimids would not sail in winter, unlike the Italians, and

---

* See Pryor, J. H., *Geography, Technology and War: Studies in the Maritime History of the Mediterranean 649–1571*, Cambridge: Cambridge University Press, 1988.
† See White, L. Jr, 'The Crusades and the Technological Thrust of the West', in V. J. Parry and M. E. Yapp (eds), *War, Technology and Society in the Middle East*, Oxford: Oxford University Press, 1975, pp. 97–112.

the very occasional capture of Italian transports by Fatimid raiding patrols was treated as a great event on the streets of Cairo.*

In the autumn of 1111, Baldwin besieged Tyre. An army under Tughtigin, the Turkish *atabeg* of Damascus, responded by raiding Frankish lands around Banyas and then crossed the Jordan and took a Frankish fortress. Tughtigin was trying to draw the Crusaders away from their siege because Tyre was the last viable trade port for Damascus – he had been offered the city as a prize for rescuing it from the Franks by its governor. Baldwin's stubborn work at Tyre's walls continued, despite Tughtigin's pillaging, and when the Franks built two siege towers Tughtigin was forced to commit to an attack to distract them and to give the city's garrison a chance to attempt to torch the towers using incendiaries. The Franks dug in and were able to both successfully repel the Damascenes and protect the towers from fire. Tughtigin then destroyed a bridge on the road that linked Baldwin's army to Sidon; when the Franks tried to bring supplies by ship from Sidon to their army at Tyre, he took a section of his army up to the coast north of the city and burnt the supply ships while they lay drawn up on the shore.

In February 1112, on the first day of Ramadan, the garrison made a sortie and attempted to raze the towers once more with Greek fire, wood and pitch. The shorter of the two towers eventually flared up and burnt down. The second tower caught fire too, but the Franks were able to put it out. A stalemate persisted until the end of the holy month, and then the Franks made another attempt with their remaining tower, but came up against a highly enterprising sailor:

> Then an officer of the fleet from Tripoli, an experienced, intelligent and observant man, thought of making iron hooks to pinion the heads and sides of the rams when they struck the wall, by means of ropes guided by men from the wall, so that the pull on them caused the tower to heel over. The Franks were forced to cut down some of the rams for fear of destroying the tower. At other times the rams would bend and break, and at other times they were smashed to pieces by two boulders roped together and flung from the walls.
>
> Again and again the rams were repaired and the tower brought up to the wall again. Then the sailor invented another weapon. A long beam of unseasoned timber was set up on the wall in front of the tower. At the top of it forming a T-bar was another long beam swung on pulleys worked by

---

* See Lev, Y., *State and Society in Fatimid Egypt*, Leiden: Brill, 1991, pp. 110–20.

a winch in the manner of a ship's mast. At one end of the pivoting beam was an iron spar, and at the other end ropes on a pulley, by means of which the operators could hoist buckets of dung and refuse and empty them over the Franks working in the tower, and so prevent their working the rams.

Then the sailor had baskets filled with oil, pitch, wood shavings, resin and cane bark, set on fire and hoisted up, in the manner described, to the level of the Frankish tower. The flames caught the top of the tower, and as fast as the Franks put them out with vinegar and water, the Muslims hurried to send over more fire buckets; they also poured small vessels of boiling oil over the tower to feed the flames.*

The fire spread and burnt the tower to the ground; Tyre's garrison then made a further sortie and this was enough to make the Franks withdraw. They burnt their encampment and many more of their ships that had been beached as protection against the winter storms. The Crusaders retired to Acre and the Damascenes withdrew. The people of Tyre repaired their walls in readiness for the inevitable return of the Franks.

Ibn al-Athir tells us that Tughtigin departed Tyre with the words, 'I did what I did for the love of God and his Muslims, not in hope of money and power' – by this point in the twelfth century, both he and his Turkish cousins in Syria and Anatolia had done a great deal more harm to the Crusader cause than the Fatimids had been able to do.

The first major success against the Crusaders came in June 1100, with the capture of *Baimand*, as the Arabic sources call Bohemond. He was besieging Afamiya and was laying waste to its farmland, when Danishmend – the Turkish lord we last met distracting Kilij Arslan from the siege of Nicaea – brought him to battle. Bohemond and his knights were caught in a hailstorm of arrows in a narrow defile and he was captured. The principality of Antioch took this in its stride and Bohemond's nephew, Tancred, took up the reins of power in March 1102. Bohemond would be ransomed and later released, but his subsequent endeavours were almost exclusively aimed at his old enemy, the Byzantines. His removal from the north Syrian theatre meant the loss of one of the Franks' best generals and hampered any concerted attempt to consolidate the lands between Antioch and the exposed outpost of Edessa. The Crusaders' failure to achieve this amalgamation during this early period of Turkish disunity

---

* Ibn al-Qalanasi in Gabrieli, pp. 30–5.

would become highly significant once the princes of Mosul began to take a serious interest in the affairs of northern Syria.

There had also been serendipitous news of the death of Godfrey, but an opportunity had been missed by Duqaq of Damascus in October 1101 to ambush the new king, Baldwin, as he travelled from Edessa to Jerusalem. Another key player, Raymond of Saint Gilles, departed the Holy Land for Constantinople.

Real success came in the summer of 1101. Kilij Arslan 'dispersed, confounded and almost totally destroyed the army of the Franks'.* This new army of Crusaders, reported to be some hundred thousand strong, had left Constantinople under the direction of Saint Gilles. The first 'wave' of this army took the city of Ankara and then advanced across Anatolia. Kilij Arslan's destruction of this force, which was very short of knights, took place near a small village named Merzifun. The ground suited the Turks as it was open and flat. It had taken several days of hit-and-run raids on the column and the poisoning of wells to steer the Crusaders to the killing field. The battle then developed over several days. The Crusaders were halted by a frontal archery assault and then surrounded. Kilij Arslan had assembled an impressive confederation of princes under him, which included Ridwan of Aleppo and Karaja of Harran. The Crusaders attempted a breakout, which failed, and they had to take refuge in a fortified village. On the fourth day the desperate Crusaders made a final effort to break the encirclement but this too was unsuccessful and, at the end of a day of slaughter, Saint Gilles and the senior knights fled the field – they saved themselves but the Turks assaulted the Christian camp and decimated the remaining infantry.

Kilij Arslan repeated his success against a second army under the command of Count William of Nevers, although the count made it easier for him due to his naiveté and tactical blunders. The Crusaders set out from Ankara and went south on a direct route for Jerusalem. This took them across the harsh dry lands of central Anatolia, which severely weakened them. They were unable to take Iconium and pressed on to Heraclea, which was a worthless prize: Kilij Arslan had poisoned every water source and left nothing in the city. The pilgrimage now became a death march as the army struggled through the desert. Then Kilij Arslan struck. The infantry was abandoned by its knights and was rapidly annihilated. Numerous women and children were enslaved. The

---

* Fulcher of Chartres, in Fink, p. 165.

knights who had fled the battle were then duped by local guides, who left them out in the desert.

Kilij Arslan completed his atonement for the failures of Nicaea and Doryaleum when he crushed a third Crusader army. This army, led by William of Aquitaine, arrived at Heraclea in September 1101. This time the knights did not abandon their infantry, but this made no difference and only William and a handful of companions escaped the debacle.

Some Latin chroniclers suggest that Emperor Alexius had informed the Turks of the Crusade's progress and there may be a germ of truth in this. Maintaining the balance of power between the Turks and the Crusaders was a key strategic point if he was to maintain a Byzantine presence in Anatolia – an important source of both taxes and recruits for the army – and to reclaim his north Syrian possessions. Alexius also used the threat of the Franks in his negotiations with the Turks. Ibn al-Qalanasi wrote that Alexius, in an embassy to Baghdad in 1111, claimed to have so far impeded the Franks but that this impediment would cease if there was no effective Muslim response to the Latin advances. It is notable that a Muslim expedition was organised from Baghdad shortly after this.

The death of these great armies was hugely important in the grand theatre of the Levant, as it starved the Crusaders of reinforcements. Edessa was so short of manpower that it turned to the Armenians for alliance. It also meant that the Italian republics increased their power in the Levant as they supplied both men and materiel across safe sea routes. After the conquest of Tyre in 1124, the Venetians took a third of the city as their share. By 1131, Pisa had also established its own little colony.

Despite Kilij Arslan's successes, there was no organised offensive against the Crusader states in the north, but this is not surprising. There was still the question of ongoing short-lived coalitions, which broke up as soon as their objective was obtained; also, at this juncture, Anatolia was still geopolitically linked with Iraq rather than with Syria. Indeed, a policy of détente with the Anatolian Turks might have served the Crusaders' interests better whilst they were subduing the Palestinian coastal cities, but just as there was little unity of purpose on the Muslim side in this period, so there was also a profound lack of any overarching strategic vision among the Franks. The King of Jerusalem's influence over the princes of Antioch and Edessa was not absolute but more like a *primus inter pares*.

It was Latin rather than Turkish aggression that got Antioch and Edessa into trouble in 1104. Tancred frequently laid waste the land from

Antioch's borders up to the walls of Aleppo, and humiliated Ridwan by forcing him to place a crucifix on the minaret of the great mosque. Bohemond was released for ransom by Danishmend and the raiding increased and widened. An agreement was made between Antioch and Edessa to reduce the city of Harran; this would then effectively encircle Aleppo. The timing was perfect as Karbuqa, the *atabeg* of Mosul, had just died and his successor, Jekermish, had not yet fully consolidated his authority and was at war with his neighbor, Suqman. The threat from the Franks, however, drove the two emirs into a union and they met the Crusaders in battle on the River Balkh in May 1104. They feigned retreat and, after a long pursuit of an apparently beaten enemy, the Franks were surrounded and massacred. Ibn al-Athir tells us that:

> Bohemond of Antioch and Tancred of Galilee were at some distance from the main body of the army, hidden by a hill from which they were to fall on the Muslims from the rear at the height of the battle. When they emerged they found the Franks in flight and their land being pillaged. They waited for nightfall and then retreated, followed by the Muslims, who killed and captured many of their number. Bohemond and Tancred, with six knights, escaped to safety. Baldwin of Edessa fled with a group of his counts. They made for the River, but their horses stuck fast in the mud and they were captured by a group of Suqman's Turcomen.*

Bohemond had obviously continued with his tactic, developed during the First Crusade, of maintaining a rearguard for late deployment in the battle, to prevent the Franks being surrounded. Here, however, it seems that the Turks moved too quickly for the stratagem to be utilised. Baldwin of Edessa remained in prison for five years until he was released by the new lord of Mosul, Jawali. Baldwin then immediately disputed Tancred's possession of Edessa and the two aimed to settle the dispute by force of arms. Both drew Turkish allies to their respective sides: Baldwin lined up with his erstwhile jailer, Jawali, along with Joscelin of Tel-Bashir, while Tancred drew Ridwan of Aleppo to his side. Tancred and his Aleppan allies defeated Baldwin, but Edessa was nonetheless returned to Baldwin after church-sponsored arbitration. Jawali lost Mosul over the affair: he was removed from power by an expedition sponsored by the great sultan in Baghdad. Ridwan had fought with Tancred through fear of a possible

---

* In Gabrieli, pp. 18–20. This 'new' Baldwin of Edessa was the cousin of the first Baldwin of that city. To add to the confusion he would later succeed Baldwin I as King of Jerusalem.

extension of Mosul's power – now he found himself in fear of the 'grand emir' Tancred, and of Baghdad.

Realpolitik broke out in Damascus and Ascalon as well: trade and agricultural rights treaties had been made between King Baldwin and both cities by 1111. The Franks were aligning themselves to Syrian politics, and Syrian Muslims started to accept the Crusader kingdom as a, perhaps unpleasant, but all too real, fact. The next stage of the Islamic 'response' to the Crusaders would come from Baghdad.

The wars over possession of Baghdad had finally burnt themselves out with the death of Sultan Berkyaruq and the absence of any further challengers to Sultan Muhammad's reign. There had also been large-scale protests in Baghdad that had included dragging the imam from his *minbar*, or pulpit, in the main mosque and then smashing it to pieces.* These were organised by *ulama* from Aleppo and refugees from Syria. However, it is clear that the sultan's expedition of 1111 was designed chiefly to regain dissident former possessions such as Aleppo and Damascus, rather than to seek revenge for the refugees on the Franks. Ridwan therefore closed the gates of Aleppo to Mawdud, the new governor of Mosul and Muhammad's general, and the sultan's army destroyed the countryside surrounding Aleppo to a far greater extent than the Crusaders had ever done. Nothing else was achieved and Joscelin of Tel-Bashir was even able to bribe some of the senior emirs to expedite the disintegration of the whole venture.

Mawdud returned in 1113 with orders to bring all the emirs of Syria together to launch an assault on the *Franj*, but the order deliberately excluded Aleppo from this union of Muslims. Mawdud established himself in Damascus, which was under the rule of Tughtigin. Tughtigin, being an *atabeg*, was effectively a ruler without a diploma from the caliph, and this lack of legitimacy probably forced him to accept Mawdud into Damascus, since the sultan effectively controlled the caliph. Tughtigin would also, however, have remembered how Jawali had lost Mosul in much the same circumstances in 1108.

Tughtigin need not have worried. Mawdud fell to the daggers of the Ismaili Assassins while he was leaving the great mosque, and the expedition disintegrated. The murder was almost certainly sponsored by

---

* This was a powerful political statement, as the *minbar* represented the sultan's power and the *khutba*, or invocation, of the sultan's name was made from it during Friday prayers in the main mosque of the city.

Ridwan of Aleppo* but Tughtigin's complicity cannot be ruled out. His actions during the 1113 expedition do not entirely match the actions of a man committed to winning all of Syria back for the Sultan of Baghdad.

The expedition had left Damascus for Tiberias. They met a force under the command of King Baldwin and Roger of Antioch, who had succeeded Tancred after his death in December 1112. In a very confused battle the Franks were defeated by three Muslim charges across the bridge of al-Sinnabrah. However, after the battle the forces of Damascus did not march on with the army of Mosul to attempt the capture of any towns: they concentrated on plundering the environs of Jerusalem and Jaffa instead. The lord of Damascus was evidently happy to see the Franks 'reined in' but he was reluctant to see Mawdud gain a foothold in the region by taking fortified towns from the Crusaders.

The sultan's final expedition set out in 1115. This time Damascene resistance to Baghdad's reach was overt. Damascus, Aleppo and Antioch allied against the sultan's forces. The sultan's commander, Bursuq, pushed towards Antioch, but Roger had mobilised early – Edessa had once again been an effective listening post for the Crusaders. Roger was west of Aleppo before the sultan's force was very far advanced in its march. Here he met the forces of Aleppo and Damascus, as well as those of Il-Ghazi of Mardin. Their forces descended to Afamiya, from where they could cover any advance by Bursuq against Aleppo, Damascus or Antioch; Roger also sent to Jerusalem for assistance. Bursuq moved against Hama and then made camp at Shayzar. Baldwin arrived with the armies of Jerusalem and Tripoli.

Bursuq moved against Roger's camp but when Baldwin's arrival was reported Bursuq retreated west; this withdrawal and Bursuq's treatment of his junior emirs weakened his force. There were desertions, and when the commander took the field again his force was under strength. Roger took the field without his Muslim allies – with only the support of Edessa, he met Bursuq in battle at Tal Danith on the Orontes. Bursuq's forces were watering their horses when they were attacked: they were completely surprised and decisively beaten. For the Syrian-Turkish princes, the campaign's result was that the status quo ante was restored and they remained free of interference from Baghdad. Usama Ibn-Munqidh, an

---

* For a full account of Ridwan's reliance on the Assassins in Aleppo, the murder of Mawdud and the sect's destructive impact on the politics of Syria in the early twelfth century, see Waterson, *The Ismaili Assassins*, Chapter Four.

Arab warrior of Shayzar, did not appear at all surprised or outraged by the 'stratagem by the governor of Aleppo' of allying with Roger.* The Saljuqs of Iraq made no more attempts to bring Syria back into the Great Saljuq fold and they ostensibly abandoned Syria to its fate.

Damascus, despite its treaties with Jerusalem and its participation in the pact against Bursuq, in fact continued to resist the Franks strongly in southern Syria. Tughtigin took on a protective occupation of Tyre in 1112 and his forces fought alongside the Fatimids at Ascalon in 1118. Meanwhile, in Aleppo, Ridwan had died and his son, who was somewhat unhinged, had been murdered by his guardian. Chaos had ensued but then the *qadi*, al-Kashab, and the leader of the city militia moved quickly to eliminate the Ismaili Assassin sect – whom Ridwan had been favouring – from the city and to invite Il-Ghazi, the governor of Mardin, to take over. However, it was not so much Il-Ghazi's experience as a soldier and leader that was of major significance – it was rather that, as at Maarrat and at Tripoli, the Sunni leaders of the *ulama* had taken control of a key resistance point to the *Franj*. A *qadi*'s religious authority was largely subordinated to the political authority of his Saljuq governor. Therefore calls for jihad from the *ulama* were always likely to fail against the indifference of a Turkish hegemony that had a strong disdain for the non-military intelligentsia. The difference here was that jihad was a perfect stalking horse for the territorial ambitions of a prince like Il-Ghazi, who was now free of fear of interference from Baghdad. Roger of Antioch was beginning a siege of Aleppo as Il-Ghazi arrived in the city. The *ulama* of the city therefore made immediate calls for the whole city to follow them, along with Il-Ghazi, in jihad against the Crusaders. It was just the stirrings of a response, but a start had been made.

---

* In Hitti, p. 105.

~ 3 ~

The Pen and the Sword
Jihad in Northern Syria

A man came to Allah's Messenger and said, 'guide me to such a deed that equals jihad.'

Muhammad replied, 'I do not find such a deed', and then he added, 'but can you while the Muslim fighter has gone for jihad, enter the mosque and pray without cease and observe a fast and never break your fast?'

The man said, 'but who can do that?'

Hadith, The Book of Jihad

Il-Ghazi concluded a hurried marriage ceremony with Ridwan's daughter and with his legitimacy thus secured, he began to gather his troops and Turcoman auxiliaries for a confrontation with Roger, who was racking up the pressure on Aleppo, confident that its internal troubles would make it easy prey. Kamal al-Din, writing in the 'post-Saladin' thirteenth century – when a lore of jihad had spread, complete with attendant myths, among the princes of Syria – tells us that:

> Il-Ghazi made his emirs swear that they would fight bravely, that they would hold their positions, that they would not retreat, and that they would give their lives for the jihad. The Muslims were then deployed in small waves, and managed to take up night-time positions alongside Roger's troops. At daybreak the *Franj* suddenly saw the Muslim banners approach, surrounding them on all sides. The *qadi*, Ibn al-Khashab advanced astride his mare, and gestured with one hand urging our forces into battle. Seeing him one of our soldiers shouted contemptuously, 'have we come all the way from our home country to follow a turban?' But the *qadi* marched towards the troops, moved through their ranks, and addressed them, trying to rouse their energy and lift their spirits, delivering a harangue so eloquent

that men wept with emotion and felt great admiration for him. Then they charged. Arrows flew like a cloud of locusts.*

Kamal al-Din's hyperbole aside, it is evident that something had changed. Whether it was the new feeling of independence from Baghdad that the princes of northern Syria had, or the union of the pen and the sword that had crystallised in Aleppo, there is a definite alteration in the way these events are recorded by the chroniclers. Commonly, Arab writers of this time differentiated between Turks and Muslims, but this practice almost ceases with Il-Ghazi's first triumph. Muslim victories are also written about in more detail and with greater accuracy, as if the writers are also engaged with the warriors' deeds, just as the *ulama* were.† Of course, to quote Count Ciano, 'victory has a hundred fathers but defeat is an orphan', and as Leo the Wise determined about Muslim armies of earlier times in the *Taktika*, '[They] enjoy war and are accompanied by many "priests".'‡ In brief then, the union was formed because the men of the pen had incited jihad against the *Franj*, the princes took on the Holy War for earthly reasons and this partnership was mutually beneficial. Of course, with success came both greater belief and a greater involvement of each party in the venture, and there was already a pre-existing tradition of the same arrangement from the Golden Age of Islam and the early conquests. The writers, who almost exclusively came from the *ulama*, proclaimed the deeds of their heroes, thus creating a 'lore' and, like every writer, also enjoyed the reflected glory of their champions.

If the above seems cynical then the antidote to such scepticism is the account of Ibn al-Qalanasi, who shows what this new union could achieve:

The Muslims charged down upon them and encompassed them on all sides with blows of swords and hails of arrows. God most high granted victory to the party of Islam against the impious mob, and not one hour of the day had passed ere the Franks were on the ground, one prostrate mass, horses and footmen alike, with their horses and their weapons, so that not one man of them escaped to tell the tale, and their leader Roger

---

* Maalouf, p. 93.

† In this early period we are heavily reliant on religious men writing of the deeds of the Turkish warriors. Needless to say, their knowledge of, and even interest in, *re militari* is negligible. Only later in the Mamluk period do we get consistent information from military men.

‡ From the *Taktika*, translated by M. Joly de Mazeroi, in Nicolle.

was found stretched out among the dead. A number of the eyewitnesses have related that they saw some of the horses stretched out on the ground like hedgehogs because of the quantity of arrows sticking into them. This victory was one of the finest of victories, and such divine aid was never granted to Islam in all past ages.*

The writer then returns to day-to-day reality when he records how Il-Ghazi was unable to follow up on this victory as his Turcomen scattered for plunder. Virtually nothing more was achieved, though arguably the destruction of Antioch's field army was in itself enough. The Battle of Ager Sanguinis, or 'Field of Blood', as it became known in the West – for the Muslims, the Battle of Sharmada – severely damaged the military power of Antioch and cast doubt on the continued existence of Edessa, as it was now a precariously exposed outpost of Outremer. Il-Ghazi's victory effectively placed the frontier zone between Antioch and Aleppo. Added to this was the fact that Roger's death then set off a protracted succession crisis in Antioch.†

It was only the generalship of the new King of Jerusalem, Baldwin II, that averted a greater disaster for the Franks. He mobilised quickly and marched to the region. Il-Ghazi managed to besiege and take the castle of Zerdana before the forces of Jerusalem arrived, and Baldwin II therefore decided to retire to Hab on 14 August 1119. Il-Ghazi dispatched troopers to harass the retreating army; the Crusaders were in column when Il-Ghazi's force made a major assault on the marching infantry, just as they had at Sharmada. They had won the archery duel against the Frankish infantry at the previous battle, and they took a heavy toll of the footsoldiers now as well. They also managed to rout the right flank of knights that were covering the column. This again was not dissimilar to what they had been able to do at Sharmada, where the remaining Franks had been made up of Turcopole mercenaries‡ who were shattered by the first Turkish charge. The Crusader left flank guard did manage to repel the Turkish assault just as their right flank had at Sharmada, but in both battles this was not significant as the

* Al-Qalanasi, pp. 160–1.
† See Asbridge, T., 'The Significance and Causes of the Battle of the Field of Blood', *Journal of Medieval History*, 1997, vol. 23, no. 4, pp. 301–16.
‡ Turcopoles, Turcoman mercenaries who were sometimes converted to Christianity, were used extensively by the Byzantines, but also by the Crusaders to fill manpower shortages.

real action was the enveloping of the Franks by swift Turkish riders. At Sharmada this was what had destroyed the Crusader army – Roger had failed to follow Bohemond's tactics and had no rearguard held back. His reserve had been deployed too early and exhausted itself in attacking a disappearing foe on the right flank. This time, however, Baldwin II had a squadron held in reserve and he was able to use this to meet attacks both in the van and in the rear of his surrounded army; Il-Ghazi's troops had to break off the attack.

Il-Ghazi died of alcoholic cirrhosis in 1122. His son briefly took the throne before being ousted by his cousin Balak, who finally ejected the last of the Ismaili Assassin sect from the city. The history of the sect as a real force in Aleppan politics was at an end. After thus charming his Sunni subjects, Balak gave them something else to cheer when he captured Joscelin, the new count of Edessa, near the city of Saruj. Then, in 1123, he went one better: Baldwin II was captured near the walls of Edessa. Both men were held in the fortress of Kharput. Joscelin was rescued by Armenians disguised as monks and then daringly crossed the Euphrates on inflated wineskins, but Baldwin II failed to escape and remained a captive.

Unfortunately for the Muslims, and in particular for the people of Tyre – from whom he had just received an appeal for aid against the Crusaders' tightening siege – Balak was killed in 1124. He was at Manbj, besieging a rebel emir, and while he was inspecting his forward mangonels he was hit by an arrow shot from the fortress. He pulled it from his neck but with the words, 'That blow will be fatal for all the Muslims', he fell dead. His rule, however, though short, was quickly woven into the lore of jihad that was continuing to grow in northern Syria and in the Jazira. Inscriptions and writings of the period reflect this. Balak's cenotaph is inscribed with his deeds in the Holy War, and contemporary writers tell us of warriors who 'bravely make it their duty to fight with heroism . . . they spill their blood for the Holy War'.*

Baldwin II obtained his freedom after the payment of a ransom to Timurtash, a second son of Il-Ghazi and Balak's successor in Aleppo. Baldwin II repaid him by gathering Bedouin allies and besieging Aleppo

* Al-Adim in Sivan, E., *L'Islam et la Crosaide: Ideologie et Propagande dans le Reactions Musulmanes aux Croisades*, Paris: Librairie D'Amerique et D'Orient, 1968, p. 41. English translation by M. McCrystall.

while Timurtash was in Mardin. Once again the 'turban' Ibn al-Khashab stepped into the breach and conducted the defence of the city. Having failed to summon help from Timurtash, he sent instead to al-Bursuqi, the governor of Mosul; the arrival of al-Bursuqi and his forces at Aleppo was enough to make Baldwin hurriedly retire in January 1125.

Al-Bursuqi took peaceful possession of Aleppo, a city he had tried to take by force in 1118, and then began to threaten Edessan territory. Baldwin II gathered an army and set out to protect his erstwhile cellmate Joscelin and his lands. The Turkish army met Baldwin II and Joscelin at the Battle of Azaz on 13 June 1125. They were unable to loose their arrows before they were engaged by the Crusaders and were drawn very rapidly into a close-quarters fight with lance and sword that they were not capable of winning. Baldwin II had also summoned troops from Tripoli, Antioch and Jerusalem, and his command numbered about eleven hundred knights and two thousand infantry. Al-Bursuqi was defeated, and Baldwin II beat him yet again at Marj al-Suffar in January 1126. However, in this second encounter the Turks were able to inflict severe damage on the Crusaders with their archery before Baldwin II managed to organise a charge that closed the battle. Al-Bursuqi was killed by an Ismaili Assassin shortly after as he left the great mosque in Mosul – Ibn al-Khashab had suffered the same fate the summer before outside Aleppo's great mosque.

Aleppo was politically rudderless once again. Assassination was a potent political weapon in the medieval period, as so much in the political arena depended on individuals and their actions. It commonly caused the complete breakdown of order in any state or principality, as it had with the Saljuq Empire in 1092. Yet, despite having to pay tribute to Bohemond II, the new ruler of Antioch, and being constantly threatened by Baldwin II, Aleppo did not fall. This was primarily because the princes of Mosul viewed it now as their protectorate – just as it had been al-Bursuqi's 'second city' when he was governor of Mosul. Freed of the fear of interference in their affairs by Baghdad after the failure of the sultan's sponsored expeditions of 1111, 1113 and 1115, they now applied themselves more to Syrian than Iraqi affairs. Antioch had also not recovered militarily from the Battle of Ager Sanguinis, and Baldwin II was frequently embroiled with Damascene affairs, as well as his southern front.

The Fatimids had first challenged Baldwin II in 1118. Al-Afdal's Damascene diplomacy had continued and Tughtigin was given robes of honour when he mustered his troops with the Fatimid army at Ascalon. A rapid mobilisation by Baldwin II was enough to prevent the coalition army from entering Frankish territory but the threat posed by the Damascene–Egyptian alliance and the disaster at Ager Sanguinis forced Baldwin II to call upon the Venetians for help. In return they were promised trade privileges throughout the kingdom, but before the promised reinforcements could arrive Baldwin II had been captured by Balak. Despite this, the Venetians sailed to Tyre, where their fleet of one hundred warships began a blockade to match the landward siege of the city by the Franks on 15 February 1124.

The city surrendered on terms on 7 July 1124 and the Venetian fleet was the key to its fall. Tyre was virtually an island and could only be approached on a narrow causeway; it was also surrounded by three strong concentric walls. Troops from Damascus defended the causeway but there was little they could do to stop the bombardment of the city from the Venetian ships. As at the first siege, the garrison used hooks to turn over Crusader battering rams, but with the failure of the Fatimid fleet to break the blockade and the death of Balak, resistance was seen as futile.

The Egyptian challenge to the Crusaders was failing fast. Their army had been decimated in 1123 at the Battle of Yibneh – during a campaign that had aimed to recapture Jaffa – because the make-up of the army was totally unsuited to the task. Its massed ranks of Sudanese foot-archers presented the Franks with a static target for their charge and the light Berber cavalrymen were not capable of defending their infantry. The battle only lasted an hour, and a hurriedly launched Damascene diversionary tactic did not distract the Franks from their task of massacring the Fatimid army.

The Egyptian navy was fading from the scene too. After the fall of Tyre, the eastern Mediterranean was dominated by Italian ships and the Fatimid fleet is barely mentioned in the chronicles, excepting some piratical raids in the 1150s. Apart from occasional raids from Ascalon, little was heard from the army either. Perhaps William of Tyre's dismissal of the Egyptians as 'effeminates' was a harsh but fair analysis, though this is not the whole truth. In fact the Fatimids' withdrawal from the war for Syria was not a direct result of Frankish victories per se, and their one victory in the second Battle of Ramla had at least exposed one weakness of the Frankish state – there were simply not enough Latin soldiers. It would take another thirty years or so for this to become fully apparent, but the loss of even a small portion of the field army was a depressing proposition for the kings of Jerusalem. Egyptian isolationism in the period immediately after 1125 was, in fact, a result of sustained political crises. The Ismaili Assassins murdered the *wazir* al-Afdal in 1121, possibly with the connivance of the Fatimid caliph, and tipped the already fragile state into a cycle of political murders and intrigues as *wazirs* and caliphs competed for the allegiances of army factions. In 1130 the caliph, al-Amir, was also killed by the Assassins. Egypt turned in on itself and became largely irrelevant to the Crusaders until they sought its conquest three decades later.

The death of Tughtigin in February 1128 could have sealed the fate of southern Syria. He had failed against the Franks in battle in January 1126 and had involved himself with the heretical Ismaili Assassins, despite being the *atabeg* of the most orthodox Sunni city in Syria – even to the extent of employing hundreds of known Ismaili sympathisers in his army. The Franks controlled the entire coast, Egypt was finished with the war and the main city of the region had now lost an experienced leader. Damascus then nearly fell to the Ismailis, as they looked to claim all that had been promised by Tughtigin. The Assassins failed to take control of Damascus simply because the Sunni revival in northern Syria – based around the embryonic jihad of Il-Ghazi and Balak, and the continuing involvement of the *ulama* in martial and government affairs – was now also taking a tenuous hold on the south. Tughtigin's heir Buri moved quickly following the old man's death. He surprised and executed his father's *wazir*, a known sympathiser of the Ismaili Assassins, and made secret alliances with the Sunni *ulama* who controlled the city militia to purge the city of the creed. Ibn al-Athir claims that there was a plot involving the *wazir*, the Ismailis and Baldwin II to hand Damascus over to the Franks in exchange for Tyre, but no contemporary chronicler reports this tale. Buri and his Sunni supporters were thorough, brutal and swift. Ibn al-Qalanasi tells us that many Ismailis took refuge with officials who had formerly been their protectors, but they were 'forcibly seized and their blood was shed without fear of consequences. By the next morning, the quarters and streets of the city were cleared of the *Batinis* and the dogs were yelping and quarrelling over their limbs and corpses.'*

---

* Al-Qalanasi p. 190. *Batini* is a common name for Ismailis in the Middle Ages as the sect claimed to be able to reveal the *batin* or hidden nature of the Quran to initiates.

The Ismailis were never able to re-establish themselves in the city and Damascus would later become the centre of the Sunni jihad that would retake Jerusalem from the Franks. The sect attempted to exact their revenge through Baldwin II by gifting him their castle of Banyas. Banyas was a strategic asset as it was close to Damascus and lay on the Jerusalem road. Using it as his base, Baldwin II gathered together forces from Jerusalem, Edessa, Antioch, the coastal cities and from the Knights Templar and began to plunder right up to Damascus's walls. Buri had to respond, and he gathered allies from the nomadic Turcomen and Arabs of the region. With his *askari* and that of the prince of Hama as a core for this rather motley force, he intercepted the Franks as they marched on Damascus, at the wooden bridge six miles from the city. He managed to get his Arab auxiliaries on all sides of the Franks and hoped to break up the column with flying raids when they restarted their march. However, Baldwin II appears to have recognised this risk and refused to move or offer battle. He would also have noted the transitory nature of Buri's forces – if there was no booty or short-term gain to be had, the Arabs and Turcomen would soon desert. Buri learnt that the Franks had dispatched a large column to Hawrun, south of Damascus, to collect provisions for a siege of Damascus. Buri, showing great understanding of the nature of his forces, dispatched a large number of his Arabs and Turcomen to surprise the column. He realised that these tribal forces were of limited utility in a pitched battle against the heavy cavalry of the Franks, but with just the *askari* of Hama to stiffen their spine they were perfect for the execution of a large-scale ambush.

The Turcomen waited for the Frank column at Leja, twenty-five miles south of Damascus, and Ibn al-Qalanasi tells us that many of the Crusaders were killed before they could even mount their chargers. The Crusaders were not able to organise a charge because they were encumbered by baggage and supply mules and were riding their palfreys rather than their warhorses. They held their ground, but repeated attacks by the Muslim forces eventually broke them. William, the constable of Jerusalem, fled the field with a party of knights, whereupon:

> The Turks and Arabs made a mighty assault and surrounded the remainder with blows of swords and thrusts of lances and showers of arrows, and ere more than a part of the day had gone they were prostrate upon the ground and befouled with dust beneath the horses' feet. The victors took from

them a spoil with which their hands were filled, consisting of horses, arms, prisoners, men-at-arms, and mules of all sorts.*

The next day Buri moved forward to engage the Crusader camp at the wooden bridge, but the Franks had already abandoned their positions and had retired upon word of the disaster at Leja. The Muslims entered the camp to find only abandoned wounded and a mass of injured horses. The *askari* of Damascus were dispatched to attack the Crusader rearguard and they killed a number of stragglers, but the Crusader retreat was generally well managed. Baldwin II tried again later the same year to take the city but appalling weather ruined his plans.

Buri fell to the vengeful daggers of Ismaili Assassins who had worked their way into his close bodyguard. He was stabbed by two guards in May 1131, as he was riding back from the baths. He survived the initial attack, but succumbed to his wounds a year later. Ibn al-Qalanasi, a citizen of Damascus, paid tribute to the saviour of his city: 'All hearts were filled with sorrow at his loss and all the eyes with tears at the fate which had befallen him.' He closed his eulogy with a statement that few warriors would argue with: 'When death with claw-like nails strikes at her prey, no amulet avails.'†

The political value of the killing to the Assassins was minimal: the Sunni revival that was taking place in Syria was by now unstoppable. Damascus remained thoroughly orthodox in its religion and its politics, and a new Sunni champion emerged from the princes of Mosul. He would come close to unifying all of Muslim Syria under him and begin the destruction of Outremer.

---

* Al-Qalanasi, p. 198.
† Al-Qalanasi, p. 209.

~ 4 ~

The Martyr Zangi
A Tradition of Jihad is Born

Paradise has one-hundred grades which Allah has reserved for the Mujahedeen who fight in his cause, and the distance between each grade is like the distance between the heavens and the Earth.

Hadith, The Book of Jihad

Just before the Assassins' attack on him, Buri had received letters from Zangi, the *atabeg* of Mosul. Zangi had taken advantage of the chaos that had ensued in Aleppo following the murder of Ibn al-Khashab to seize the city. He then wrote to request the assistance of Damascus against the Franks. Five hundred men were sent from Damascus's *askari* to join the *askari* of Hama, which was commanded by Buri's son. Zangi quickly created trumped-up charges against Buri's son and imprisoned all the men of Damascus and Hama. He then seized Hama and demanded ransom from Damascus.

Buri knew Zangi's history and was not comforted by it. Zangi had been the governor of Basra in 1127 when the caliph had taken advantage of the inexperience of a newly enthroned Saljuq sultan to re-establish his power around Baghdad. He had rebelled against the Saljuqs and the new sultan could do little to stop him, as his throne was also under attack from his own family. He had therefore called on Zangi to make war on the commander of the faithful. The caliph was soundly beaten by the professional soldier Zangi; in reward, Zangi was given the city of Mosul and a free hand in the Jazira. The sultan also gave him diplomas of authority over the whole of Syria.

Buri was therefore dealing with the region's new strong man and he paid the ransom. By now, Zangi had moved his base of operations from

Mosul to Aleppo. He married the now thrice-wedded daughter of Ridwan and transferred his father's remains to the city – a highly symbolic act among Turkic peoples. Every Turkish prince in Syria knew that the union of Mosul and Aleppo under Zangi was a huge challenge to their continued independence. Certainly, the Franks suffered at his hands, but as the actions of the early years of Zangi's Syrian campaign make clear, he was just as partial to war with Muslims as he was with Latins.

In 1130, Bohemond II of Antioch was killed in battle by the son of Danishmend, the man who had captured the unfortunate Crusader prince's father. Bohemond's head was sent to Baghdad as a gift for the caliph; perhaps it cheered him somewhat after his first failed revolt against the Saljuqs. Bohemond's princess, who was also King Baldwin II's daughter, then rebelled against a proposed union of Antioch with the Kingdom of Jerusalem. The princess was half Armenian and the Greeks and Armenians of the city rallied to her cause against the Latins. Zangi sent raids into Antioch's territory but his attempts to exploit the situation ended when Baldwin II brought an army from Jerusalem to Antioch to rein in his recalcitrant offspring. The Muslims gained nothing from the episode, but it was a portent of what would occur over the next half century to Outremer. Ibn al-Qalanasi tells us that, following the death of Baldwin II 'the little' in August 1132, there was, 'none left amongst them possessed of sound judgement and capacity to govern'.★ He was succeeded without incident by Fulk of Anjou, but the Latin state was fragmenting, just as Muslim Syria had on the eve of the Crusaders' arrival in 1097, and the idea of a single state in which Antioch, Edessa and Tripoli were client states of the Kingdom of Jerusalem rapidly eroded. In 1139, soon after Zangi had started campaigning against him, Raymond of Antioch recognised the Byzantine emperor as his overlord. Tripoli and Edessa also slipped away from royal control.

Zangi was distracted by Iraqi affairs during the early 1130s. The caliph had rebelled again and was more successful this time. Zangi, concerned over his position should the Saljuq sultan lose Iraq, formed an army and marched on Baghdad. The caliph met him at the head of several thousand men at Tikrit on the Tigris. Zangi was heavily defeated and only escaped the battle with his life after being saved by a Kurdish trooper of the Ayyubid clan. In Baghdad the sultan now did homage to the caliph. In June 1133, the caliph, hoping to extinguish Zangi as a small

★ Al-Qalanasi, p. 230.

but continuing threat, marched on Mosul. However, he met such fierce resistance from the city's garrison that he still had not reduced the city even after a three-month siege – this failure was fatal to his plans. He was deserted by the emirs who had previously supported him, and by 1135 he was once again the captive of the sultan.

Zangi also had concerns in Anatolia. The region was disturbed from 1130 onwards by the Byzantine emperor, John II, who had begun to campaign against the Danishmend Turks. Much of the land lost after Manzikert was regained by the Greeks and they once again had to be counted as an important power in Anatolia and northern Syria. There was, however, a small advantage for Zangi in the Byzantine advances, in that they effectively ended the power of the Danishmendids of western Anatolia and reduced the risk of Turcoman alliances being formed against him.

Zangi's 'Damascus policy' centred on taking advantage of the death of Buri and the political chaos that Tughtigin's mad heir had caused in the city. However, he was militarily frustrated by the city's commander, and politically stymied by the judicial murder of the insane prince and his replacement with a puppet prince by Tughtigin's dowager. He got nominal recognition of his suzerainty over the city but little else. Throughout the 1130s, he therefore looked for easier opportunities in northern Syria and this inevitably brought him into conflict with the Franks of Antioch, Tripoli and Edessa. By 1135, he had taken Atharib and Maarrat al-Numan without having to engage any Crusader field armies. In 1137, he went back to his assaults on Damascus and its possessions.

The city of Homs had always been dominated by either Damascus or Aleppo, and Zangi set out to bring it back into the Aleppan fold in a June campaign. Its emir called on the *Franj* for assistance and as Homs sat on the edge of the county of Tripoli, its knights responded quickly to the request. Zangi rapidly made a truce with Homs and then besieged the Frankish castle of Barin. Tripoli now called on King Fulk for support: he attempted to break the siege, but his forces ran into a perfectly timed ambush. Fulk and Raymond of Tripoli pursued a fleeing group of Turkish cavalrymen, but were surprised by the main body of Zangi's forces and cut to pieces. Ibn al-Qalanasi tells us that the infantry were mown down and the baggage train was taken with incredible rapidity. Then, as Fulk tried to rally his men in his now devastated encampment, Zangi's *askari* routed him once more and Raymond was killed. The king fled to Barin to join the besieged, and suffered the furious bombardment of Zangi's *manjaniqiyin.* Supplies ran out before a relief force could reach the king and he surrendered to Zangi on terms. Barin went to Zangi and the king was released for fifty thousand dinars.

Zangi had released Fulk on these easy terms because the Byzantine emperor was active again – this time he was in northern Syria, which was very much Zangi's backyard. By early 1137 John II had the conquests of Tarsus and Adana from the Armenians to add to his vassalage of Tripoli. John II used this realignment of loyalties to bring a Byzantine-Crusader army, with forces drawn from Antioch and Edessa, into the field in the spring of 1138 – to attack Hama, Aleppo and the castle of Shayzar, which was controlled by the clan of Munqidh, just north of Hama. Zangi responded to this challenge – in an area he considered as his dependency – with a rapid, wide-ranging and effective diplomatic operation, and an impressive local military response. He stirred up the Anatolian Turkish emirs into assaults on John II's recently regained territories, and ensured that there was enough turmoil produced in Baghdad by its *ulama* to ensure that the sultan was chagrined into sending troops to Shayzar's defence. His military clerks then sent letters to all the major cities still under Muslim control in Syria to come to the aid of Shayzar. He was able to do this because, despite his skulduggery against Damascus and his long campaigns against his Muslim neighbours over the last few years, he was now the hero of resistance to the *Franj* and to the emperor of the *Rum*,* the Muslims' oldest enemy.

How had this transformation taken place? Simply because Zangi was now engaged in jihad as it was defined by the Sunni scholars of the time: jihad is a discrete action in Sunnism. Zangi was now engaged in a project that was pan-Islamic, as the many alliances he sought to form were all aimed solely at defeating the *Franj*. Such coalitions were central to the 'spirit' of jihad. Zangi also took on the mantle of a fighter for the faith – a *ghazi* or *mujahid* – and whilst there was a culture of Arabic poetry eulogising the exploits of *ghazis* of the age of conquests, Zangi's reputation was chiefly built by religious propagandists. Another key element of jihad is that social justice must also exist in the community that undertakes Holy War. There is certainly evidence of this in Zangi's government of Mosul and Aleppo. He controlled his army through iron discipline, and crucified transgressors of his laws. Al-Isfahani tells us that

---

* *Rum* is the Arabic transliteration for Rome, and Rome in this period was of course Byzantium.

Zangi was 'tyrannical and indiscriminate',* which in fact probably meant that he was harsh but fair and impartial in his justice. Ibn al-Athir tells us that, 'under his government the strong dared not harm the weak',* and that after he retook cities from the Franks he would return land and property to any claimant with deeds, and if these deeds had been lost then he would have the local land registers examined to decide on entitlement. The high opinion of Sunni jurists was vital, so maintaining the *sharia* was also essential for Zangi's position as the leader of jihad in Syria to remain unchallenged. Any prince undertaking Holy War had to work within these 'traditions' of jihad in order to maintain their legitimacy. Jihad was, and remains, an ideological war. Jihad gave Zangi legal and moral authority, even if his ventures were self-aggrandising.

Zangi's personal qualities also made him a natural leader of men and soldiers. He had the endurance to travel the length and breadth of Syria for eighteen years on campaigns, and his charismatic leadership and personal bravery were the keys to keeping his army in the field. The Turcomen, for one, would not have followed a weak leader for such a protracted period of time. In the Crusades period, prior to Zangi, no Muslim leader had managed to achieve such a prolonged union of forces nor to use it with such acumen or dash.

Zangi's local military response to John II's incursion was a brilliant delaying tactic, which bought him time for his diplomacy among the Anatolian Turcomen, with the sultan and with the emirs of Syria. He reinforced Shayzar as much as he was able and then deployed the small number of forces available to him to harass the enemy's flanks, though not to attempt a full engagement. John II made no progress in the siege and broke camp to make a thrust towards Aleppo, but Zangi quickly re-deployed and thwarted the Byzantines' ambitions once more. A sortie from the city then inflicted a defeat on the emperor's troops; during the Byzantine-Crusader army's retirement, the *askari* of Aleppo inflicted further casualties on them. Turcoman expeditions started across the Euphrates against the Byzantines, and the forces of Damascus and Aleppo turned John II back from his second attempt on Shayzar. His army recrossed into his own territory and the forces of Antioch and Edessa returned home on 22 May. It had been an unhappy union of forces, marred by suspicion between the Christian allies, which had been fuelled by Zangi's agents.

---

* In Hillenbrand, p. 113.

Zangi returned to the miasma of Turkish-Syrian politics. Damascus was once more in political turmoil in June 1138, with the stabbing to death of its prince in his bedchamber by three of his slaves. By this point, Zangi had married the prince's mother and it seemed inevitable that the city would fall into his hands. It was not to be, however, thanks to a rapid installation of the prince's brother by the senior emirs of Damascus, who also quickly moved to reinforce Baalbek, the fortress that lay halfway between Homs and Damascus. Zangi only brought fourteen mangonels with him to the siege of Baalbek, but he ensured that they battered away all night and day – the constant attacks that Zangi threw at the garrison and the completeness of his blockade brought the fortress to surrender. He secured the capitulation of troops holding out in the last tower with promises of safe passage to Damascus. However, he quickly reneged on this pledge and had every man of the group crucified.

Despite his double-dealing and the fact that he was making war on Muslims, Zangi was still able to utilise jihad propaganda during his assaults on Damascus in late 1139. He began a siege of the city, and initially he was wary of causing too much destruction: he needed to tread a cautious line and avoid excessive violence against Muslims. He learnt of an apparently terminal illness that had struck Jamal al-Din, the new prince of the city, through one of his spies. He offered Jamal an exchange of Damascus for another city, but the offer was refused; there was an engagement between Zangi's vanguard, which was moving up from the Biqa valley, and an advance guard of Damascene troopers. Jamal al-Din's men were defeated and Zangi moved into Damascus's environs. The reluctance of the Damascenes to accept Zangi, the great hero of the jihad, as their new prince is attested by the fact that the city militia and a company of peasants next engaged his men, with an almost predictable result:

> There was wholesale slaughter. Survivors were killed or imprisoned. Those who could, whether or not they were wounded, fled to the city. That day, but for God's grace, the city would have fallen. Zangi took his prisoners back to camp and for the next few days undertook no operations. He sent out messengers and exerted himself to obtain peace by courtesy and diplomacy, offering the Prince of Damascus Baalbek and Homs and other towns. Jamal al-Din would have preferred to accept these terms and to come to a peaceful agreement without bloodshed in a way that would bring peace and prosperity to the people but his advisers rejected this view. For several days Zangi sent out his troops in raiding parties without deploying

his full force or completing the blockade in order to avoid violence and to act like a man restrained by peaceful intentions and a reluctance to indulge in bloodshed and pillage.*

Jamal al-Din died, despite the attentions of 'medicine and magic art', on 29 March 1140 and Zangi brought his troops closer to the city in hopes of fomenting dissent among the senior commanders within Damascus. He was frustrated in this, though, by the orderly succession of Jamal's son, and resistance continued. However, the leaders of Damascus gifted him a propaganda victory when they allied themselves with King Fulk, who received both monies and hostages from the Damascenes.

The Frank–Damascus strategy was fairly simple. The Franks would attack Zangi's possessions in the vicinity of Damascus and thus draw him off from the siege and allow the Damascenes the opportunity to counter-attack and force him into a war on two fronts. Zangi was initially able to counter this approach through the mobility of his forces and by calling in Turcoman irregulars to harry the Crusaders' operations. He was able to draw nomadic Turks to his colours because 'his' preachers were proselytising the jihad. The Crusader–Damascene commanders then switched strategy and besieged Banyas. They knew that this fortress was vital to Zangi's blockade, as it sat on the road from Damascus to Acre and possession of it denied Damascus access to the Palestinian ports. The coalition hoped, therefore, to compel Zangi to abandon his siege of Damascus. He sent more Turcomen to Banyas, but in insufficient numbers to break the siege – if he was gambling that Damascus would fall before the fortress, then he lost his stake. Banyas fell in early June and a display of strength before the walls of Damascus at the end of the month failed. Zangi raided every district of Damascus's environs before he withdrew: for the sake of revenge and in order to pay his troops. He had, therefore, only a light curtain of troops watching the city's gates when its militia once again came out to meet his troopers in battle. This time the citizen soldiers were more successful, and while there was no precipitate flight from the battlefield, Zangi's men retreated with some haste. We are told that they took away a vast haul of booty with them.

It is surprising, given the distractions of Damascus, that Zangi ever returned to the jihad and it is sometimes hard to see a distinct pattern to the Syrian jihad prior to the Mamluk dynasty, simply because Muslim

---

* Ibn al-Qalanasi in Gabrieli, p. 46.

princes spent so much time reacting to events and opportunities rather than actively planning. Indeed, it is possible that Zangi's return to jihad was as much by accident as design, and that his assault on Edessa was pure opportunism – based on the death of Fulk in late 1143, the subsequent regency of Queen Melisende to the child king, Baldwin III, and a developing enmity between Joscelin II and Raymond of Antioch. There was, however, certainly a 'culture' of jihad flourishing under Zangi's aegis. Dedications on Aleppan buildings from the period before his assault on Edessa name him as the 'tamer of the infidels and polytheists, leader in the holy war, helper of the armies, protector of the Muslims'.*

These 'credentials' allowed Zangi, once more, to call on the *ulama* to legitimise his war and to call warriors to the jihad. In November 1144, knowing that Joscelin II was absent from Edessa, he attacked the city. The city's fall resulted in some members of the religious class going further than simply extolling Zangi's actions in the Holy War: they began to propagandise not just for the jihad but also for Zangi's dynasty. For Zangi, the conquest of Edessa effectively galvanised the support of the intelligentsia for his clan. Ibn al-Qalanasi tells us of his call to jihad and the subsequent victory:

He sent to summon the aid of the Turcomen in fulfillment of their obligations in the Holy War. Large numbers answered his appeal and they completely surrounded the city, intercepting all supplies and reinforcements. It was said that even the birds dared not fly near, so absolute was the desolation made by the besiegers' weapons and so unblinking their vigilance. Mangonels drawn up against the walls battered at them ceaselessly and nothing interrupted the remorseless struggle. Special detachments of sappers from Khurasan and Aleppo began work at several suitable places, digging into the bowels of the earth until their tunnels, propped up with beams and special equipment, reached under the towers of the city wall. The next step was to light the fires and they applied to Zangi for permission. This was given after he had been into the tunnels to inspect them and had admired their imposing work. The wooden supports were fired; flames spread and devoured the beams, the walls above the tunnels crumbled and the Muslims took the city by storm. The city was taken at dawn on Saturday 23 December, 1144. Then the looting and the killing began, the capturing and the pillaging. The hands of the victors were filled with money and treasure, horses and beauty enough to gladden the heart and to make the soul rejoice. Then Zangi

---

* In Hillenbrand, p. 110.

ordered that the carnage should come to an end and began to rebuild the walls where they had been damaged. He appointed suitable men to govern and defend the city and to look after its interests. He reassured the inhabitants with promises of good government and universal justice. Then he left Edessa for Saruj, to which the Franks had fled and took it. Indeed every region and town through which he passed was immediately handed over to him.*

William of Tyre tells us that the city fell rapidly because the population was made up of 'Chaldeans and Armenians, unwarlike men, scarcely familiar with the use of arms', and that 'the city was entrusted solely to mercenaries.' He also tells us that, 'the continual shooting of arrows tormented the citizens incessantly; and the besieged were given no respite.' The city fell so rapidly that Queen Melisende's relief force never had a chance of saving it. William also tells us that the Turks poured in through a gaping breach in the wall made by Zangi's sappers that was over one hundred cubits wide.† Abu-l-Faraj, a Syrian bishop of Edessa, tells us that the attack cost the Muslims many men and it is certain that the final assault was dangerous. Ibn al-Athir tells how Zangi continually inspired his men through his own bravado and courage:

> 'No one', he said, 'shall eat with me at this table unless he is prepared to hurl his lance with me tomorrow at the gates of Edessa.' The only ones who dared to come forward were a solitary emir and a youth of humble birth, whose bravery and prowess were known to all, for he had no equal in battle. The emir said to him, 'what are you doing here?' But the *atabeg* intervened: 'Leave him, for his, I can see, is not a face that will be lagging behind me in battle.'
>
> The army set out to and reached the walls of Edessa. Zangi was the first to charge the Franks but the young man was at his side. A Frankish knight lunged at Zangi from the side but the youth faced him and transfixed him with his lance and Zangi was saved.‡

Joscelin II attempted a stand in the city of Turbessel. Fortunately for him, Zangi was distracted once more by Damascene affairs and Ibn al-Qalanasi recorded in early 1145 that he was, 'mustering levies for the

---

* In al-Qalanasi, pp. 266–8.
† William of Tyre in Brundage, J., *The Crusades: A Documentary History*, Milwaukee: Marquette University Press, 1962, pp. 79–82. One hundred cubits is approximately forty-five metres.
‡ In Gabrieli, pp. 51–2.

purpose of the raid and the Holy War, and stories were circulated that he would probably march into the territories of Damascus and besiege the city'. He was distracted from an attack on the city by trouble in Edessa from Armenians attempting to betray the city to Joscelin II. Zangi marched north and rapidly crushed the conspiracy. The 'guilty parties were seized, hunted out, and requited therefore with punishments, such as slaying, crucifying, and scattering throughout the land.'*

This was followed by a revolt at the fortress of Jabar on the Euphrates. Zangi was three months into a siege of its rebellious emir when he was murdered on 14 September 1146 by a Christian slave, as he lay drunk in his tent. His army quickly dispersed and his senior commanders each made for a fortified city, to claim a share of the spoils. The treasury was raided and Damascus took advantage of Zangi's death to seize Banyas once more. Raymond of Tripoli raided up to the walls of Aleppo. Every act seemed designed to prove the truth of Ibn al-Qalanasi's encomium:

> His treasures now the prey of others,
> by his sons and adversaries dismembered.
> At his death did his enemies ride forth,
> grasping the swords they dared not brandish whilst he lived.†

All this occurred before either of his sons, Nur al-Din and Sayf al-Din, could consolidate their positions against their father's emirs or against each other.

Civil war and a regaining of the initiative by the *Franj* seemed the most likely outcome of Zangi's sudden death, but this did not occur and this was in part because Zangi's sons were able to acquire a major city each – Mosul for Sayf al-Din and Aleppo for Nur al-Din – and chose not to interfere with each other's ambitions in their respective spheres of the Jazira and Syria. Furthermore, the *Franj* lacked the manpower to take advantage of Zangi's death. Their numbers had been seriously degraded following the annihilation of the Crusade of 1101 and had been further diminished by the second Battle of Ascalon in 1103, the Battle of al-Sinnabrah in 1113 and by Ager Sanguinis in 1119. Fielding an army was becoming more and more difficult and there was an increasing reliance on mercenary forces. These cost money, and the loss of territory

---

* Al-Qalanasi, pp. 269–70.
† In Maalouf, p. 139.

to Zangi in the 1130s had meant that petty lords could no longer afford to commit substantial funds to the defence of the Latin lands.

The weakness of the Franks and the reluctance of Zangi's offspring to make war on one another were key factors in the holding together of the Muslim state in northern Syria after the death of the region's strongman. However, they were not enough, in themselves, to explain why internecine conflict did not break out among the warriors that Zangi left behind. Zangi's dominion did not disintegrate because his capture of Edessa had effectively made him a *shahid*, or martyr. The exploits of Il-Ghazi and Balak had caused a lore of jihad to evolve in northern Syria, and Zangi's martyrdom brought this to maturity. Certainly jihad had been a stalking horse for his ambitions, just as it had been for those earlier princes and it would now become a centripetal force that his son, Nur al-Din, would apply to bring all of Muslim Syria together under his command and to continue his father's war on the *Franj*. It is not without reason that Ibn al-Athir recorded in his *Perfect History* how: 'A holy man saw the dead Zangi in a dream and asked him, "How has God treated you?" And Zangi replied, "God has pardoned me because I conquered Edessa."'★

★ In Gabrieli, p. 53.

~ 5 ~

The Pure King, Nur al-Din
Institutionalised Jihad

Verily Allah hath purchased from the Believers their lives and their goods in return for their possession of Paradise. They shall fight in the Path of Allah, and they shall slay and be slain. It is a promise that is binding on Him in the Torah, the Gospel and in the Quran. And who is truer to his covenant than Allah?

Quran: Sura 9, v. 111

Nur al-Din was twenty-nine years old when he succeeded his father in Aleppo, and whilst we should discount a good deal of Ibn al-Athir's attempt to write a hagiography of him, it seems that he was pious and reserved and entirely more trustworthy than his father. These features explain much of his success, which went far beyond the battlefield, and why he was able, so successfully, to harness religious propaganda and the *ulama* to his cause.

His first concern was an attempt made by Joscelin II to recover Edessa. Nur al-Din's forced march from Aleppo – the sheer pace of which killed a number of horses – at the head of his *askari*, was enough, however, to deter Joscelin II from trying to hold on to the city. The Crusaders were attacked during their withdrawal by Nur al-Din's Turcoman auxiliaries and they were driven to hole up in a water tower. This was swiftly mined by the Turcomen, but then the tower fell onto its besiegers and a few Crusaders escaped. They were undoubtedly lucky as, 'the sword blotted out of existence all those of the Christians of Edessa that the Muslims laid hands on.'*

---

* Al-Qalanasi, p. 275.

The speed with which Nur al-Din established himself in north Syria made him an attractive proposition as a son in-law for Muin al-Din, the senior emir of Damascus, and a marriage contract to the emir's daughter was swiftly concluded. The union encouraged Muin al-Din to attempt to recover Sarkhad and Bosra from a garrison commander who had rebelled against Damascus and was trying to use the support of the Franks to maintain his independence. Muin al-Din besieged both fortresses in the spring of 1147, but then he received threatening communications from the Franks, telling him to retire from the fight. Muin al-Din therefore called on Nur al-Din, who arrived at Bosra on 28 May. At first, it seemed that the sight of Nur al-Din's cavalry bodyguard – 'no finer *askari* than his was ever seen, in appearance, equipment and numbers' – was going to be enough to bring the garrison of Sarkhad to surrender, as their commander quickly offered to negotiate. However, this was only a delaying tactic as there had been word of the Franks' advance from Jerusalem. The *Franj* arrived under the command of their sixteen-year-old king, but were roundly beaten in what almost appears to have been a portent of what would happen to the field army of Jerusalem some forty years later at Hattin:

> The combatants drew up eye to eye, and their ranks closed up to one another, and the *askari* of the Muslims gained the upper hand over the polytheists. They cut them off from watering place and pasture ground, they afflicted them with a hail of shafts and death-dealing arrows, they multiplied amongst them death and wounds, and set on fire the herbage on their roads and paths. The Franks, on the verge of destruction, turned in flight, and the Muslim knights and horsemen, seeing a favourable opportunity presented of exterminating them, made speed to slay and to engage in combat with them.*

Whilst the military union between Damascus and Aleppo that had brought this victory was only one of convenience and was soon dissolved, a degree of détente was beginning to evolve between the two cities. This was a frightening prospect for the *Franj*, since dissent between Aleppo and Damascus had been pivotal to the Crusaders' success in the early years of their invasion. In Europe, the fall of Edessa had made for an unpleasant inauguration gift for the new pope, Eugenius III. He responded with a papal bull on 1 December 1145, and by the spring of

---

* Al-Qalanasi, p. 278.

1146, King Louis of France made a commitment to a Crusade. The Holy Roman Emperor, Conrad, also, if somewhat tardily, committed himself to the venture in December 1146. The pope issued indulgences for the Crusade, though significantly these were also granted for an expedition into Slavic lands to the east, and for the knights of the Reconquista in Spain. This divergence from the original notion of Crusading being solely the defence of Jerusalem, to it being participation in *any* church-sponsored war, would be significant later – when the Latins of Outremer were being pushed into the sea by the Mamluks and no assistance worth speaking of could be drawn from Europe. However, the major problem for the Latins of Outremer in 1148 was the fact that a king and an emperor had responded to the pope's call. Neither would listen to the Orientalised Franks of the Levant and their ambitions would not end with the simple defence of Jerusalem. They were monarchs after all, and medieval monarchs enjoyed conquest. They could also only be a temporary addition to the forces of Outremer. Rulers, as Richard of England would later discover, could not leave their realms for too long.

Notwithstanding the above problems, it must be said that the armies of the Second Crusade were very impressive and Ibn al-Qalanasi describes the initial fears of the Muslims when news of their arrival at Constantinople came to Damascus:

> In this year a succession of reports was received of the coming of the Kings of the Franks from their lands, amongst them being Alman and the son of Alphonso, with a company of their nobles in number innumerable and equipment incomputable. They were said to be making for the land of Islam, having issued a summons throughout their lands and strongholds to set out on expedition thither and hasten towards it and to leave their own territories and cities empty and bereft of protectors and defenders. They brought with them amounts beyond reckoning of their monies, treasuries and weapons, until it was said by some that their numbers amounted to a million horse and foot and by others to be even more.*

Conrad, with about twenty thousand men, arrived in Anatolia in October 1147. On the 25th of the month, as his army approached Dorylaeum and his knights were watering their horses, they were attacked by Turcomen. Thus began the slow destruction of the Second Crusade, which is given only a short passage in Ibn al-Qalanasi's chronicle:

---

* Al-Qalanasi, pp. 280–1. Alaman was Conrad, the emperor of Germany, and the latter individual was Bertram, the grandson of Raymond of Toulouse.

When the news of their approach became known and their purpose was bruited abroad, the governors of the neighbouring lands and of the Islamic territories in their proximity began to make preparations for warding them off and to muster their forces for engaging in the Holy War. They repaired to their outlets and mountainous defiles which hindered them from crossing and debouching on the land of Islam, and assiduously launched raids upon their fringes. Death and slaughter commingled with the Franks until a vast number of them perished, and their suffering from lack of foodstuffs, forage and supplies, or the costliness of them if they were to be had at all, destroyed multitudes of them by hunger and disease. Fresh reports of their losses and of the destruction of their numbers were constantly arriving until the end of the year 542 [1148], with the result that men were restored to some degree of tranquillity of mind and began to gain some confidence in the failure of their enterprise, and their former distress and fear were alleviated in spite of the repeated reports of the activities of the Franks.*

This first encounter was a slaughter. Kilij Arslan, who had failed at this very place against Bohemond, was revenged on the *Franj* through his son. The Anatolian Turks' destruction of the Franks was so rapid that they were unable even to heave together for defence. Nightfall gave respite and Conrad fled back to Byzantine-controlled Nicaea, but he had left almost his entire army on the killing field of Dorylaeum. One odd result of this carnage was that knights in Germany, when they heard of the battle, were so impressed by the martial prowess of the Turks, that they commonly forged genealogical tables and legends to give themselves Turkish-German origins.

Conrad returned to Constantinople a sick man, but later embarked by ship for Palestine. Louis's army reached Nicaea in November and set off on the overland route. They were beset by storms and therefore tried to shorten their journey to Antioch by leaving Greek territory and climbing over the Taurus Mountains. They had too few supplies for the task and many stragglers were picked off by Turcomen. The army was soon showing signs of total disintegration due to the march and the Turkish harrying of its rearguard and flanks. Then its van lost contact with the main body of the army because the troops at the head of the column were in a hurry to reach a valley in which to camp for the night. The Turks cut off the army's main body from its vanguard just as night was coming on. Once more the Franks were routed by

---

* Al-Qalanasi, pp. 281–2.

the sheer rapidity of the assault and by the volume of shots delivered from the Turks' composite bows. Louis spent the night in a tree, surrounded by what was left of his bodyguard, but many of his other troops deserted the field only to be hunted down by Turcomen and killed. Louis scraped together the remainder of his forces and marched to Byzantine-controlled Attalia. From there he sailed to Saint Simeon in March 1148, with only his household: the rest of Louis's army remained encamped around Attalia, where they continued to be the target of Turcoman raids. The infantry attempted to march to Antioch and over half of them died en route.

At Antioch, Raymond attempted to swing Louis in favour of an attack on Aleppo as a step to recapturing Edessa but Louis was not convinced. The number of men already lost without even a glimpse of Jerusalem played heavily on his mind and he was still awaiting the arrival of his infantry from Attalia. Louis rejected the plan and marched to Palestine, having heard that Conrad was already in Jerusalem. Raymond and Joscelin II stayed in the north and this division of forces ensured that Nur al-Din's dominions around Aleppo were safe from attack.

The Crusade's belligerence was instead directed at Damascus. Many historians have suggested that the Crusaders remained secure from the risk of a united and belligerent Muslim Syria until this abortive campaign against Damascus, and that the Damascenes were effectively forced by the Franks' actions to abandon their policy of non-alignment. There is a degree of truth in this, but Nur al-Din had already shown that he was not averse to short-term coalitions with the Damascenes against the Crusaders, and he now had a marriage connection with the effective ruler of Damascus. Furthermore, Damascus did not actually succumb to the combination of charm and threat that Nur al-Din employed until six years after the Crusade's defeat.*

In fact, the targeting of Damascus, despite the treaties that existed between it and Jerusalem, was not as foolish as hindsight makes it appear. Damascus was the closest, potentially belligerent, Turkish-controlled city to Jerusalem. Egypt might have been a better choice – particularly given the Franks' later attempts to take it with far weaker

---

* See Hillenbrand, p. 117. Muin al-Din had placed a puppet on the throne and had received robes of honour and a caliphal diploma from Baghdad in 1147. He also received a gift of horses and a diploma from the Shiite caliph of Egypt. The bond between the Fatimids and Damascus was still very much alive.

forces than they had available in 1148 – but Egypt was quiescent at this
point, and the Turks, by virtue of their successes, had made themselves
the prime threat to the Franks.

The real blunder was therefore not the choice of objective, but the
execution of the plan to take it. The Crusaders arrived in the environs
of Damascus on 24 July and immediately found themselves able to
invest only a fraction of the long walls. They therefore set themselves
the limited task of securing the western wall, from its southern corner
to its most northern point, the citadel. Muin al-Din had already been,
'fortifying the places where their attack was feared, setting men to
guard the roads and passes, cutting off the movement of supplies to
their stations, filling up the wells and effacing the water sources',*
and according to the Arabic sources the Crusaders were immediately
affected by a lack of water. As the Franks moved through the suburbs
and gardens outside the western wall, they were met by a furious
assault made up of a hotchpotch force of Turcomen, city militia, *ghazis*
and even a elderly lawyer named al-Findalawi, who shrugged off all
attempts to make him desist from jihad and who was eventually killed
in battle. This force was badly beaten by the Franks, who advanced
through a cemetery west of the city and were able to use the trees found
in the orchards and gardens to begin building siege towers. They came
up close to the walls at various points and William of Tyre gives a vivid
picture of the limited resistance they met with:

> With the ingenuity which is characteristic of those suffering misery and
> adversity, they had recourse to desperate devices. In all the sections of
> the city which faced our camps they heaped up huge, tall beams, for they
> could only hope that while our men were working to tear down these
> barriers they might be able to flee in the opposite direction with their
> wives and children.†

Muin al-Din had sent letters to all the governors of Muslim-controlled
southern Syria, and more Turcomen began to arrive in the city through
the Aleppo and Baghdad city gates, which had not been blockaded.
These new forces assembled on 25 May and made a dawn attack on
the Crusader positions. They were held at a distance by the Franks'

---

* Al-Qalanasi, p. 284.
† All quotations from William of Tyre are from the *Historia Rerum in Partibus Transmarinis
Gestarum*, translated by J. Brundage, in *The Crusades: A Documentary History*, Milwaukee:
Marquette University Press, 1962, pp. 115–21.

crossbowmen, but were at least able to lay down a harassing fire that lasted until Muslim infantry bowmen from the Biqa valley were deployed to cover their retirement from the field. The next day the Muslims took the field again. The orchards in which the Crusaders were camped impeded any concentration of forces and a dispersed battle was fought, in which individual Turcoman cavalrymen and infantry archers, supported by mangonels mounted on the city wall, destroyed the Crusaders' engines and barricades with *naft*. Irregulars were also deployed from the city and ambushed the Franks as they tried to move from one position to another. William of Tyre tells us that:

> There were men with lances hiding inside of the walls. When these men saw our men passing by, they would stab them as they passed, through little peepholes in the walls which were cleverly designed for this purpose, so that those hiding inside could scarcely be seen. Many are said to have perished miserably that day in this way. Countless other kinds of danger, too, faced those who wished to pass through those narrow paths.

These men were paid for each head that they returned to Damascus with.

On 27 May, the Crusaders attempted a retirement but came under sustained attack; the chronicler of Damascus recorded that the Franks lost many of their 'magnificent horses' in this retreat. The Crusaders revenged themselves by burning down the suburb of al-Rabwa during their retreat, but they must have begun to feel by this point that the entire enterprise was doomed.

On 27 July, the Franks moved their entire operation to an assault on the south-eastern wall of the city. This was either an act of desperation or, as William of Tyre suggests, it was because the Damascenes,

> began to work on the greed of our men. With consummate skill they proposed a variety of arguments to some of our princes and they promised and delivered a stupendous sum of money to them so that the princes would strive and labour to lift the siege. They persuaded these princes to assume the role of the traitor Judas. By impious suggestions they persuaded the kings and the leaders of the pilgrims, who trusted their good faith and industry, to leave the orchards and to lead the army to the opposite side of the city.

There was no viable water source for the new encampment, thanks to Muin al-Din's preparations, but this was of little consequence as the

Crusaders knew they needed either to take the city quickly or to give up on the siege. Sayf al-Din and his brother Nur al-Din* were already marching from Aleppo and Mosul and would arrive within only a few days. However, the planned assault on the city never took place because the army's morale was broken and their commanders could not agree on the action to be taken, with many of them refusing to lead their troops into what seemed certain defeat. The next day the Crusaders began a retreat, during which they lost many more men to Turcoman raiding parties. William of Tyre's vitriol over the campaign is reflected in the fact that he tells his readers that the city's name means 'bloody' or 'dripping with gore'.†

Louis and Conrad accrued most of the blame for the failure and they left Outremer with their troops in 1149. Young King Baldwin III had lost the esteem of his vassals and now had neither the men nor the required prestige to ride to Antioch's aid when Raymond's army was virtually annihilated by Nur al-Din on 29 June at the Battle of Fons Muratus. A repeat of his grandfather's rescue of Antioch's territories after Ager Sanguinis was simply impossible. Raymond had managed to force Nur al-Din to raise a siege of the fortress of Inib, but had then made a terrible mistake by camping in open country instead of returning to one of his fortified cities. Nur al-Din's reconnaissance patrols soon reported that this isolated force was receiving no reinforcements, so the Turks confidently surrounded Raymond's camp. The next morning a general attack was made and Ibn al-Qalanasi tells us that the Franks managed one charge before being 'attacked from various directions', and that barely a man survived. A Kurd, Shirkuh, of the same Ayyubid clan as the soldier who had saved Zangi's life, took Raymond's head. It was sent, like that of his father-in-law, to the caliph in a silver box. Ismaili Assassin irregulars had fought with Raymond and were also slaughtered to a man; the man who took the head of their leader was rewarded handsomely by Nur al-Din. The Sunni jihad not only had Crusaders in its sights: heretics too had much to fear from it.

---

* Ibn al-Athir tells us that Muin al-Din wrote to Sayf al-Din rather than Nur al-Din for support. Perhaps the theory that the Second Crusade drove Damascus into Nur al-Din's embrace needs some revision given this fact. Damascus could quite easily have continued playing off the princes of Aleppo and Mosul against one another and, indeed, could even have fully repaired its relationship with the *Franj*.

† In fact Damascus or *Dimashq*, the watered abode, draws its name from an early Semitic dialect.

Joscelin II was the next prince to suffer at Nur al-Din's hands as the north of Syria slipped away from Crusader control. He was captured while raiding Muslim lands and was blinded and imprisoned until his death ten years later. Baldwin III secured the city of Antioch following a swift march, but virtually all its lands and fortresses were lost. Joscelin II's widow sold all her possessions beyond Antioch to the Byzantine emperor, as Muslim raiding had made her position untenable. Baldwin III closed the deal with the emperor and arranged the evacuation of Latins from the region. Baldwin only had about five hundred troops to cover this column of non-combatants as they marched from Tel Bashir to Antioch. Nur al-Din's troopers were therefore able to harass the column almost at will and to repeatedly cut off those marching at its rear. Baldwin III, however, managed the task with exemplary skill – though his baggage train soon looked like a porcupine as it was so covered in arrows – and the column survived the march in fairly good order.

The army of Jerusalem spent the next three years defending Antioch. Meanwhile, Muin al-Din's death in 1150 meant that Nur al-Din was distracted from northern Syria by the opportunity of capturing Damascus. However, the city's senior emir, Abaq, concluded a new truce with the Franks in an attempt to counter Nur al-Din's ambitions. In 1153, with the north stabilised – if nowhere near returned to its status quo ante – Baldwin III launched a major attack on Ascalon and called on the populace of Jerusalem, as well as pilgrims visiting the city, to join him. He was thus able to invest the whole city. Ascalon was still wealthy and William of Tyre tells us that when the city was finally taken there was plenty of treasure for these irregulars. However, despite having a strong Italian fleet blockading the port, and a large land force applying itself to the city's walls, the Franks could not bring the siege to a rapid conclusion and it dragged on for months.

The Fatimid navy was enjoying something of a last hurrah at this time and it caused the Crusaders a great deal of trouble. A fleet of seventy ships had raided up the Syrian coast in 1152 and had attacked Jaffa, Acre, Beirut and Tyre and had burned several Frankish and Greek ships. The fleet also bravely ran the Italian blockade a number of times and resupplied Ascalon. However, despite these courageous efforts, it eventually became obvious to the city's Fatimid garrison that no relief force was coming from Egypt, and that their tenuous naval supply route might be broken at any point. They therefore surrendered on terms on 10 August 1153. Nur al-Din had attempted to bring the

Damascene forces and his own to the relief of the city in April, but this united front broke down quickly; fighting erupted between the troops of Damascus and Aleppo before a planned assault on Banyas. This last failure of the Damascenes to join the jihad seems to have finally settled Nur al-Din's mind: he had to take the city, even if a campaign against Muslims was required.

Ascalon was an important victory for Baldwin III. It ensured that a frightened Damascus would maintain its non-aggression pact with the Franks, and it improved his prestige among his vassals at a time when the military orders were accruing more and more influence within the state. Finally, of course, Ascalon was a stepping stone on the road to Egypt, and Egypt would soon become the chief strategic focus for the Crusaders and Nur al-Din.

Meanwhile, Nur al-Din's designs on Damascus slowly came to fruition. He had already secured the mention of his name in the *khutba* at Friday prayers in the great mosque, and coins were minted in his name in the city. He was winning over the *ulama* with his piety, and the peasantry with his propaganda, along with the fact that even when he brought his army to the walls of Damascus to impose his will on the city's leaders there was no damage done to smallholders' crops. He even seems to have gained credit for the falling of rain after a long drought, as it coincided with his arrival. The actions of Abaq – inviting the Franks to the gates of the city, and even allowing some senior knights to enter the city to counter Nur al-Din's presence in the city's environs – only served to further isolate the leadership from the populace. Nur al-Din also chipped away at the loyalties of the city's senior emirs and of the militia. Abaq was finally left with only the support of a small clique of officers, whom he then turned on after being fed false information that they were plotting to remove him; several of them were imprisoned or executed. Interruptions to the food supply of the city then began, and Abaq, rather than Nur al-Din, was blamed for the shortages, even though it was the forces of Aleppo that were intercepting the wagons.

Nur al-Din turned to a 'gentle' besieging of the city on 18 April 1154. He had been bombarding the city with propaganda that shamed its leaders' reluctance to engage in the jihad three years previous to this show of strength. The tone of these letters was never incendiary enough to upset Damascene pride, but was rather cajoling and encouraging: 'There is no need for Muslims to be slain by the hands of one another, and I for my part will grant them a respite that they might devote their lives to the struggle with the polytheists.' He was also aided by the fact that Frankish raids continued throughout the area despite the Damascus–Jerusalem accord:

> I seek nothing but the good of the Muslims, and to make war against the Franks and to rescue the prisoners who are in their hands. If you will support me with the *askari* of Damascus and we aid one another in waging the Holy War and matters are arranged with a single eye to the good my desire and purpose will be fully achieved.*

Nur al-Din did not in fact need the *askari* of Damascus that much any more, but he did need the wealth of the city to pay his burgeoning army. He had attracted a vast number of Turcoman and Turkish mercenaries to his banner by virtue of his success and reputation. Even back in 1152, when he had encamped his forces south of Damascus, his army's tents had stretched the full length of the city's walls.

Abaq sent to Baldwin but Nur al-Din quickly moved to an attack on the eastern walls of the city before the king could react. There was some skirmishing with the regular city garrison and militia beyond the city's walls and Nur al-Din pressed his attacks daily. Then on 25 April, the Damascene *askari* rode out in force to counter Nur al-Din's early morning assault. They had to try to break the siege as the city was extremely short of grain, but the attack severely denuded the walls of troops. Nur al-Din's superior forces outflanked the Damascenes and pushed them back to the gate leading to the city's Jewish quarter. They then made an attempt on the walls and were assisted by an elderly Jewish lady who lowered a rope to one of the foot soldiers below. Nur al-Din's standard went up on the wall and a woodcutter followed the old lady's example by smashing the lock of the East Gate and allowing the Aleppans easy entry. There was no resistance and then the Christian quarter's gate was thrown open too. Abaq fled to the citadel, but was coaxed out with promises of a general amnesty. Nur al-Din had his city and a united Syria was called into existence.

The new Sultan of Syria immediately granted the Franks a one-year truce, in complete contradiction to his recent jihad propaganda. However, this action was necessary – unifying Muslim Syria was one thing but consolidating one's hold over it was quite another. The truce that Nur al-Din granted the Franks has a specific legal position within jihad: the

---

* Both quotes from al-Qalanasi, pp. 302 and 309.

hudna is a truce that can interrupt jihad only if there is an advantage to be gained by a cessation of hostilities against the infidel. In this case, it allowed Nur al-Din to eliminate a rebel emir in Baalbek and to intervene in a dispute between the Turkish emirs of Anatolia. He knew that any confrontation in that region could rapidly spill over into his northern territories and might also draw Byzantine armies back into Anatolia, with an attendant risk to Aleppo. The *hudna* was also only granted to Jerusalem and not to Antioch: operations could continue against the *Franj* there without interruption.

The Kingdom of Jerusalem was assaulted in 1155 in a highly unorthodox manner by the Fatimid navy. They had appointed a gifted and unorthodox commander:

> He selected a company of seamen who spoke the Frankish tongue, dressed them in Frankish dress and sent them forth on a number of vessels belonging to the fleet. He himself went out to sea to investigate various places and hiding places and the routes usually taken by the vessels of the Greeks and to obtain information about them. Thereafter he repaired to the Harbour of Tyre, on information which had come to him that there was a large Greek galley there with many men and a great quantity of riches. He made an assault upon it, seized it, and killed those who were in it and took possession of its contents. After staying for three days, he burned the vessel and went out to sea again, where he captured some vessels with Frankish pilgrims and having slain, taken prisoner, and plundered, returned to Egypt with his booty and his captives.*

The Fatimid fleet was still showing some fight at this stage, when it could slip between the Latin ships that were now crowding the eastern Mediterranean, but its limited successes really just made Egypt a more attractive prize for both the Crusaders and the new Sultan of Syria.

Nur al-Din set out for Aleppo in April 1156 to repel Antiochene raiders, but his Aleppan *askari* had already performed the task for him before he arrived, and this was the last military action before a series of earthquakes struck northern Syria from September onwards. Shayzar took the brunt of the shocks, but Hama and Afamiya were also hit. Simply keeping government going in the region preoccupied both sides for nearly six months, but the arrival of pilgrims in February 1157 encouraged the Franks to make a successful raid on Banyas. This action went temporarily unpunished, because another great earthquake struck

---

* Al-Qalanasi, pp. 323–4.

in early April 1157. Hama and Homs were all but destroyed and Shayzar's ruling family was virtually wiped out. Once again, the reordering of government in the region consumed all the attentions of Nur al-Din. His Aleppan troops took control of Shayzar after both the Franks and the Ismaili Assassins had attempted to acquire the city's remains themselves. Perhaps the severe damage wreaked on Antioch by the earthquake boosted his morale a little during this trying time.

Despite all the problems that nature had caused him, Nur al-Din was ready in mid-April to begin operations against the Franks again. He created a festival to celebrate the reignition of the Holy War, with a series of parades and spectacles that lasted seven days in Damascus. The citadel was decorated with banners and weapons taken from the *Franj*; troops and citizens and, more importantly, Turkish lords were invited to join the festivities and of course to join the jihad. Nur al-Din was now operating through lieutenants, rather than fighting the Franks directly as his father had, and he was now more like a field marshal conducting a campaign rather than a general. His brother Nusrat al-Din destroyed a Frankish army made up of Hospitaller and Templar knights as it was on route to Banyas, through a series of ambushes and feigned retreats, at the end of April.

Meanwhile, Shirkuh the Kurd had brought Turcomen into the field in the north and had been attacking the fortresses and lands of Antioch. Shirkuh and his Turcomen were then dispatched by Nur al-Din to a siege of Banyas, while the sultan returned to Damascus to arrange logistics and reinforcements and to whip up enthusiasm for the jihad. He called for *ghazis* from Damascus and from beyond the city to join the venture. He brought mangonels, supplies and the volunteers to Banyas on 18 May and received news of a further defeat of a Frankish column from Banyas by a composite force of Arabs and Turks under the leadership of Shirkuh. The heads of the Crusaders, their equipment and horses were dispatched back to Damascus to further provoke the populace's zeal for the Holy War. A carrier-pigeon dispatch from Shirkuh then announced to the sultan that Banyas was close to falling: a tower had been mined and fired at dawn and the Muslims had taken every part of the city except the citadel. Baldwin III reacted quickly, however, and his arrival took the Muslim besiegers by surprise.

The Franks of Banyas were saved, but they had to abandon the city; while they were encamped between Banyas and Tiberias they were attacked by Nur al-Din and his *askari* on 19 June. He totally surprised them and his troops had time to dismount quietly, in order to increase the accuracy of their archery. The Franks were still trying to don armour as the attack developed and their slaughter was complete. Ibn al-Qalanasi tells us that, 'we overpowered their horsemen with slaughter and captivity and extirpated their foot soldiers.'* There were even rumours that Baldwin III had fallen on the field. The captured knights were paraded through Damascus on camels, each with his banner attached so the crowds could recognise them. The infantry and Turcopoles were simply roped together in fours and marched through the cheering throngs.

More operations were planned for July 1157, but continuing earth tremors put these on hold. Then, in late July, Antioch was threatened by Kilij Arslan II, the sultan of Iconium. Nur al-Din responded by entering into a truce with Baldwin III to allow for support to be given from Jerusalem to Antioch. This, at first glance, is not the action of a leader of jihad against the *Franj*, but Nur al-Din, like every other Turkish prince, had his clan to think of and he regarded the conquest of Antioch to be the right of his family alone. 'Ownership' of the jihad was therefore vital to the ambitions of the Zangid clan. Furthermore, Byzantine claims on Antioch had never been rescinded and the fall of Antioch to Turcomen would be bound to provoke a response from Constantinople, and this would greatly complicate Nur al-Din's Syrian affairs. On 11 August, Nur al-Din set out with a large force that arrayed itself before Antioch and essentially created an exclusion zone around the city, through which neither the Franks nor the Turks of Anatolia could pass.

It was now clear that Nur al-Din was the most powerful sovereign in the region, and when he fell seriously ill in October 1157 there was a very real danger of a power vacuum. However, command was successfully delegated to Nusrat al-Din and Shirkuh, and despite a few odd rumours of his demise, there was no serious trouble while he recovered. The sultan was back in charge, though still in fragile health, by the turn of 1158, but his illness had given some hope to the Crusaders after the disasters of the last two years. They began raiding the districts surrounding Damascus with relative impunity until Nur al-Din rode out to engage them on 11 May on the Tyre road. He quickly met with and destroyed a foraging party, but was then engaged by a large body of Franks. His own force quickly gave way, leaving only Nur al-Din and his personal bodyguard on the field. This small group of men was able to kill enough of the Franks'

---

* Al-Qalanasi, p. 326.

horses during the Crusaders' charges, with a fierce archery fusillade, to allow them to retire to the safety of their camp where the sultan's anger was released upon his subordinates. Nur al-Din remained in the field until the end of August 1158, whilst unsuccessfully trying to secure a new peace treaty with Baldwin III. He also received envoys from the Fatimids with gifts of horses and treasure.

Unwelcome intelligence then arrived that, despite all his efforts to prevent it, a Byzantine army was being mobilised for service in Anatolia. Nur al-Din therefore wrote to all the Muslim leaders of Anatolia, warning them of the likelihood of war, but he was unable to do more as his health worsened again and he didn't recover fully until March 1159. He received gifts from Manuel, the Byzantine emperor, of mules and rich fabrics, but as if to prove the old adage, *Timeo Danaos et dona ferentes*, Nur al-Din also got word of a rapprochement between Manuel and Baldwin III and that not only Antioch but other cities, some of them Muslim held, were in the sights of the emperor. He therefore mobilised and moved to the north in an impressive show of strength, designed to deter the Greeks from molesting Muslim lands. His strategy worked to a degree, and a prisoner exchange of Frankish leaders held by Nur al-Din was enough to secure both good relations with the emperor and the Greeks' withdrawal from Anatolia. This diplomatic success was celebrated at a banquet held by the sultan, for which a multitude of horses, cattle and sheep were slaughtered.* However, the Greeks still had designs on Antioch and the emperor had also secured suzerainty over several Anatolian Turkish lords.

The Greek presence in Anatolia and the risk of their interference in Syria had therefore severely limited Nur al-Din's offensive options in the north. Another potential offensive route against the *Franj* had, of course, been advertising itself in recent years through small successes at sea against the Franks and through raids on Outremer's south-western border. Furthermore, the Crusaders had also realised that they could not hope to recover their losses to Zangi and Nur al-Din without the resources of Egypt. The campaign for the ailing Fatimid state and its treasure, army and navy would be between Nur al-Din and the new King of Jerusalem, Amalric, who succeeded his dead brother, the childless Baldwin III, in February 1162.

---

* Even the urbanised Mamluks of Egypt continued to consume horses as late as the nineteenth century. This was a cultural link to their steppe origins that all Turks tried to maintain.

Amalric felt, despite his state's ongoing manpower problems, that it was possible to take Egypt, and he was encouraged by the fact that, despite its small naval successes, Egypt remained in crisis and politically rudderless. The Ismaili Assassins' murder of the caliph, al-Amir, had begun a process of disintegration in 1130, and by the 1160s Egypt was paying tribute to the Franks just in order to stave off invasion. It had also gone through fifteen different *wazirs*: every one of the *wazirs* had been involved in deadly standoffs with the caliphs and only one of them had survived his tenure. The cliques of military officers that backed the various candidates for the *wazir*'s office broke the state apart. It was unfortunate for Amalric that Shawar, one of the losers in the deadly competition for the *wazirate*, fled not to the Frankish king, but to Nur al-Din's court to seek aid against his successor. Amalric reasoned, however, that fear of an intervention by Nur al-Din on Shawar's behalf could mean a welcome for the Franks from one or other of the factions now fighting for power in Egypt. He also had a *casus belli* because the tribute due to Jerusalem had not been paid by Shawar. Amalric invaded Egypt in September 1163 and got to the wetlands of Pelusium, where he defeated a force sent against him by the new *wazir*, Dirgham. However, when he pushed on to Bilbays and started to besiege it, his hopes were literally washed away when the Nile flood dykes were broken open by the Egyptians and his army's camp was flooded. A hasty retreat from the mud of the delta back to Palestine soon followed.

In Damascus, Nur al-Din hurried to organise a response to Amalric's grab for Egypt, and Shawar enthusiastically told the sultan that all expenses for the expedition could be met from the Egyptian treasury. He selected his trusty lieutenant Shirkuh to lead the mission, although some contemporary writers suggest that the whole thing was Shirkuh's idea and that Nur al-Din was badgered by his deputy on a daily basis about the venture. Nur al-Din would have been right to show reluctance. *Franj*-controlled Ascalon was only a three-day march from the cities of the Nile delta, the political and commercial heart of Egypt. Nur al-Din's expedition would have to negotiate enemy territory in Palestine or take a long circuitous route, almost to the Red Sea, in order to enter Egypt without harassment.

Nur al-Din commenced a diversionary attack on northern Palestine in April 1164 to pull Amalric away from his Egyptian preparations and to allow Shirkuh and his nephew Saladin, along with a small force, a window of opportunity in which to return Shawar to the *wazir*'s palace.

They took a long route down east of the Jordan to the point where the roads out of Arabia met the Red Sea before running across the Sinai to Bilbays. They captured the city on 24 April and were at the walls of Cairo by 1 May. Their sudden appearance seems to have paralysed Dirgham's responses and the city fell bloodlessly. Shawar was put back in office whilst the body of Dirgham was left in the streets to rot.

Shawar then showed how he had been able to survive in the cut-throat world of Fatimid politics by rapidly double-crossing Shirkuh and ordering him to leave Egypt. Shirkuh, having seen the condition of the Egyptian army and believing that Shawar could not garner much support from the Egyptian emirs, called his bluff. Unfortunately Shawar had one ace up his sleeve to back his bluster, and so in July 1164 Almaric and the army of Jerusalem marched on Egypt again, this time at the invitation of the *wazir*. Shirkuh abandoned his barracks at Cairo, knowing that if he was going to stop the Franks then it would have to be where the delta ran out and the desert began. He was able to hold the Crusaders from newly prepared positions at Bilbays for a few weeks but the situation looked hopeless unless something could be done to pull Amalric away from Egypt. Nur al-Din therefore wrote to all the emirs of Syria, calling on them to bring their *askaris* into the field, and struck at Harim, one of Antioch's remaining possessions. This was risky, as Antioch was under the suzerainty of the Byzantine emperor and Harim bordered Byzantine-controlled lands. Nur al-Din's attack also pulled Thoros, the most powerful Armenian prince in the region, into a coalition with the Byzantine governor of Calaman and Bohemond III of Antioch.

On the approach of this large force, Nur al-Din raised the siege of Harim and began a withdrawal. His retreat was taken by the coalition's leadership as an opportunity to obtain a meaningful victory. In their pursuit, however, they lost touch with each other's forces and Nur al-Din was therefore able to beat the forces ranged against him in two separate battles on 10 August 1164. In both encounters the coalition's cavalry was also separated from their infantry and their columns were so badly organised that Nur al-Din was able to isolate and massacre the foot soldiers and then do the same to the knights. Harim then fell easily. Ibn al-Athir claimed the encounter showed Nur al-Din's tactically brilliant use of the feigned retreat and ambush, but in fact the coalition forces' blunders were so gross that Nur al-Din's skilful exploitation of his enemies' errors is what should be praised. Amalric wrote in a letter to Louis VII of France that they had achieved all they had needed to do on the day and that their pursuit of the Turks had been pointless. What the king meant, of course, was that with the bulk of the kingdom's forces committed to Egypt, limited warfare was the only option for the Franks. The wisest of his successors consistently followed this dictum and the rashest ignored it to great cost.*

Nur al-Din sent a selection of the heads of the slain Franks to Bilbays to cheer Shirkuh. The news of the defeat, and that Bohemond III had been captured, certainly didn't do anything for Amalric's humour. He was, however, still facing an inferior force and he still did not have full intelligence on the disasters in Syria. He therefore forcefully negotiated with Shirkuh for a mutual withdrawal of forces, and both armies left Egypt in October 1164. Amalric went straight to Antioch to defend the city. He managed to secure the situation there, but then had to march south to try to relieve his own possession, the fortress-city of Banyas, which was now under attack by Nur al-Din. He arrived too late and Nur al-Din took the town.

Things were going well in Syria and Nur al-Din did not intervene directly in Egypt again until he was provoked to do so by Shawar. The *wazir* had concluded a treaty of mutual assistance with Amalric and Nur al-Din took this as a virtual capitulation of Egypt to the *Franj*. Another expedition led by Shirkuh and Saladin was therefore dispatched in early 1167. Shawar got wind of these preparations and appealed to Amalric for help. Both armies took almost the same routes they had followed in 1164, but Shirkuh steered his forces further to the south of Cairo and crossed the river upstream of the city. This effectively sited his forces on the west of the city and meant that Shawar and his Frankish allies were arrayed on the wrong side of the river to engage him. He hoped to split Shawar away from Amalric and the river was a formidable barrier that bought him time to send promise-filled dispatches to the *wazir*. These unfortunately failed and drove Shawar to make a formal treaty with Amalric.

Amalric crossed the Nile in early March, but Shirkuh denied him battle and fled up the Nile valley. Amalric set off in pursuit with only his mounted forces, as his infantry could not keep up with the pace of Shirkuh's retreat. The chase continued until 18 March when Shirkuh halted his forces, having found ground suitable to his aims. The Battle

---

* For the Latin text of Amalric's letter, and a masterly account of the limited warfare option in the Latin kingdom, see Smail, R. C., *Crusading Warfare 1097–1193*, second edition, Cambridge: Cambridge University Press, 1995, pp. 133–5.

of al-Babayn was fought on the fringes of the desert where soft sand and the steep slopes of the dunes made the Crusader charge of limited value. Amalric had about four hundred knights with him and a large contingent of Egyptians and Turcopoles. He made a charge at Shirkuh's centre with a contingent of his knights, but the troops positioned there and under the command of Saladin quickly retreated from him. Amalric then found himself under an archery assault from two charging wings and also cut off from the rest of his forces. He managed to cut his way out of the melee of injured and dying knights that his force had become, and returned to his main force. Shirkuh's *askari* was by now concentrating its efforts on the Egyptians and Turcopoles and on the Franks' baggage train. It is a credit to Amalric that he was able to hold the field and then to lead small groups of knights into a battle that rapidly became a series of small engagements in which virtually none of the participants knew whether the day was won or lost. The king eventually rallied as many men as he could around his standard, formed them into a close-order column, cleared the field, and headed back to Cairo. Shirkuh had not secured a victory per se, in that Amalric had not been denuded of his force, but the king had lost about one hundred troopers and knights – given that Shirkuh's own forces were numerically inferior at the outset of battle, it was a good result for the general.

Shirkuh then marched back up the Nile valley but completely avoided Cairo and headed instead for Alexandria. Shirkuh's reasons for this move seem to have been: he had beaten Amalric and wanted something to show for it; Alexandria was openly hostile to the alliance with the *Franj*; and simply that Shirkuh had the heart of an adventurer. Amalric and Shawar immediately besieged Alexandria and within a month the city was close to famine. The situation worsened when a Pisan fleet arrived and prevented any supplies reaching the city from the sea. This forced Shirkuh to gamble further. He took a body of his best troops and broke out under cover of night from the city, leaving Saladin in charge of the remaining men. He headed for Upper Egypt again, where he tried, with some success, to foment rebellion against Shawar; he hoped to unnerve Amalric by the straightforward principle that the Frank king could not possibly know what the Kurd was going to do next. Amalric was also under pressure again from Nur al-Din in Syria, and after the disaster at Harim the king was dubious about the abilities of any of his lieutenants. A protracted war in Egypt with Shirkuh's men acting as guerrillas was the last thing he needed. He tightened the siege of Alexandria a little by adding in a daily mangonel bombardment, but it was obvious that little else could be achieved except by negotiation; he was at least, at present, negotiating from a position of strength. Saladin was held as a hostage during these negotiations and he became friendly with the Crusader Humphrey of Toron. A ransom was paid for him and all Frankish prisoners were released. The Syrian army was allowed to leave Egypt unmolested and Amalric left soon after in August. He had secured an increased tribute to Jerusalem and the right to have troops and a military attaché garrisoned in Cairo itself from Shawar.

Amalric's demands on the Egyptians for tribute required huge tax increases. Coupled with the presence of *Franj* troops in Cairo, this ate away at Shawar's support and there was a very real chance that the factions ranged against him would call on Nur al-Din for support. A Crusader army led by Count William of Nevers also arrived in Palestine in the summer of 1168, and with these new forces Amalric made another attempt on Egypt in October. He took Bilbays in November, but the slaughter that ensued during the city's reduction hardened the Egyptians' will to resist the Franks. While Shawar opened protracted negotiations with the king and sent to Nur al-Din once again for aid, Cairo prepared to repel the Franks. The old city, which comprised much of the housing of the poor, the graveyards and markets, was razed to the ground in a fire that lasted over fifty days because it was undefendable and in order to deny the Franks its shelter and food. The Fatimid caliph, al-Adid, also sent letters to Nur al-Din – this was enough to bring Shirkuh and Saladin once again to Egypt in December 1168, but this time with an army larger than Amalric's. The arrival of these forces in Egypt, and the unpleasant facts that besieging Cairo had proved unfeasible and that 'camp sickness' was killing his men was enough to force Amalric's withdrawal. He led his army back out of Egypt on 2 January 1169. Shirkuh took the position of *wazir* with the support of the Fatimid caliph and executed Shawar. Shirkuh did not, however, enjoy the pleasures of the *wazirate* too long, as he died in his bath in March 1169.

At the outset of this final campaign Saladin had demurred when told by Shirkuh that he was to campaign in Egypt once more:

> I answered that I was not prepared to forget the sufferings endured in Alexandria. My uncle then said to Nur al-Din. 'It is absolutely necessary that Yusuf go with me'. And Nur al-Din thus repeated his orders. I tried to explain the state of financial embarrassment in which I found myself. He

ordered that money be given to me and I had to go, like a man being led off to his death.*

However, now he had been catapulted to the head of the state that Shirkuh and he had, essentially, conquered. Ibn al-Athir suggested that Saladin was chosen by the Fatimid caliph's advisers to replace Shirkuh simply because he was the youngest and most immature of the possible candidates and therefore likely to be the most easily led. This might lead to the conclusion that Saladin was an innocent youth surrounded by devious enemies, but he was in fact a mature thirty-year-old, and was already a seasoned warrior and politician. What he had inherited, however, would sorely test even his undoubted talents. He was *wazir* to a Shiite-Ismaili caliph and had only a small body of Syrian troopers to counter the still large, if virtually unmanageable, forces of the Fatimid army.

Despite all his later achievements, what he managed to do in Cairo, in these early years, may have been Saladin's finest deeds in terms of simple political acumen. He started by seizing lands and properties from senior Fatimid emirs, whilst still maintaining his loyalty to the Fatimid caliph. He then used the funds and property he garnered from this to buy the services and loyalties of the Turkish Mamluks of the Fatimid army, and to supply his own men with *iqtas* in Egypt. By these actions, he increased his own forces and tied both Syrian and Egyptian troops to his personal fortunes. However, he pushed the black troops of the Fatimid army, some thirty thousand men, into a revolt because of his, possibly intentional, indifference to their welfare during the summer of 1169. Their chief sponsor in the Fatimid palace was a senior eunuch named al-Khilafa, and he started an intrigue against Saladin with the Crusaders, in which he claimed he would co-ordinate a revolt among the black troops with any Frankish invasion of Egypt. His messenger to Amalric dressed in peasant rags in order to slip by Saladin's Turkish guards, but he neglected to remove his palace slippers. A guard became suspicious of a peasant wearing such fine footwear and arrested the man. Inside the slippers was the incriminating letter, which was taken to Saladin. The *wazir* bided his time, but then in August 1169 Saladin had al-Khilafa killed. Ibn al-Athir tells us what happened next:

The Africans became furious on account of the killing of their protector. They gathered until their numbers increased to over fifty thousand. They

* Ibn al-Athir in Maalouf, p. 169.

intended to battle Saladin's army. They fought one another between the two palaces. Many were killed on both sides. Saladin sent troops to the Africans' lodgings and set fire to their possessions, killing children and women. When the news reached the African troops they fled. Saladin attacked them with swords and closed their escape routes. After many of them had been killed, the Africans asked for peace. Many of them then left Egypt for Gaza. Turanshah, Saladin's oldest brother, crossed over to Gaza with an army and cut the Africans to pieces. There remained among them only a few fugitives.★

Saladin had gambled but he knew that he had bought enough loyalty among the Turkish cavalry to crush the Sudanese troops. Furthermore, the role of infantry in Muslim armies had declined from the eleventh century onwards, and would continue to do so as the mounted and heavily armoured archer increasingly dominated the battlefield. The defeats that the Fatimids had endured made it plain to a talented professional soldier like Saladin that the Sudanese were, in crude terms, more trouble than they were worth. This said, the street fighting that ensued during the revolt was hard fought and damaging. In 1173, Africans who had fled to Upper Egypt joined a general revolt aimed at restoring the Fatimid dynasty. This time Saladin sent his brother al-Adil against the Africans. Their threat was finally extinguished within the next year.

In order to pursue his ambitions in Egypt Amalric had reached out to Byzantium. The emperor, Manuel, was married to Amalric's cousin, Maria of Antioch, and in 1167 Amalric had contracted to marry Manuel's grandniece. The follow-on to these political nuptials was the forming of an alliance aimed at the conquest and partition of Egypt, and in July 1169 Saladin got word of a joint Crusader–Byzantine expedition. Given the limited naval resources available to him, he was unable to guarantee the safety of the Egyptian coastline, but he endeavoured to have at least forward intelligence of any maritime operations that would be launched against him. He therefore sent a number of patrolling ships out along the likely routes to be taken by any Byzantine or Crusader fleet. One of his squadrons returned with the news that Emperor Manuel had dispatched a fleet of 230 ships, including large transports capable of carrying cavalry straight to the point of battle – an important consideration in

---

★ In Bacharach, J. L., 'African Military Slaves in the Medieval Middle East: The Cases of Iraq (869–955) and Egypt (868–1171)', *International Journal of Middle East Studies*, November 1981, pp. 471–95.

the Nile delta – as well as an army to Palestine. A campaign against Egypt was beneficial to Manuel because it would distract Nur al-Din from Byzantine ambitions in northern Syria, and because Egypt could become the bread-basket of Constantinople again, as it had been in the seventh century, before the Arab invasions.

The attack was due to be launched from Ascalon during the campaign season, but fortunately for Saladin it was delayed by protracted negotiations over division of the spoils between Manuel and Amalric, and by Amalric's slow gathering of his troops. It was also slowed by the Franks' insistence on marching to the Nile delta rather than being carried by the Byzantine transports. The force did not therefore reach Damietta until mid-October, at which point the Byzantines found that access to the port was barred by a giant chain, and the best the invaders could do was to settle in for a siege of the city, which commenced on 27 October. Still, coming as it did in the midst of the suppression of the black troops' revolt, and in the light of Saladin's short tenure of power, the enterprise still looked hopeful. However, Damietta's garrison was well supported with money, mercenaries and supplies by Saladin via the Nile, and it showed no signs of disloyalty to their new *wazir*; Nur al-Din also sent levies from Syria to bolster its defence. The Crusaders were therefore met by a fierce resistance. They subsequently worsened the situation for themselves by refusing to cooperate with their Byzantine allies in almost every area, and by arguing once again over spoils – before they had even been won. Amalric's supplies began to run low and Saladin knew that winter was closing in on the Greeks and Latins. Amalric made a fruitless assault on the city, and then attempted to negotiate for a peaceful withdrawal. The weather smiled on the defenders: rains destroyed the Franks' morale and the ensuing mud made movement almost impossible. They withdrew after thirty-five days and a severe storm destroyed half the Byzantine fleet during its return to Constantinople.

Saladin took the offensive in 1170. Whilst we can dismiss William of Tyre's statement that he brought forty thousand mounted troops into the field with him, it is evident that, by this point, he had moulded the Egyptian Turks into his own personal army. He raided *Franj* lands in Gaza and took the Crusader fortress-city of Ayla at the head of the Persian Gulf, near modern-day Aqaba. The latter venture had required the dismantling of many ships and transporting them across the Sinai to the Red Sea, where they were rebuilt, launched and joined the assault on the port. These raids may have been aimed at showing Saladin's loyalty to Nur al-Din, as Amalric had been very publicly trying to draw him into a pact against his overlord. Certainly relations between the *wazir* of Egypt and the sultan of Syria were beginning to show signs of strain. What seems more likely, however, is that Saladin was already thinking about the weakness of Egypt in terms of attacks from the sea and the risk of blockade – both of its supplies and its trade from India. In this he was extremely far-sighted. The Portuguese entered the Indian Ocean many years later in the fifteenth century and began to do battle with the Muslims in the Red Sea, both in an attempt to blockade Egypt and to take control of the trade of the sub-continent.

By 1171, Nur al-Din was placing increasing pressure on his lieutenant to finish the Fatimid line and impose Sunnism, with adherence to the Abbasid caliph, on Egypt. Saladin's admiring biographers claim that he could not bring himself to kill the sickly young caliph, al-Adid, but it is obvious that he was also attempting to maintain Egypt as a satellite to, rather than a province of, Nur al-Din's sultanate. His hand was nearly forced in September 1171, however, by a citizen of Mosul who was visiting Cairo. This gentleman, who was apparently very wealthy, entered the Friday mosque, climbed the pulpit ahead of the regular Ismaili preacher, and said the *khutba* in the name of the Abbasid caliph. There was no protest from the congregation and absolute quietude on the streets over the following days. The gentleman's largesse may have had something to do with the way that the Fatimid dynasty died so quietly, and almost without grieving on the part of its citizens. Its last caliph also died, in his sleep, only a few days later and the women and men of the ruling house who survived him were separated so that the line, which claimed descent from the Prophet Muhammad's daughter, might die out naturally.

After that, the political action of the Levant began closely to resemble that of 1097. Saladin assisted Nur al-Din in the sultan's campaigns against the Franks – as a vassal he could not refuse, but he realised that the Crusaders were effectively distracting Nur al-Din from a march on Egypt and dividing Muslim Syria from Saladin's state. The Fatimids' old tactical design of a Crusader state that protected them from the Turks still had some life in it, but Saladin also realised just how dangerous this game was: in February 1174 he sent his brother to Yemen to clear it of Fatimid supporters and to secure it as a possible sanctuary for the Ayyubid family should he should fail in his dangerous balancing act.

Saladin and Nur al-Din did attempt joint campaigns in 1171 and 1173, when Saladin attacked Karak and Shawbak, two great Crusader fortresses in the Transjordan, but in both ventures the two armies failed to join up. Ibn al-Athir blames Saladin for withdrawing early from the second campaign and for letting the Franks escape serious defeats. However, other evidence suggests that Saladin's advance into the area was only aimed at Bedouins who had been raiding Muslim territory with the Franks, and that Nur al-Din was delayed in rendering aid, as he was engaged in what can only be described as a turf war with Kilij Arslan II in northern Syria. Therefore, whilst there was certainly mistrust between the two men, Saladin was a reasonably loyal vassal. Indeed, Nur al-Din was credited with Saladin's actions in Nubia and North Africa in letters to the Abbasid caliph, and there were no complaints from Nur al-Din over his initial share of the booty of Egypt.

Ibn al-Athir states that Saladin's usual 'excuse' for not undertaking lengthy campaigns in support of Nur al-Din was an ongoing concern over the political stability of Egypt. Saladin's concern was, however, proved to be correct in early 1174 when a grand conspiracy was discovered. Remnants of the black troops had been retained in the palace guard and they had linked up with Armenian Mamluks, who had formerly been dominant in the state but who had become political losers of late, as well as with diehard loyalists of the Fatimid line. The plotters also opened negotiations with the Franks and, if a letter from Saladin to the caliph is to be believed, with the Ismaili Assassins of Syria. Saladin's secret police discovered the plot and, acting quickly, he was able to round up all the ring leaders and have them crucified.

Meanwhile, Nur al-Din was becoming convinced that his lieutenant was starting to be too strong and that Egypt's tax revenues, needed for the Syrian jihad, were being salted away by Saladin. Nur al-Din always viewed Syria as the main theatre of the war, and the conflict between the sultan and Saladin certainly had a strategic component to it, as Saladin always put the safety of Egypt ahead of the Syrian campaign. Nur al-Din sent an inspector to Egypt to check the tax remittances and the inspector duly submitted a fairly damning report to the sultan. Mosul and Aleppo were immediately abuzz with rumours that Nur al-Din was mustering his forces for an attack on Egypt. Saladin's response to all this has been recorded by Baha al-Din, Saladin's army *qadi*:

> Some reports reached us of a possibility that Nur al-Din might come down to Egypt against us. All our friends were of the opinion that we should oppose him and break off our allegiance to him, and I was the only one of

the opposite view, saying nothing of this kind must either be said, but the controversy continued until we had heard of his death.*

Nur al-Din died on 15 May 1174 following a heart attack brought on by a polo match. He had always been a gifted and aggressive player of the game, much as he had been a gifted politician and an aggressive military leader. He was about sixty when he died and he was rightly remembered by the populace of Muslim Syria as the man who had taken away the very real fear that the *Franj* would conquer Aleppo and Damascus. He was eulogised by the writers of the time and vigils were kept in the major cities of Syria with readings of the Quran being made in his memory. Nur al-Din was only one man and sometimes the heroes of the past are blown up by historians to greater levels of importance than they deserve, but, as Oliver Wendell Holmes once observed, 'a great man represents a strategic point in the campaign of history, and part of his greatness consists of his being there.'† The unification of Muslim Syria was Nur al-Din's contribution to history, but his gift to the Syrians was far larger than that, and contemporary poems mourning his death show how important he was as a beacon of hope:

> Religion is in darkness because of the absence of his light
> The age is in grief because of the loss of its commander.
> Let Islam mourn the defender of its people
> And Syria mourn the protector of its kingdom and its borders.‡

Nur al-Din morally rearmed the Sunnis and gave their jihad material strength. His victories on the battlefield were, of course, a major element of this accomplishment, but justice in his cities and the piety and modesty of the Holy War's leader were also vital components. Amongst his throne names we find 'al-Malik al-Adil', perhaps of all his titles this meant the most to Nur al-Din Mahmud Ibn Zangi, as it named him the 'Just King'.

---

* Baha al-Din in Gibb, H., *The Life of Saladin*, Oxford: Oxford University Press, 1973, pp. 14–15.
† Bent, S., *Justice Oliver Wendell Holmes*, New York: Vanguard Press, 1932, p. 248.
‡ Abu Shama in Hillenbrand, p. 166.

~ 6 ~

Fortune Makes a King
The Achievement of Saladin

Vidi quel Bruto che cacciò Tarquino,
Lucrezia, Iulia, Marzïa e Corniglia;
e solo, in parte, vidi 'l Saladino.

I saw that Brutus who expelled Tarquin,
Lucretia, Julia, Marcia, and Cornelia,
and I saw Saladin, by himself, apart.

Dante, L'Inferno, Canto IV: 127–9

Al-Salih, the son of Nur al-Din, was still a child when his father died. Almost every senior emir in Syria offered to take on the protection of the youth and we might cynically suggest that their motives were not born entirely of simple affection for the child of their master. With the regency of al-Salih came power, and Saladin – who viewed himself as the true heir both to Nur al-Din's mission and to his powerbases – attempted early on to secure his right to act as the child's *atabeg*. In the summer of 1174, he wrote to the emirs of Syria after hearing of a 'united front' being formed against him in Damascus:

> If our late king had detected among you a man as worthy of his confidence as me, would he not have entrusted him with the leadership of Egypt, the most important of his provinces? You may be sure that had Nur al-Din not died so soon he would have designated me to educate his son and to watch over him. Now, I observe you are behaving as though you alone served my master and his son, and you are attempting to exclude me. But I shall soon arrive. In honour of the memory of my master, I shall perform

deeds that will have their effect, and each of you will be punished for his misconduct.*

He couched his argument in slightly different terms once he had intelligence about the breakaway of Mosul under Nur al-Din's cousin and the removal of al-Salih to Aleppo by Gumushtigin, Nur al-Din's eunuch, who now seemed to consider himself the young man's *atabeg*. Saladin now spoke of unity for the cause of jihad and not just simple rights by virtue of service:

> In the interests of Islam and its people we put first and foremost whatever will combine their forces and unite them in one purpose. In the interests of the house of [Nur al-Din] we put first and foremost whatever will safeguard its root and branch. Loyalty can only be the consequence of loyalty. We are in one valley and those who think ill of us are in another.†

His message was, however, essentially the same. Only the Sultan of Egypt had the power to reunite the Muslim Levant and thereby to oppose the *Franj*. Furthermore, failure to unite under Saladin was a betrayal of Islam and the jihad. Saladin was, in fact, at a disadvantage in the scramble for Syria, by virtue of his possession of Egypt. For example, he was unable to mobilise to Syria to counter a move made by Amalric against Banyas in June 1174, as he was under the threat of an attack by a Sicilian fleet and events moved too quickly in Syria for him to intervene. The emirs of Damascus concluded a truce with Amalric, but then the King of Jerusalem, known as 'Morri' to the Muslim chroniclers, died on 11 July 1174 of dysentery while attempting to forge a stronger Muslim–Crusader alliance against Saladin.

This was the first of many fortunate events that would favour Saladin in the early part of his reign. His genius, like that of all great leaders and military commanders, was to exploit fully such pieces of luck. In October he received an appeal for assistance against the Franks from Damascus's governor, the city having been abandoned by the emirs of the Zangid clan, who had fled to the north for fear of the ruler of Egypt. Saladin took only seven hundred men with him to Damascus since he knew he needed to move quickly to secure the city before its independent-minded citizenry decided – as they had so often in the past – that they preferred autonomy to a sultan's control. The gates were opened to him by members of his

---

* In Maalouf, p. 180.
† In Gibb, p. 16.

clan, the Ayyubids, and there was virtually no opposition. Nor was there any real interference from the *Franj*. Again, Saladin was fortunate in that Amalric's son, Baldwin IV, was a thirteen-year-old minor who suffered from leprosy. Factions formed in Outremer regarding the succession to this boy-king, who was expected to be a weak, short-lived monarch who would not sire an heir. Jerusalem was politically paralysed and the kingdom's later fatal divisions began with Baldwin IV's accession.

Saladin was therefore relatively unhampered as he continued on his quest to bring all of Muslim Syria under his control. Some contemporary chroniclers criticised him sharply for this war on Muslims,* but the situation now faced by Saladin was entirely similar to that which had faced Nur al-Din upon his accession to the government of Aleppo in 1146. The first task of Nur al-Din, Saladin and every successful monarch who prosecuted jihad after them had to be bringing Syria fully under their control. The turning point in Nur al-Din's campaign against the Franks had been his occupation of Damascus, since its government had, time and time again, allied with the Crusaders. Now Aleppo, Homs and Hama, under the Zangids, were doing the same. Saladin's war against the Zangids was also carried out under the pretence of carrying out his legal duties of suzerainty to, and guardianship of, al-Salih. It is notable in this respect that he did not move to occupy Aleppo until after the death of al-Salih in 1181. Saladin also had to act against the 'rebel' emirs simply because their ambitions threatened to involve the whole of Syria in a vicious contest for the regency. Saladin's intervention averted a destructive internecine war amongst the petty princes. Furthermore, after September 1176, with his marriage to Nur al-Din's widow, Khatun, and his obvious pre-eminence among the emirs, it also followed accepted custom.†

Saladin's main aim in the years between 1174 and 1186 was, therefore, not the jihad per se, but instead the bringing under his aegis of Syria's Muslim cities and their forces. In terms of simple army building this makes perfect sense. Saladin was almost exclusively, and unlike his mentor Shirkuh, a cautious general. He rarely gambled and always looked to have superior numbers in any engagement. The war that was being fought

---

* Indeed, some modern writers have also criticised him. See Ehrenkreutz, A. S., *Saladin*, New York: State University of New York Press, 1972. His verdict on the sultan was that he was nothing more than a calculating opportunist who 'compromised religious ideals to political expediency'.

† See Paine, L., *Saladin: A Man for All Ages*, London: Hale and Co., 1974.

against the *Franj* was now, after all, not one of desperate resistance but rather a slow grinding one that would be concluded through attrition of their fortified places and destruction of their field army. Battle is always a risky venture and Saladin was keen to pursue it only if the odds were stacked absolutely in his favour. At this point, risking battle without securing every available advantage would have been tantamount to dereliction of duty for any leader of the jihad. Saladin's slow building of his forces also fitted with Ibn Zafar's advice on the application of *quwwa*. What he learnt in his first few years as sultan was to use *tadbir*, and more importantly *hila*, to bring the Franks to the field under conditions that totally favoured his troops and allowed him to utilise his force fully.*

A preponderance of numbers could not be achieved in Syria without the accession to his army of the standing forces of every city, including those of Mosul. His general reluctance to engage the Franks before this process was completed therefore makes perfect sense, especially given the mauling that he received from the Crusaders at Mont Gisard in 1177, the fact that the combined *askari* forces of Damascus and Egypt only amounted to six thousand troopers and that the Zangids retained at least the same number of men in arms right up until the recognition of Saladin's claims on Mosul in 1186. Saladin's position was only secure enough to make full commitment to the conquest of Jerusalem after Mosul was secured.

In early 1175 Saladin invested Aleppo. He had already subdued Homs, excepting the fact that its citadel continued to hold out against him. Gumushtigin, now *atabeg* of Aleppo and guardian of al-Salih, responded with a little asymmetrical warfare. He made contact with Sinan,† the Ismaili Assassin grand master, and persuaded him to make an attempt on Saladin's life. The Ismaili Assassins had struggled to survive in Syria during Nur al-Din's reign, but in the confused political landscape of the 1170s they reached out from their mountain strongholds and bid once again for political power in the cities of northern Syria. A group of Assassins, disguised as ordinary soldiers in Saladin's army, tried to gain access to the sultan's tent, but they were challenged by an emir. They stabbed the emir and one Assassin got into the tent, only to have his head

---

* Dekmejian and Thabit, pp. 125–37.

† The Crusader sources called him the 'Old Man of the Mountain' and he certainly lived to a ripe old age before succumbing to natural causes – a perhaps surprising but not uncommon end for Assassin grand masters. For further detail on his extraordinary history and that of the sect in Syria, see Waterson, *Ismaili Assassins*, Chapters Four, Six and Eight.

slashed off by a guard's sabre. More Assassins then forced their way into the tent, but so did a number of Saladin's close bodyguards and senior officers, who killed them to a man.

Gumushtigin also called on Raymond of Tripoli to distract Saladin from Aleppo by attacking Homs, as well as calling on Mosul to stand with Aleppo against the Ayyubid usurper. Saladin successfully negotiated with Raymond for a truce, with Humphrey of Toron acting as an intermediary, but he still withdrew from Aleppo's environs in March 1175. However, he had been able to secure the citadel of Homs, despite a bloody resistance by its garrison during which his sappers mined and fired one of its walls.

This partial success encouraged Gumushtigin to widen his attacks on Saladin: after allying himself with Mosul and other minor emirates, he attacked Hama. This was a mistake, because much of the army of Mosul was already committed to the reduction of Sinjar in the Jazira and Saladin's ranks had been swollen by Turcoman irregulars and the troops of Hama: they now numbered some seven thousand troopers. This was small compared to the number of troops now called to the banners of Aleppo, but troops from the Egyptian regiments were also close by. On 13 April 1175, Saladin crushed the combined forces of Mosul and Aleppo at the Battle of the Horns of Hama, near the River Orontes. One cavalry charge was enough to clear the field of the Aleppan *askari*, and the baggage train and the infantry were both abandoned to their fate. The Mosul contingent was particularly badly, but courageously, led. Saladin said of its leader, Izz al-Din, that he was, 'either the bravest man present on the field that day or a complete fool'.*

Saladin concluded a truce with Gumushtigin that left him in undisputed possession of Damascus and a large part of northern Syria, including Homs, Hama and Baalbek. He also achieved virtual suzerainty over Aleppo, in that its forces were obliged to join with him in jihad whenever they were called upon to do so. By this he neutralised the risk of alliances between Gumushtigin and the *Franj*. However, he failed to achieve full caliphal recognition of his rights in northern Syria, despite sending envoys to Baghdad in the summer of 1175 – such recognition was vital for him to be able to claim unchallenged leadership in the Holy War. There was a further challenge to the rights he had gained at the negotiating table, following a battle in the spring of 1176 when Sayf

---

* In Gibb, p. 22.

al-Din brought troops from Mosul to once again ally with Aleppo against him. The rise of Saladin the Kurd, in a theatre dominated by Turks for over a hundred years, may have been the reason for the ongoing animosity of the Zangids – though it is just as likely that seeing Nur al-Din's former subordinate now holding more than the 'Just King' had ever held as sultan, was just too galling for the emirs of these cities. Their spleens were never to be vented, though, and they were routed once more at Tall al-Sultan. The emirs may have been cheered a little by Saladin's return to them of some of the booty raided from their camp, made up as it was of caged parrots and nightingales. A short note advising their commander to amuse himself with such trivia and stay well clear of the military arts was also sent with the birds.

In May 1176, Saladin was besieging Azaz – one of several fortresses that defended Aleppo. While he was resting alone in the tent of one of his emirs, an Ismaili Assassin rushed in and struck at him with a dagger. He was only saved by the close-fitting mail coif that covered his head and neck. The Assassin then slashed at his throat, but Saladin, who was a small but extremely powerful man, struck his attacker's arm and slapped the blow away. One of Saladin's emirs heard the commotion and rushed into the tent and the Assassin was overpowered and killed. At that point, another Ismaili plunged into the tent and attacked Saladin. Fortunately, the sultan's guard had now arrived and the Assassin was hacked to pieces. When the Assassins' bodies were examined it was found that they were both members of Saladin's close personal bodyguard.

Saladin closed the siege of Aleppo by another round of negotiation with Gumushtigin. He had taken Aleppo's fortresses, Azaz and Manbj, by storm, but it was obvious that taking the city itself would be logistically and technically difficult, given Aleppo's impressive citadel and walls, and might well turn out to be counterproductive. The bloodletting that the city's conquest was guaranteed to require would have driven the senior emirs of Syria away from Saladin at a time when he was attracting more and more of them to his banner, including Nur al-Din's old army commander. Saladin also had concerns over maturing Aleppan–Frankish negotiations. The Aleppans had been in contact with Baldwin IV and had released both Reynald of Châtillon and Joscelin of Courtenay* as

---

* Both had been captured by Nur al-Din. Reynald had, of course, been lord of Antioch but had now lost that title. Joscelin was titled as lord of Edessa but the fiction of that title had become fairly obvious by 1176.

part of a mutual support pact. Saladin had also received intelligence on an extensive raid to be made by Baldwin IV into the Biqa valley. He warned his brother Turanshah, who was now governor of Damascus, of the coming of the Frankish king, and he once more gave the Aleppans easy terms, so that he could quickly extricate himself from the siege.

Saladin had not forgotten the two attempts made on his life by the Assassin grand master Sinan and he set out to besiege the forbidding Ismaili castle of Masyaf in August 1176. He was riding through a forest with his bodyguard towards the fortress when an Assassin dropped from a tree in a further attempt to murder him. Fortunately for Saladin, the Assassin's timing was off and he landed on the rump of the sultan's horse, fell backwards to the ground, and was trampled and hacked to death by the bodyguard riding close behind. Saladin began a siege of the castle, but he had misread the Ismaili grand master totally. Sinan was more than just a knife for hire. Saladin, with his mission to unite all of Syria in the Sunni jihad, would leave no room for any heretical groups, and the Ismailis' response to all such threats was always assassination. They could only hope to survive during political chaos. Sinan could not, therefore, be bought off by the sultan or cowed into submission. Saladin's only real choice, if he wanted to close the affair quickly and maintain his own safety, was to negotiate with this intractable adversary. Until this occurred he always had to be on his guard: he even went so far as to have a tall wooden tower built, in which he would sleep at night, and was never seen without mail during the day.

Saladin finally agreed to receive an ambassador from Masyaf in his tent. The Ismaili emissary was surrounded by the sultan's close guard and searched for weapons before being allowed into Saladin's presence. However, he then refused to deliver his message in the presence of guards and Saladin dismissed them all except two Mamluks whom he had raised from boyhood in his own household. Still the emissary insisted on a one-to-one meeting, but Saladin stated that the two men never left his side and that they were as sons to him. The Ismaili then turned to the two Mamluks and said, 'If I ordered you, in the name of my master, to kill this sultan would you do so?' Their simple response was to draw their swords, saying, 'Command us as you wish.'

This affair, along with threats against his entire household, ensured that Saladin was suddenly very inclined to make peace with Sinan.*

---

* Lewis, B., 'Kamal al-Din's Biography of Rashid al-Din Sinan', *Arabica. Revue D'Etudes Arabes*, vol. XIII, fasc. 3, 1966, pp. 231–2.

An agreement was struck that ensured the safety of the Assassins' enclaves from the sultan's army and allowed Saladin to continue with the prosecution of his campaign against Aleppo and indeed gave him the opportunity to employ Assassins for his own political ends. He almost certainly used them against the house of Zangi soon after, but his secret relationship with Sinan would bring its greatest benefit to him at the end of his reign.

Saladin returned to Egypt in 1176 having fixed a truce with Jerusalem. He then began to address the naval problems of that state and to rearrange the internal affairs of Syria, which basically meant placing his relatives in charge of the key cities. However, his nephew, Tapi al-Din Umar, showed little interest in the Levant and went off adventuring with his *askari* into the *Maghrib*.* This quest for new lands, which Saladin unofficially permitted, would initially benefit the sultan, but would cause enormous problems at the closing stages of his reign. Saladin also began work on rebuilding the citadel and walls of Cairo.

The loss of Ascalon in 1153 had meant that Egypt was totally without any forward base for its navy and therefore without any early warning system for raids on Egypt itself. In 1154, the Normans had sailed from Sicily past Alexandria to raid the city of Tinnis; they repeated the exercise in 1155, only this time they added Rosetta and Alexandria to their itinerary of places to plunder. Information on the damage done to the Fatimid navy by these raids is patchy, but it must have been significant, both physically and psychologically, as all three cities were industrial centres and Ibn al-Qalanasi tells us that Fatimid sailors only ventured to raid in Latin areas of control when they could disguise themselves as Franks. The contemporary writer Abu Shama also tells us that, whilst in 1152, before these Norman raids, the Fatimid navy still had a raiding fleet of seventy vessels, by 1155 it could only send a small number of ships to attack Crusader possessions.†

Saladin had been on the receiving end of the Franks' ability to assault Egypt from the sea at Alexandria during the Pisan blockade of 1167 and had witnessed the galling spectacle of his wounded being evacuated from Alexandria by Frankish merchant vessels. Then in 1168, in support of

---

* The Arabic word *maghrib* denotes North Africa and the 'West' generally and is also the word for sunset.

† In Ehrenkreutz, A. S., 'The Place of Saladin in the Naval History of the Mediterranean Sea in the Middle Ages', *Journal of the American Oriental Society*, April–June 1955, pp. 100–16.

Amalric's offensive, twenty Frank ships had sailed up the eastern branch of the Nile and were only prevented from travelling up to Cairo by a blockade of sunken ships that had been hastily assembled by the Egyptian army. The immolation of the old city of Cairo by the Egyptians during their defence of the new city in 1168 had also destroyed a significant portion of the Fatimid fleet, which was at anchor in the old port. The debacle of the Byzantine–Crusader operation against Damietta in 1169 brought a short period of calm in the naval war, as Sicilian-Norman animosity to the Byzantines restrained the Greeks from further assaults on Egypt. The confrontation between Sicily and Constantinople also benefited Saladin, in that he was given fair warning by the Greeks of a coming Sicilian seaborne invasion via Alexandria in July 1173. However, when the Norman fleet hove into view, the sultan's forces were nowhere to be seen. The Normans were able to manage an orderly disembarkation and seize control of the quay, but then Saladin, who had been raiding in Gaza, appeared at the head of his *askari*, and after three days of heavy fighting the Normans were forced back to their ships. They had, however, done an enormous amount of damage to the port during their occupation and the Egyptians had also been forced to burn many of their own war and cargo ships to prevent them falling into the Normans' hands.

The Normans returned in 1175 to raid Tinnis, but were repulsed after only two days. They were more successful in 1177 as they totally surprised the garrison of Tinnis, occupied it for several days, carried out a brutal sack and secured a number of Muslim vessels, which they then towed back to Sicily.

Restoring and re-manning the navy was going to be a complex and difficult task and the threat to Egypt's ports was ongoing. The Normans of Sicily had abandoned the last of their North African coastal possessions in 1160 after the rise of the Almohad dynasty. They were likely to try to reclaim these losses elsewhere now, and Egypt had shown itself to be a lucrative target many times before. Saladin also had a dearth of materials with which to repair the fleet and the treasury was stretched, but then it always was: Saladin's reputation as a spendthrift ruler began, perhaps, with his shipbuilding programme.

In fact, his generosity to the navy had begun back in 1172, when he had raised sailors' wages. The navy's morale had been at an all-time low during this period and press-ganging was common. By increasing the wage, he not only encouraged Egyptians to stay with the navy, but encouraged many men from further along the North African coast to

1. Mounted Turkish troops carried only small bucklers as any larger shield would have impinged on their archery. Fatimid infantry, however, carried long shields, not dissimilar to the European 'kites'. (*National Museum of Syria*)

2. The great mosque of Damascus was the scene of the murder of the leader of the Sultan of Baghdad's commander by the Ismaili Assassins in 1113. The sultan had sent an army to challenge the Franks but also to bring the independent Muslim princes of the region back under his control. The murder led to the collapse of the sultan's jihad and several of these princes may have collaborated in planning the murder. The great mosque was also, however, the starting point for the Muslim expedition that finally extinguished Outremer in 1291. (*Author*)

3. (*Above, left and right*) Impressive Crusader castles were a major obstacle to the jihad, and also cut across Muslim communication channels. The Crusaders excelled in the science of fortification. This is the curtain wall of Karak castle in Jordan. The astounding strength of the castle is indicated by the thickness of the walls surrounding this arrow slit. (*Author*)

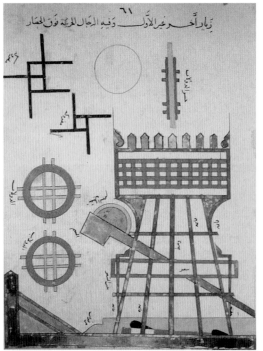

4. A counterweight trebuchet for firing quarrels or artillery-size arrows, from a treatise of al-Zardakus. Extensive written works on siege engines were produced by *manjaniqiyin* – the engineers who designed them for the sultans. Sultan Zangi brought a mere fourteen mangonels to his siege of Edessa in 1144. At the fall of Acre to Sultan Khalil in 1291, however, some ninety mangonels were arrayed against the city, including one named al-Mansura, 'the Victorious', the largest siege engine ever built in the Middle East. (*Sharjah Museum of Islamic Civilization*)

5. (*Left*) Muslim siege engineers had a range of different mangonels: this is a *qarabugha* (black bull), but there were also the *shaqtani* (devilish), *al-Lasib* (playful) and *Franj* (Frankish); from a treatise of al-Zardakus. (*Sharjah Museum of Islamic Civilization*).
(*Below*) Reconstructed mangonel from the Cairo citadel. (*Author*)

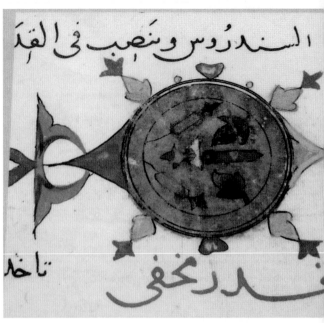

السندروس ونصب فى القد

تاخذ

...در يخفى

6. Early grenades often contained scorpions and snakes; later versions, however, employed *naft* (Greek fire) to create incendiary devices. (*Sharjah Museum of Islamic Civilization*)

7. (*Above, left*) The Mamluk sultan Baybars had virtually crushed the Crusader kingdom out of existence by the time of his death. This is his tomb in Damascus. (*Author*)

8. (*Above, right*) Saladin has two tombs in the great mosque of Damascus. An ornate marble one was donated long after his death by Kaiser Wilhelm. The sultan has been idealised in the West as the epitome of chivalry, and he was certainly the greatest hero of the jihad. (*Author*)

9. (*Below*) The lion was the emblem of Sultan Baybars. The motif reflects the power of a sultan who defeated the Mongols and who was essentially the founder of the Mamluk dynasty that ended the Crusader kingdom. (*National Museum of Lebanon*)

10. (*Above, left*) The classic Egyptian film *al-Nasir al-Saladin*, released in 1963 shortly after the dissolution of the United Arab Republic of Syria and Egypt, both laments this loss of unity among the Arabs and equates the military disasters of 1948 and 1956 with the Crusader successes before the rise of Saladin. It is also notable that 'al-nasir', meaning victorious, was also the name of the Egyptian president: the champion of pan-Arabism, Gamal Nasser.

11. (*Above, right*) Saladin remains a potent icon for unity and resistance in the Arab world, despite the sultan being a Kurd. This film poster advertises, 'The Search for Saladin'.

12. A Crusader church, converted into a mosque after Beirut's fall to the Mamluks. Other churches were demolished and their arched doors and windows were used in the construction of mosques and sultans' mausoleums in Cairo. (*Author*)

13. (*Above, left*) Damascus's walls thwarted the Second Crusade in its attempt to take the city. However, when Nur al-Din's troops made an attempt on the city, the populace greeted them warmly: the city, including the citadel shown here, fell more or less without resistance. (*Author*)

14. (*Above, right*) After the death of his father, Zangi, Nur al-Din became lord of Aleppo. By the end of his reign he had taken Damascus, conquered Egypt and unified the men of the pen with the men of the sword through jihad. (*Author*)

15. (*Below*) A somewhat idealised nineteenth-century view of Jaffa. Fighting against Richard Lionheart in virtually the last action of the Third Crusade, the Muslim army rebelled against Saladin and refused to attack Richard's camp. Maintaining an army in the field for over five years, against both the Crusaders of Acre and against Richard, was the sultan's greatest achievement.

16. (*Left*) Folio from a *Shahnama* (The Book of Kings) by Firdawsi, showing the siege of a Turanian stronghold by the forces of Kay Khusraw; Turkoman period, Iran. Early attempts at taking Crusader castles failed, due largely to the inability of Muslim leaders to maintain their composite armies in the field for sufficient lengths of time – that changed with the advent of the Mamluk sultans, and the Crusader castles fell one after another. (*Freer Gallery*)

17. (*Below, left*) A scene depicting Khusraw and Shirin in the hunting field, from *Khusraw u Shirin* by Nizami; Timurid period, Tabriz, Iran. Note the composite bows and the 'Parthian shot' of the archer on the right of the hunt. The Turks, like the Mongols, engaged in massive hunts with hundreds of horsemen taking part. The hunt allowed practice in movements which would be transferred to the battlefield. The hunt would end with encirclement, a tactic the Turks employed against the Crusaders at the Battle of Ager Sanguinis (Field of Blood). (*Freer Gallery*)

18. (*Above*) 'Saladin the Victorious', from a nineteenth-century engraving. The reputation of the sultan in the West as the avatar of chivalry had begun as early as the thirteenth century and was complete by the time that Sir Walter Scott penned *The Talisman*.

19. (*Left*) A polo game: an illustration from the poem 'Guy u Chawgan' (The Ball and the Polo-mallet); Safavid dynasty, Tabriz, Iran or Turkey. Both Nur al-Din and Sultan Baybars were renowned players of polo. Baybars would play twice a week in Damascus and in Cairo, and Nur al-Din died playing the game. The training potential of polo for cavalrymen, with its requirement for fast turns and close control, is obvious. (*Freer Gallery*)

20. (*Below, left*) Canteen; Ayyubid period, the Jazira. Items like this were often made for Crusader patrons. This is one of the rare examples, beyond the extensive transfer of military technology, of cultural exchange between the Muslims and Crusaders, despite nearly two centuries of war, détente and trade. (*Freer Gallery*)

21. (*Below, right*) Plate; Fatimid period, Egypt. The Shiite Fatimid dynasty, in its early history, personified jihad, in that its princes were adored imams and the state's *raison d'être* was to spread its creed across the entire world. However, by the eleventh century the dynasty's energies were spent and the Fatimid armies were repeatedly defeated in Syria by Crusader forces. (*Freer Gallery*)

22. (*Above, left*) A detail from a Mamluk glass vessel, showing a Mamluk emir enjoying hunting with falcons. The pastimes of Muslim military men and the knights of Outremer were entirely similar. (*Author*)

23. (*Above, right*) A Turkish prince on a decorated dish; Saljuq period, Iran. The face of the prince indicates his central Asian origins. The Saljuq Turks were seen as oppressive aliens by the Arab populace of Syria until the union between them and the religious classes of Aleppo and Damascus in jihad against the Crusaders. (*Freer Gallery*)

24. (*Below*) The Arab mare was the warhorse par excellence of the Mamluk troopers of Egypt. The sultans would offer horses from Medina, purportedly the best horses in the Islamic world, as prizes in martial games. This is one of their descendants at an annual horse fair in Dubai. (*Author*)

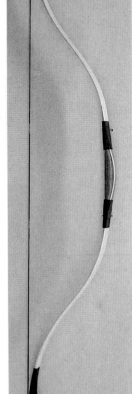

25. (*Above*) Folio from the *Tarikh-i alam-aray-i Shah Ismail* (The World Adorning History of Shah Ismail): the battle between Shah Ismail and Abul-khayr Khan; Safavid period, Isfahan, Iran. Note the bow quivers and wide-mouth arrow quivers at each rider's side. The People's Crusade, contingents of the Crusade of 1101 and of the Second Crusade, were all annihilated by Turcoman archery fusillades. Mamluk troopers could loose three arrows in under one and a half seconds: their archery assault was even more impressive than that of the Mongols. (*Freer Gallery*).

(*Top, right*) An unstrung Turkish bow in the Topkapi Sarai treasury, showing its 'pretzel' shape. (*Author*)

(*Right*) A twenty-first-century Turkish bow, handmade with traditional materials by Csaba Grózer.

26. (*Above, left and right*) Statue of Saladin; Damascus. This statue was erected in 1992 and shows the sultan urging his horse forward into battle. Its sculptor wished to represent Saladin as a leader embodying a wave of popular feeling against the *Franj*. Hence the presence of both a *Sufi*, representing the religious classes, and an infantryman, representing the city militias. We might call this popular feeling the essence of jihad in this period. At the back of the sultan's horse, virtually under its hooves, lay King Guy, holding his ransom, and Reynald of Châtillon, who exhausted and demoralised, looks down at his fallen sword after the Crusaders' crushing defeat at the Horns of Hattin. (*Author*)

27. (*Below, left and right*) The Mamluks rebuilt the citadel of Damascus and left their blazons on their work. The lion of Baybars can be seen here and the goblet would have been the insignia of a senior emir. (*Author*)

28. The citadel of Aleppo, seen from the south. The city's impressive fortifications repulsed Muslim armies from Baghdad in 1111 and 1113. The city's Saljuq prince, Ridwan, even allied himself with the Crusaders in 1115 against a Baghdad-sponsored army in order to preserve his independence. (*Author*)

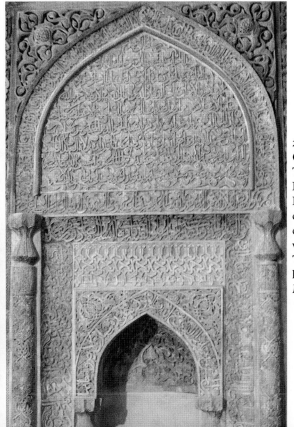

29. The *mihrab* of the Mongol Ilkhan Oljeitu in the great mosque of Isfahan. The Mongols of Persia converted to Islam in the early fourteenth century. During their invasion of Muslim lands, culminating in their killing of the caliph of Baghdad and invasion of Syria, they were entirely antagonistic to the religion. The Crusaders hoped, in vain, that the khans would be their saviours from the Muslim jihad. (*Author*)

30. The Dome of the Rock was purified by Saladin and its floor covered with rose petals after he retook Jerusalem for Islam in 1187.

31. The Church of the Holy Sepulchre in Jerusalem. The tombs of the Latin kings were destroyed during a sack of the city by the Khwarazmians in 1244. The sequel to this desecration was the mustering of the largest Crusader army to take the field since the Horns of Hattin, and its destruction by the army of Egypt at the Battle of Harbiyya.

32. The walls of Antioch incorporated much of the lower slopes of Mount Silpius. It is ironic that the Mamluks, when they took the city back from the Crusaders in 1268, broke in along this section of wall. The Crusaders had entered the city during their assault of 1098 at almost exactly the same defensive point.

33. The Gate of Herod and a section of the walls at Jerusalem. The Fatimids retaking of Jerusalem from the Saljuq Turks in July 1098 was certainly an error of judgement, as they failed to consolidate the region surrounding the Holy City before the Crusader army began its march into Palestine. The city fell to the Franks in July 1099.

34. A highly idealised portrayal of the Battle of Ascalon, 1099. Poor generalship and the fact that the Fatimid army massed together and formed a perfect target for the Crusader knights' charge were chiefly responsible for the debacle that ensued. The Fatimids repeatedly challenged the Crusaders in southern Palestine throughout the first decade of the twelfth century but were unsuccessful in virtually all these encounters.

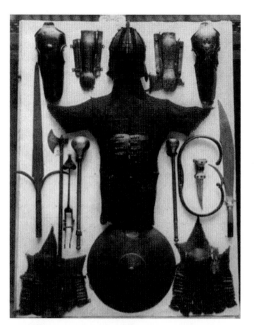

36. Muslim helmets were designed to cover the wearer's turban. The finials and plume holders helped with the recognition of individuals in the heat of battle.

35. The *askari*, or bodyguards, of Islamic princes were heavily armed. Chamfrons for horses, heavy chain-mail armour and maces became the standard equipment for royal Mamluks in the thirteenth century.

join up. Obtaining shipbuilding material in a country that had virtually no forests required Saladin to cut cards with the devil, and he secured a trade agreement with Pisa, whose navy had caused him such misery in 1168, for the importation of wood, wax and iron. Meanwhile, Saladin's adventurous nephew, Tapi al-Din Umar, had been reasonably successful in his invasion of Muslim lands to the west of Egypt – this benefited Saladin, as it increased the coastline west of Egypt that could be controlled with short-range sailings and would therefore 'buffer' Egypt to a degree from Sicilian raids. There were also the forests of North Africa, which could now begin to supply Egypt's shipyards, as well as the plundering of ports and harbours along its coast by Tapi al-Din Umar for ships and smaller craft. Finally, of course, this enhancement of Saladin's name as a powerful sultan encouraged North African sailors to serve in the slowly recovering Egyptian navy.

The formal call to build a fleet was proclaimed by the sultan in Alexandria in March 1177, but a damper was placed on the optimism this produced by news that the Byzantines were preparing once more to try to take Egypt. Saladin's espionage system then reported more heartening news that the Crusaders had rejected Manuel's overtures of finance for an overland expedition backed by a Byzantine fleet of seventy galleys. Court intrigues in Jerusalem had paralysed the project, but Manuel had also lost a lot of prestige in the last year after failures in Anatolia and this had made him an unattractive ally.

In fact, it was suggested in court circles throughout Europe that Emperor Manuel had not recovered his nerve after his defeat at the hands of Kilij Arslan II on 17 September 1176 at the pass of Myriokephalon. Manuel, like Romanus Diogenes in 1071, had brought a large army of some twenty-five thousand men into Anatolia to punish the Turkish emirs of the region for raiding Byzantine lands; he also intended to reduce Iconium and his troops were burdened with siege equipment and engines. His column, like that of his predecessor, was unwieldy and over ten miles long and he failed to send advance parties out to look for his foe. Kilij Arslan II set a perfect ambush and his Turcomen tore the Greek column apart with arrows and charges. All the siege equipment was destroyed and it was reported that Manuel had panicked and had required assistance to leave the field. The losses to the army were surprisingly not that heavy, but the Byzantines were forced to retreat from central Anatolia; from this point on, the pattern of movement in the area would be of Turks to the west and not of Greek advances to the east.

Saladin, like Manuel, was defeated due to uncharacteristic recklessness on 25 November 1177 by Baldwin IV, who, despite his leprous condition and the divisions within his court, would prove to be a tenacious, committed and often skilful defender of the Holy Sepulchre. The truce of 1176 had clauses in it that allowed Jerusalem to support any Crusading noble. This was, of course, tantamount to saying that any visiting prince could attack Saladin's possessions and the lords of Outremer could aid him. However, this was not a lapse of scrutiny on Saladin's part. We have to remember that agreements in the Middle Ages were made between individuals and not states, and also that a certain degree of elasticity was built into every treaty, as there was a sure expectation that minor raids and settling of scores by lesser lords and emirs would always occur. Such 'trivial' affairs should not be allowed to bring monarchs into conflict.

Under these conditions then, the arrival in August 1177 of Philip of Flanders on crusade to Outremer and Baldwin IV's support of his assault on Hama were perfectly legitimate. The Crusaders were repulsed from the city by local troops, and when they moved north to besiege Harim, Saladin saw an opportunity to strike in the south. He had invested heavily in his army by buying more elite Mamluk slave soldiers and he had also been improving both the condition and numbers of the *halqa* or regular Turkish and Kurdish cavalry. He therefore brought a sizeable force into Gaza with him. Baldwin IV, following a precept that he tried always to maintain, refused to allow this force to roam through his lands unchallenged. He returned to Palestine and confronted Saladin; upon the sultan's advance, he then retired to Ascalon. Unfortunately, this 'retreat' may have made the sultan and his troops overconfident and Saladin headed for Jaffa and Ramla, allowing his troops licence to plunder the countryside. Baldwin IV, with a dogged dedication to duty and defence that characterised his wise approach to war, followed at a distance. Then, near Ramla, at Mont Gisard, he struck at Saladin's *askari*, which he knew would be the rallying point for the army once they realised that they were under attack. The *askari* Mamluks were thrown into complete confusion by the Crusaders' charge and the panic spread. Huge casualties were taken by every part of the Muslim army, which was impeded from forming up to mount a response by baggage animals and cattle they had raided from the Franks. This plunder was all lost and Baldwin IV pursued Saladin until nightfall. The retreat to Egypt hardly went any better: it was undertaken in heavy rain and under constant attack by Bedouins. It was the heaviest loss in battle that Saladin would ever endure and he learnt much from the debacle.

The disaster of Mont Gisard also kept Saladin from taking the field in 1178 and he spent the year building up his navy and restoring his army's strength. He started a trend that would continue through the later Ayyubids: of an increasing reliance on Mamluk Turks who, almost exclusively, hailed from the Caucasus. These would be the men who would eventually take the sultanate of Egypt from the Ayyubids.

In the spring of 1179, the new model Egyptian fleet took sail. Its complement of ships had doubled and now included sixty *shini* (galleys) and twenty *tarrida* (transports) and an assortment of small patrol vessels and coastguard vessels. The fleet's resources were now back to the levels that the Fatimids had achieved at the height of their power. The force was divided into a defensive arm of fifty ships and an offensive arm of about twenty vessels. The offensive fleet reached Byzantine waters off Cyprus in June 1179 and then sailed back down the coast of Syria, making several raids on its ports and capturing two cargo vessels. It returned with this booty, along with a thousand prisoners. Abu Shama recorded the ecstasy of the people of Cairo over the victory. Then, on 14 October, Acre, the Frankish state's most important port, was raided. Muslim ships entered the harbour under cover of darkness, and before the Crusaders could respond, they managed to take control of every ship in the harbour. The Muslims held the Franks at bay for two days with archery fire from their galleys' decks and demolished parts of the harbour and fired a number of the Frankish ships. The deaths of three Egyptian captains were recorded in the engagement; the deaths of ordinary seamen were not recorded. Abu Shama was once again overjoyed: 'Our fleet once destroyed, became in turn the destroyer of the enemy. Never a similar victory was achieved by a Muslim fleet, neither in the past centuries, nor even at the time of our naval supremacy and the weakness of our enemies.'*

Saladin also looked to revenge himself for Mont Gisard on land. He took his rebuilt army into Syria in March 1178 with the intent of attacking Crusader forces besieging Harim, but the Zangids of Aleppo had paid the Franks off before he could reach the city. Philip of Flanders's retirement from Outremer then required that the truce be re-established and Saladin was denied the conflict he was looking for with the Franks. It seems almost redundant to state that the Franks viewed Saladin as their most dangerous adversary at this juncture, but it was also vital to Saladin that this remained so. He had to keep the mantle

---

* In Ehrenkreutz, 'The Place of Saladin in the Naval History', p. 106.

of the leader of jihad against the infidels, simply because it identified him as the legitimate Muslim ruler of the Levant. Jihad gave him 'instrumental sanctity'* and political sanction in what might very easily have become a bloody turf war between Muslims as he battled with the Zangids. The Franks' and Zangids' *modus vivendi* was serendipitous for the sultan, as it increased Saladin's esteem in the eyes of the *ulama*. He attracted the caliph of Baghdad's treasurer to his cause early on, and several of Nur al-Din's *qadis* deserted the Zangid court and came to work under Saladin in Damascus. The traveller Ibn Jubayr tells us that Saladin's name was held in awe by pilgrims in Mecca as early as 1183. It was also evident that opinion outside of the *ulama* was sliding toward him, even among the Turkish military men of Syria, who were repelled by the Zangids' arrangements with the infidels. As a Kurd, in a period when clan and kin were the common xenophobic limits of loyalty, he could never hope to win over the Turks fully, and even after his triumph at Jerusalem in 1187 he was evidently not universally beloved. Ibn al-Athir gives us the *sotto voce* words of a Turkish emir who was helping the sultan onto his horse: 'Have a care son of Ayyub, what sort of death you will come to – you who are being helped to mount by a Saljuq prince and a descendant of the *atabeg* Zangi!'†

The Franks broke the truce in August 1178 with an attack on Harim, though it was beaten off by its garrison. All the prisoners captured were executed for their breach of the armistice: such treatment of prisoners seems at odds with Saladin's image in the West. However, it must be remembered that this representation of Saladin was propagated by romantic constructions – such as Dante's unbaptised but spotless soul placed among others whom the poet admired but could not place in his *Paradiso*, or Scott's *Talisman*, where the sultan is portrayed as a chivalrous and clement Muslim knight. Saladin was a professional soldier and politician, and politics in the Middle Ages had as much to do with the sword as it did with the pen. There was also, of course, pure

---

* See Crone, P., *Slaves on Horses: The Evolution of the Islamic Polity*, Cambridge: Cambridge University Press, 1980, p. 89. Jihad gave rulers a legal and moral authority; the leader who took up jihad could also expect the support of the clerical class and the populace even if his ventures were self-aggrandising. A passage from a Mamluk war manual of the fourteenth century captures perhaps more succinctly how success in jihad gave the right to rule: 'An arrow from a warrior shot at an unbeliever counts more than the endless prayers said by a pious hermit.'
† In Gibb, p. 22.

rage at times: as in 1186, when Reynald of Châtillon's men raided in ships down the coast of Arabia almost to Mecca. By order of the sultan, among the men captured there must not: 'Remain among them neither an eye capable of seeing nor a single man capable of indicating or even knowing the route from this sea.'* This rage was not simply confined to Christian wrongdoers either. In the Muslim chronicles we can also read of the sultan's intolerant attitude towards unorthodox Islam:

> He hated philosophers, heretics, materialists and all the opponents of the Law. For this reason he commanded his son-in-law al-Malik al-Zahir, prince of Aleppo, to punish a young man called al-Suhrawardi who called himself an enemy of the Law and a heretic. His son had the man arrested for what he had heard of him and informed the sultan, who commanded that he be put to death. So he was killed, and left hanging on the cross for several days.†

In 1189, Saladin would use clemency as a political weapon, just as Caesar had, in order to speed the submission of Crusader cities to him and it seems beyond doubt that he was a humane man by the standards of the day. It is his actions after the fall of Jerusalem, perhaps more than anything, that have encouraged the Western view of him as the avatar of chivalry, but in the final analysis, he was a leader of jihad and as such, his ultimate goal was the destruction of Outremer. If that task had required the extermination of its entire populace, then that would simply have been the unfolding of God's will.

Saladin was then distracted from the *Franj* by the internal affairs of Syria and by his family, which basically amounted to the same thing. His brother, Turanshah, had been mismanaging Damascus and was also far too friendly with Aleppo. He was therefore removed from office and replaced by Saladin's nephew, Farrukhshah, but demanded

---

* Abu Shama in Barber, M., 'Frontier Warfare in the Latin Kingdom of Jerusalem: The Campaign of Jacob's Ford, 1178–79', Chapter Two in *The Crusades and their Sources: Essays Presented to Bernard Hamilton*, edited by J. France and W. G. Zajac, London: Ashgate, 1998; also available at www.deremilitari.org.

† Baha al-Din in Gabrieli, p. 90. Though it is hard to get an intimate picture of the minds and personal morals of the great men of this period we do know that Il-Ghazi and Zangi were both heavy drinkers, and that Nur al-Din was similarly likely to imbibe, until a number of setbacks seem to have convinced him that the drink really was from the devil, whilst Saladin was teetotal throughout his life. Whether this means that the evolving jihad personally affected these men is, however, a difficult question. See Irwin, pp. 38–9.

compensation in the form of Baalbek. This required Saladin to allow his brother to invest and take Baalbek, even though this was held by one of his own emirs. The emir then had to be paid off with lands in the north of Syria. This distraction, as well as an ongoing drought and famine in Syria, kept Saladin busy until the spring of 1179. His 'easy' attitude towards his family has often been criticised and the Ayyubid dynasty at times shamed his legacy, but as noted above, kith and kin were often all a leader had to fall back on during crises and even for day-to-day governance in twelfth-century Syria.

Farrukhshah justified the trust his uncle had placed in him with a signal victory in April. Baldwin IV had mobilised and was preparing to raid across Muslim territory near the fortress of Belfort. Farrukhshah was engaged by the Franks while he was trailing them with part of his *askari*, and lighting beacons to show their progress so that Saladin might intercept them with a larger force. The Franks forced the issue with Farrukhshah because they wanted to plunder cattle that were grazing in the valleys nearby, and thought they had beaten him off when his force fled before them. However, the main body of his Mamluks was hidden in the narrow rocky valleys of the area and they emerged in small groups at the gallop and assaulted the disorganised Franks with showers of arrows. The Crusaders retreated in disarray and Humphrey of Toron was killed whilst protecting Baldwin IV from the rain of arrows that was falling all around them.

The months after this were spent containing the Franks. Imad al-Din describes how this was done and why it was so important:

> In this year the Franks resolved to disturb the Muslims from all sides at the same time, in order to prevent their concentration at a single point. As the prince of Antioch [Bohemond III] had violated the truce in invading the country of Shayzar, as had the count of Tripoli in attacking a troop of Turcomen after having accorded them a truce, the sultan placed his nephew Taqi al-Din on the frontier of Hama, adding to him Shams al-Din and Sayf al-Din. He also posted Nasir al-Din on the frontier of Homs in order to oppose the count of Tripoli. Beyond this he wrote to his brother al-Adil, who was his lieutenant in Egypt, to detach a squadron of fifteen hundred Egyptian horsemen to reinforce the army of Syria which was going to attack the enemy.*

---

* Recorded by Abu Shama in Barber. Al-Adil is known more commonly in the West as Sayf al-Din or Saphadin.

Saladin took the field with these fifteen hundred Egyptian troopers in June 1179. He brought his forces out of Damascus and beyond Banyas and sent contingents as far as Sidon to raid. He also recruited starving Arab tribesmen on the way and sent them to raid around Beirut with heavy cavalry in support. Famine had struck Syria, so Baldwin IV was forced to respond to these raids on his croplands; he also hoped to repeat the victory of Mont Gisard, as Saladin's forces were dispersed once more in search of booty. He watched the movements of the Muslim army for some time, before bringing his forces quickly down from the low coastal hills near Toron to surprise the sultan's forces on the plain named Marj Ayyun or 'Field of Springs'. Baldwin IV was able to defeat several Muslim detachments as they returned piecemeal from their raids, but this was his undoing because his men, rejoicing in their easy victories, paid more attention to dividing the spoils than to Saladin's rapidly approaching force. Furthermore, Baldwin IV's mounted troops had taken up a position on the high ground to the west of the plain, but could not see Farrukhshah's *askari* as it rode towards them up a gorge. The Franks were then caught between Saladin's force arriving from the east and Farrukhshah's from the north. The survivors fled the field and took refuge in the castle of Shaqif Arnun. Over 270 knights and numerous infantrymen were captured.

Saladin moved on to besiege, storm and destroy the fortress of Chastellet, at Bait al-Ahzan, or Jacob's Ford, on the upper Jordan on 24 August 1179. The fortress had only been founded the year before by the Templars and had been intended to dominate one of the key points of ingress into the Kingdom of Jerusalem along with the already established Templar castle of Safad, which lay about half a day's journey to its south-west. Over one thousand men were killed inside Chastellet when Saladin's troops mined one of the walls and broke in. Numerous horses and coats of mail were also seized and one hundred Muslim slaves were freed.

Back in 1178, Saladin had offered one hundred thousand dinars to the Franks if they agreed to cease their building but they had refused. He had attempted to take the castle a little later but, after losing one of his senior emirs in the attempt, he had withdrawn. The Battle of Marj Ayyun had effectively opened the door to its capture because, after the battle, the Franks were in no position to relieve the castle if it was besieged. The walls were so thick that initially the sultan's sappers made a miscalculation with the length of their tunnel and lit the supports of their mine too early.

The fire was extinguished after Saladin offered a dinar for every goatskin of water brought to the mine. The sappers then went to work again and at dawn on 29 August the wall came down. Imad al-Din described the storming of the castle:

> The Franks had piled up wood behind the wall which crumbled; the current of air which penetrated at the moment of its fall spread the fire, their tents and several combatants were prey to the flames; the remainder who were in the region of the fire implored amnesty. As soon as the flames were extinguished, the troops penetrated the place, killing, taking prisoners, and seizing important booty, [including] one hundred thousand pieces of iron arms of all types and victuals in quantity. The captives were taken to the sultan, who executed the apostates and the bowmen; of around seven hundred prisoners, the greater part were massacred en route by the volunteer troops, the remainder were taken to Damascus.*

Al-Fadil wrote excitedly of how the commander of the castle died: 'When the flames reached his side, he threw himself into a hole full of fire without fear of the intense heat and, from this brazier, he was immediately thrown into another.' He also tells us that Saladin ordered the complete destruction of the castle and even tore at the stones of its walls with his own bare hands.† Saladin took two weeks to destroy the fortress completely and then rode on to raid around Tiberias, Tyre and Beirut before returning to Damascus. In April 1180 Farrukhshah entered Galilee, where the castle used to stand, and devastated the region around Safad. The whole frontier region of the Kingdom of Jerusalem was now virtually uninhabitable for the Franks and the kingdom lay open to Saladin's armies.

This series of defeats, in combination with the newly revitalised Egyptian navy's capture of more Frankish shipping, was enough to bring the Franks to the negotiating table, and a two-year truce was agreed in May 1180. Saladin needed the truce, as drought and famine in Syria had made it logistically almost impossible to keep an army in the field and also required that he supply Syria's great cities with grain from Egypt. The *hudna* also allowed Saladin the opportunity to reorganise and refurbish his navy further, create a new ministry – the *diwan al-ustul*, entirely devoted to the fleet – and to renew his coastal defences in Egypt. Damietta was furnished with a new chain, to close the mouth of the port,

---

* Recorded by Abu Shama in Barber.
† Recorded by Abu Shama in Barber. The 'other brazier' is Hell.

and new fortifications, as were Tinnis and Suez. Under the terms of the truce, the Latin-controlled city of Tortosa received no guarantee of safety. It was raided repeatedly by Muslim ships and marines from the island of Arados, which sat opposite it.

It is an old adage that men make history and they may realise that they are doing so, but they can never fully know the history they are making. After his defeat and miserable retreat from Mont Gisard, Saladin is reported to have said, 'again and again we were on the verge of destruction, nor would God have delivered us if it were not for some future duty.'* Saladin's victories against the Franks in 1179, and especially his destruction of the castle at Jacob's Ford, seem to have made him realise that he was now able to make history – for medieval men, both Muslim and Christian, history unfolded according to God's will. There was a strong belief in destiny and God's control over a man's fate among Muslim military men. The twelfth-century soldier Usama Ibn Munqidh summed up this attitude in one statement: 'The hour of one's death is not brought nearer by exposing oneself to danger nor delayed by being overcautious.'† In short, Saladin at this point felt the hand of God, or what we might call history, guiding him. Saladin's war and his war aims changed from being opportunistic and at times simply reactive, to a jihad that would unite Muslim Syria and expel the Franks from the Levant. The reasons for this change are not difficult to find. The destruction of Chastellet was a severe blow to the expansionist castle strategy of the Franks – it had been an excellent platform for the Templars' pillaging of Muslim caravans. The Kingdom of Jerusalem was placed, to a great extent, on the defensive after this point, and even defence was now increasingly difficult for the Franks as so many troops had been lost during the Battle of Marj Ayyun, and the sack of Chastellet and the subsequent massacre or enslavement of the prisoners taken. The sultan's morale and that of his men was now also sky-high following these three victories. Before 1179, the initiative had been with the Franks, as they exploited the divisions in Muslim Syria, but after Chastellet's fall, Saladin and his lieutenants could raid almost at will into Galilee, complementing his naval raids on the kingdom's coast.

The year 1180 saw the conclusion of a truce with the new Byzantine emperor, Alexius II, who was struggling to assert himself in

* In Gibb, p. 24.
† In Hitti, p. 194.

Constantinople. He only lasted until September 1182, when he became the puppet of Andronicus Comnenus, who initiated his reign with the massacre of Latins living in Constantinople. The obvious anti-Latin policy of Andronicus boded well for Saladin's campaign against the Franks; even though he was killed in 1185, the subsequent emperor, Isaac Angelus, continued with the same strategy. Saladin was later able to negotiate for the resumption of legal Muslim prayers in Constantinople and, in 1187, a new mosque was built in the capital of Orthodox Christianity. By forging diplomatic and trading links with Byzantium, Saladin ensured that Outremer became increasingly isolated.

The Franks of Ascalon broke the truce in the summer of 1181 and raided Tinnis. They managed to capture one Muslim cargo ship, but were prevented from raiding the port by the new fortifications, and were chased off by the prompt arrival of a Muslim fleet. Egypt's navy was beginning to perform well.

The drought and famine in Syria dragged on; in May 1182, Saladin set out from Egypt with a train of caravans to bring relief to the cities. He would not return to Cairo again.

The *Franj* assembled an impressive force at Karak and prepared to strike at the column, but to do so they had taken troops from all over the kingdom. Farrukhshah, finding that there was no opposition worth the name in Jerusalem, ravaged the lands around Tiberias and Acre, and took Daburiya. He returned with one thousand civilian prisoners and twenty thousand animals; more importantly, he diverted the Franks from their chief mission and made it evident to them that they were now restricted to very limited operations. Saladin followed this success with his own raids around Tiberias and Baysan in July 1182, and made an attempt on the castle of Belvoir, which had been strengthened by the Franks as a response to the loss of Jacob's Ford. In August 1182 came a real test for the Muslims, as they attempted a combined land and sea siege of Beirut. Possession of a port on the coast was vital to the retaking of Syria, and the conquest of Beirut would severely hamper communications between the northern and southern states of Outremer. Thirty galleys were committed to the siege, but the port's defences had recently been bolstered and attempts to disembark a force failed completely. Saladin's land forces retired after the failure of the amphibious landing and the arrival of thirty-three Latin galleys was enough to make the Egyptian fleet abandon the siege and sail for home. They perhaps gained more than they deserved by their flight from the enemy when they intercepted a ship full of Venetian refugees fleeing Constantinople. They also captured some seventeen hundred Apulians who had been sailing to join the Crusader armies in Palestine and who had been marooned off Damietta.

The Crusaders had successfully defended Beirut but had very few offensive options. It was this that decided Reynald of Châtillon, now the lord of Karak, to target the caravans that travelled between Syria and Arabia. He had started as early as 1181, with very effective raids against Muslim trade-traffic between Syria and Egypt, but in January 1183 he stepped up his campaign of economic warfare by launching a small flotilla of vessels on the Red Sea. He besieged Ayla with two ships and initially his policy was successful, as he sank some sixteen Muslim vessels and captured two more. The Muslim chroniclers tell us that he wanted to strike at Mecca, but his actions were more probably aimed at harming Egypt's finances. Either way, his success was short-lived, as a portion of the defence fleet was taken overland from Cairo and very rapidly destroyed Reynald's ships off Ayla, before moving on to hunt down and destroy the rest of his small fleet. The Egyptian fleet then added insult to injury by carrying out a very successful campaign that mimicked Reynald's piracy off the coast of Syria. Transports carrying timber, shipwrights, knights and rich merchants were all taken back to Alexandria as plunder.

For the Crusaders, 1183 turned ever more sour, as Aleppo surrendered to Saladin on 12 June. Obtaining the city had looked to be too difficult at the end of the 1170s: it had continued to stand with Mosul, and the Saljuq sultan of much of Anatolia, Kilij Arslan II, had also begun to interfere in north Syria. In 1179, the sultan had demanded small cities bordering his lands that Saladin had won from the Zangids in earlier campaigns. Taqi al-Din was sent north from Hama with his *askari* and secured an important victory over superior forces in early 1180. Then the emir of the fortified town Hisn Kaifa appealed to Saladin for assistance against Kilij Arslan II, even though he was technically a vassal of Mosul. Saladin handled the situation with deft political skill, to his own advantage. By a show of strength he brought Kilij Arslan II to the negotiating table and an alliance was formed between the two sultans. Mosul was essentially being sidelined from Syrian affairs by a process of military muscle and diplomacy, but the city's new emir, Izz al-Din, saw an opportunity – with the death of al-Salih in Aleppo on 4 December 1181 – to force his way back in. The army of Mosul should have been prevented from crossing the Euphrates by Taqi al-Din and Farrukhshah, but the latter was engaged in countering Reynald's caravan raids and the army of Hama could not possibly match that of Mosul. Izz al-Din placed his brother, Imad al-Din, in command of Aleppo and returned to Mosul uncontested.

Saladin wrote to the caliph complaining that while he had been defending Medina and Mecca from Reynald, a province that had been granted to him had been stolen away. He was also in no doubt that the re-attachment of Aleppo to Mosul would seriously stall his jihad. His manpower was simply insufficient to match any aggression from the two cities and take on the Franks, especially now that Reynald was increasing the geographical range of the war. Following the unsuccessful assault on Beirut in 1182, he therefore led his troops to Aleppo to besiege it. He was then encouraged by a group of minor emirs from the Jazira to bring his army of five thousand troopers across the Euphrates, with guarantees that he would meet little opposition. Izz al-Din attempted to bring together forces to prevent Saladin's incursion into lands that Saladin held by caliphal decree, but which Mosul had always traditionally held. However, he failed to draw the region's emirs to his standard.

Saladin went on to besiege Mosul and in desperation Izz al-Din appealed to the Saljuq Sultan of Persia, who was by this juncture very much the foe of the caliph, the caliph's possessions in Iraq having grown at the cost of the Saljuqs. His mission failed, however, which is not surprising given the cataclysmic events that had occurred in the East in the second half of the twelfth century, which we will review a little later. Izz al-Din then appealed to the caliph. The caliph ordered negotiations, to which Saladin agreed, but he continued to press the siege and also invested Sinjar, an allied city of Mosul. Sinjar capitulated on 30 December 1182 and Saladin went into winter quarters in the Jazira. In early spring 1183, Izz al-Din tried once again to gather allies, but his coalition simply melted away when Taqi al-Din advanced from Hama. Saladin next tried for what should have been an impossible prize, the purportedly impregnable fortress of Amid, but it fell within three weeks – simply because the terms offered were so generous that continued allegiance to Mosul was simply without benefit. Saladin then wrote once more to the caliph, describing how, whilst he held no territorial ambitions on Mosul, he needed the city to heed the call to jihad: 'This little Jazira is the lever which will set in motion the great Jazira; it is the point of division and centre of resistance, and once it is set in its place in the chain of alliances, the whole armed might of Islam will be coordinated to engage the forces of unbelief.'*

The Turkish emirs of the cities around Aleppo now began to come to Saladin to proclaim their loyalty and soon the main city was bereft of allies. Saladin invested it on 21 May 1183, but was reluctant to fight the *Nuriya*, the old guard of Nur al-Din. Equally, Imad al-Din was quite happy to accept the governorship of Sinjar, along with safe passage, as recompense for the loss of Aleppo. Saladin attempted to woo the old *askari* of Nur al-Din with fine words about their courage and how they were 'the soldiers of the jihad, who had in the past done great services for Islam . . . whose gallantry and courage had gained his admiration'.† The *Nuriya* were, however, determined to have their day of battle and the sultan was unable to restrain his young Mamluks, who wanted to show both their loyalty to Saladin and to show that they were the new *corps d'élite*. Saladin's brother, Taj al-Muluk was killed in a fierce clash between the two sides, but this did at least finally bring the two sides to the negotiating table. Imad al-Din gained all he had wished for at the outset of the siege, and Saladin obtained the prize he had coveted for so long. The emir of the nearby fortress of Harim tried to call on the Franks for aid, but his garrison quickly arrested him on 22 June. Saladin completed his work in the north by concluding a peace treaty and Muslim prisoner release with Bohemond III of Antioch, and then he went to war with Jerusalem.

Jerusalem was ill-prepared for a contest. Raymond of Tripoli had been guiding the state, since Baldwin IV had gone into a terminal decline, but a faction under Baldwin IV's new brother-in-law, Guy of Lusignan, along with Reynald of Châtillon was contesting this control and accusing Raymond of plotting against the kingdom. On 29 September 1183, Saladin crossed the Jordan and entered Galilee with his forces and it was as if he was entering a land of ghosts. The entire region had been abandoned by its Latin inhabitants. The small cities of Baysan, Kerferbela, Zarin and Jinin, previously flourishing centres of agriculture and trade, fell to the Muslims without a single Frankish soldier being seen. The army of Jerusalem did not come out to challenge him and seemed paralysed instead. Guy had managed to get himself named as

---

* Imad al-Din in Gibb, p. 44. Saladin is likening a reconquered Syria to a *jazira* or island, as his desire was evidently to push the Franks into the sea and make the Levant entirely Sunni.
† Ibn al-Athir in Gabrieli, p. 117.

regent over Raymond before this incursion – his failure to challenge the sultan, as Baldwin IV would have, lost him the regency. This humiliation would later lead him to a catastrophic error of judgement.

Reynald continued to be a thorn in Saladin's side with his raids on trade-traffic from Karak. These required Saladin to finance military escorts for caravans, and Reynald maintained a very real threat against the holy cities of Arabia. The sultan therefore made attacks on Karak in both November and December, but the city's massive fosse and walls repelled his troops and kept his engines at a safe distance. The famous story of the wedding of Reynald's daughter taking place whilst the sultan's mangonels pounded at the walls, and wedding fare being offered to the besieging army, who chivalrously agreed to avoid pounding the tower where the newlyweds were sleeping, was the high point of a disappointing time spent before the castle's walls. Saladin's diplomacy with Mosul also failed at the end of this year, and the city remained nearly as committed an opponent as Karak.

The absence of the sultan from Cairo during these years reduced the volume of attacks that the fleet undertook, or at least reduced their reporting. There was only one raiding cruise launched in May 1184; in 1185 there was an episode of rioting in Alexandria with Christian sailors being attacked. It would be convenient to argue that Egyptian sailors were caught up in the passion of jihad, but, as we have seen, jihad in this period was very targeted and generally allowed 'trade relations' to continue. Instead, we might suggest that it was just indiscipline in the absence of the sailors' master that caused the unrest. This is an important point, as it indicates just how important Saladin's personality was to the maintenance of both the army and navy. Without him at its helm, it is unlikely that the state could later have survived the challenges that would be laid upon it with the arrival of the Third Crusade.

In August 1184, Saladin once again returned to besiege Karak but with no success. He did, however, have the opportunity of operating with all the elements of his coalition army during the campaign against the fortress, and through raids into Frank territory. This display of the sultan's army's capabilities was enough to convince the regent Raymond that he needed to secure a truce with Saladin, and a treaty was signed in early 1185, as Baldwin IV lay dying. The king died in March, and as Saladin besieged Mosul over the winter of 1185 he too came close to death from a contagion that spread through his camp.

Saladin had been warned that he would face a gigantic army of Azerbaijani Turcomen if he interfered with Mosul, but nothing came of these threats when he besieged the city in August 1185, or when he moved north of the city to restore his authority at Mardin and Amid, following the death of the two cities' princes. He then returned to Mosul's siege, and despite his extreme ill-health, kept his troops at the walls until 25 December. Then, following his reception of a delegation of Zangid princesses from the now desperate Izz al-Din, which he had initially rejected, Saladin agreed to negotiate. The depredations wrought by his own allies, the Azerbaijani Turcomen, who had done nothing to protect Mosul but had pillaged much of its environs, were a major factor in Izz al-Din finally taking suzerainty under Saladin. The agreement was struck on 3 March 1186; the grand coalition was now finally complete and Outremer was in dire peril.

The new king, Guy of Lusignan, was not the man to save a kingdom. Raymond of Tripoli was forced to seek a treaty with Saladin, but not simply for fear of the sultan's army. Ibn al-Athir's statement that Saladin agreed to make Raymond 'King of all the Franks' in the agreement is untrue, and Raymond had, in theory, no need of an agreement with the sultan as he had already secured an accord for all of Jerusalem when he was regent. However, by this new treaty he gained the guarantee of Saladin's support against his own king, who was mustering troops to attack Raymond's capital, Tiberias. The treaty forced Guy to think again and it allowed Saladin to transit troops across the strategically important region west of the Sea of Galilee, and to garrison troops in Tiberias.

Then the *casus belli* came. Reynald's continuing attacks on Muslim caravans from Karak breached the truce at the end of 1186. Guy was unable to force Reynald to return the booty and Saladin's response was both vengeful and effective. He personally escorted the next pilgrimage caravan to pass by Karak with the troops of Egypt and sent his son, al-Afdal, with the forces of Damascus to Tiberias to threaten the coastal cities and thereby prevent Guy from bringing the Latin field army to Reynald's aid. After the pilgrims had passed in safety:

> Saladin marched on al-Karak and sent his raiding parties throughout the regions of al-Karak, al-Shawbak and elsewhere, pillaging, breaking and burning, while the prince was besieged and powerless to defend his lands, and fear of al-Afdal's army kept the other Franks immobilized at home. So Saladin was free to besiege and pillage, burn and ravage the whole region, which he did.*

---

* Ibn al-Athir in Gabrieli, p. 119.

Al-Afdal then raided in Tiberias and was met in battle by a rather foolhardy contingent of Templars and Hospitallers, who had ignored Raymond's advice to avoid conflict with the superior Muslim forces. They were caught by al-Afdal's troopers at Saffuriyah on 1 May and annihilated. The master of the Hospital died with his men.

Saladin reviewed the army in May 1187. He now commanded about twelve thousand regular troopers and the chroniclers indicate that a significant number of volunteer fighters or *mujahideen*, auxiliaries and Turcomen were also attracted to his standard. The entire force probably numbered about twenty thousand men. During the review, emirs were given specific positions in either the left or right wing to which they would bring their contingents when the army opened up into its battle formation. The sultan's Egyptian *askari* always formed the centre. Saladin addressed the army and whipped up its morale before the march began:

> 'When we enter the enemy's terrain this is our army's battle order, our method of advancing and retreating, the position of our battalions, the place where our knights rise up, where our lances are to fall, the paths by which to direct our horses, the arenas for our coursers, the gardens for our roses, the site of our vicissitudes, the outlets of our desires, the scene on which we shall be transfigured.' When the ranks were drawn up and the arms distributed he made gifts of warhorses and scattered largesse, devoted himself to making donations and giving coveted prizes . . . distributed bundles of arrows, of which the soldiers received more than a quiverful. He made chargers gallop and brought forth an ample harvest of troops. He spurred on brave coursers and called on the witnesses to bear witness, he drew up in succession his squadrons' virtues and won over to his side the sympathies of the swords. He strengthened the cutting blades, gave drink to the terrible lances and returned to his tents happy and contented.*

On 26 June the army entered Palestine, and on 2 July Saladin began a siege of Tiberias and quickly took the lower town. The army of Jerusalem lay not far off at Saffuriyah, as it had been shadowing Saladin's progress. Guy had also called upon mercenaries and knights from Antioch to rally to him. Raymond warned Guy not to engage Saladin, but in truth the king's army was roughly equal in size to the sultan's and Guy still had the haunting memory of 1183 and his loss of the regency to spur him into action. The Muslim chroniclers describe the discussion between

---

* Imad al-Din at his hyperbolic best in Gabrieli, p. 126.

Guy and Raymond in an interesting manner. Imad al-Din, in fact, has Raymond advocating *for* battle while Ibn al-Athir puts the following speech in Raymond's mouth:

> By God, I have observed the armies of Islam over the course of the years and I have never seen one equal to Saladin's army here in numbers or in fighting power. If he takes Tiberias he will not be able to stay there and when he has left it and gone away we will retake it. For if he chooses to stay there he will be unable to keep his army together, for they will not put up for long with being kept away from their homes and families. He will be forced to evacuate the city and we will free our prisoners.*

Certainly Ibn al-Athir was closer to the truth. Time and time again the Muslims had shown themselves incapable of holding a force together after a victory for long enough to exploit it fully. Ibn al-Athir then has Reynald of Châtillon accusing Raymond of treachery, which seems very likely, but he then leaps into fantasy when he describes the patriarch of Jerusalem berating Raymond for having converted to Islam. Both writers have Saladin showing a cheerful anticipation at discovering that Guy intended to seek battle, but as the accounts were both produced after the battle, this characterisation of the sultan's demeanour should be taken fairly lightly. There was still a great deal to do if the Franks were to be beaten, and defeat would have been as catastrophic for Saladin's coalition as it was to be for the *Franj*. As at Mont Gisard, Saladin had no fortified point to withdraw to and would have had to make a hazardous and protracted retreat; the opposite was true for the Crusaders. They had been defeated many times before, but their army had always been preserved and the Muslims had been denied a conclusive victory by the proximity of a Frankish castle or fortified town to which the Franks could withdraw. Saladin's greatest achievement of the campaign of 1187 was to trap the Christian army away from any sources of security – in exposed country, where a near liquidation of the flower of Jerusalem's chivalry could be achieved.

The Crusaders broke camp and marched to the relief of Tiberias on 3 July. They knew that they would be passing through arid country without water sources, although they were headed to a fertile region on the banks of Lake Tiberias, where they could restock and rest before attempting to break the siege. They never made it there, because Saladin used the tactics that had often brought victory in the past, to their optimum effect.

---

* Ibn al-Athir in Gabrieli, p. 120.

His Turks and Kurds harassed and harried the Crusader column with fast attacks and volleys of arrows, with the consistent aim of breaking up the Crusaders' marching order and detaching their rearguard. Eventually, the Templars at the rear of the column could no longer sustain a defence against Saladin's troopers while continuing with the march. It was also impossible for the infantry, who were suffering particularly badly in the summer heat, to up the pace of the march to escape the attentions of the raiders. Saladin's men forced the Franks to a halt and the Crusaders could now see that their route to Tiberias was blocked by the sultan's army. They made camp on a low hillside named the Horns of Hattin. In the Muslim camp, Saladin ensured that extra arrows were distributed to his men. Al-Tarsusi tells us that, under 'normal' circumstances, endless camel-loads of arrows were deployed with the army, so for the chroniclers to mention 'extra rations' is significant and indicates that Saladin knew how the coming battle would develop.

The next morning dawned with the *Franj* in a fearful condition. They were almost mad with thirst and any will to fight had been extinguished by the gruelling march the day before. Ibn al-Athir tells us how the battle was won:

> Saladin and the Muslims mounted their horses and advanced on the Franks. They too were mounted and the two armies came to blows, the Franks were suffering badly from thirst, and had lost confidence. The battle raged furiously, both sides putting up a tenacious resistance. The Muslim archers sent clouds of arrows like thick swarms of locusts, killing many of the Frankish horses. The Franks, surrounding themselves with their infantry, tried to fight their way toward Tiberias in the hope of reaching water, but Saladin realised their objective and forestalled them by planting himself and his army in the way. He rode up and down the Muslim lines encouraging and restraining his troops where necessary. The whole army bade his commands and respected his prohibitions. One of his young Mamluks led a terrifying charge on the Franks and performed prodigious feats of valour until he was overwhelmed by numbers and killed. When all the Muslims charged the enemy lines and almost broke through, slaying many Franks in the process, the count [Raymond] saw that the situation was desperate and realised that he could not withstand the Muslim army, so by agreement with his companions he charged the line before him. The commander of that section of the Muslim army was Taqi al-Din Umar, Saladin's nephew. When he saw that the Franks charging his lines were desperate and they were going to try to break through he sent orders for a passage to be made for them through the ranks.

One of the *mujahideen* had set fire to the dry grass that covered the ground. It took fire and the wind carried the heat and smoke down onto the enemy. They had to endure thirst, the summer's heat, the blazing fire and smoke, and the fury of battle. When the count fled the Franks lost heart and were on the verge of surrender, but seeing that the only way to save their lives was to defy death they made a series of charges that almost dislodged the Muslims from their position in spite of their numbers, had not the grace of God been with them. As each wave of attackers fell back they left their dead behind them; their numbers diminished rapidly while the Muslims were all around them like a circle about its diameter. The surviving Franks made for a hill near Hattin where they hoped to pitch their tents and defend themselves. They were vigorously attacked from all sides and prevented from pitching more than one tent, that of the king. The Muslims captured their great cross called the True Cross which they say is a piece of the wood upon which, according to them, the Messiah was crucified. This was one of the heaviest blows that could be inflicted on them and made their death and destruction certain. Large numbers of their cavalry and infantry were killed or captured. The king stayed on the hillside with five hundred of the most gallant and famous knights.

I was told that al-Malik al-Afdal, Saladin's son, said: 'I was at my father Saladin's side during that battle, the first that I saw with my own eyes. The Frankish king had retreated to the hill with his band, and from there he led a furious charge against the Muslims facing him, forcing them back upon my father. I saw that he was alarmed and distraught, and he tugged at his beard as he went forward crying: "Away with the devil's lie!" The Muslims turned to counter-attack and drove the Franks back up the hill. When I saw the Franks retreating before the Muslim onslaught I cried out for joy: "We have conquered them!" But they returned to the charge with undiminished ardour and drove our army back toward my father. His response was the same as before and the Muslims counter-attacked and drove the Franks back to the hill again. I cried: "We have beaten them!" My father turned to me and said: "Be quiet, we shall not have beaten them until the tent falls!" As he spoke the tent fell and the sultan dismounted and prostrated himself in thanks to God weeping for joy.'*

Two manuscripts, 'Persecutio Salaardini' and 'Jerusalem a Turcis obsessa capitur', now held in the Vatican Library, tell us that King Guy had been counselled by a knight named John, who 'having long served in Turkish armies' was acquainted with them and that he had advised the king to 'direct his army's charge against the centre of the opposing

---

* Ibn al-Athir in Gabriel, pp. 121–3.

army, where stood Saladin'.* He suggested that if they succeeded in
routing this section, the battle was won. The story is interesting, not
only because John had fought with the Muslims and had then returned
to Crusader service, but also because it gives credence to the account
of Saladin's son, recorded by Ibn al-Athir, that the Franks charged
at least twice at the sultan's *askari* and pressed them back onto his
rearguard. Taqi al-Din Umar's act of letting Raymond flee the field
without hindrance was a key element in the Muslim victory. Raymond's
'desertion' fatally weakened the Franks' numbers and, more importantly,
their will to fight on. Al-Ansari's fourteenth-century war manual also
vindicates Taqi al-Din Umar's action: 'No soldier should get in front of
a routed army, nor seek to shunt it from its path of flight.'†

As the main body of the Muslim army rode up to the collapsed tent,
they found Guy, Reynald and an exhausted group of Templars and
Hospitallers lying prostrate from fatigue on the ground. The site of
the king's tent would later be marked by a *Qubbat al-Nasr* or 'Dome
of Victory'. It was only a small building with a humble inscription, 'In
gratitude to God and in remembrance of his victory'.‡

The number of prisoners was so large that groups of thirty were led
on ropes by their captors and their value as slaves was reckoned, under
the normal market conditions of supply and demand, at only three dinars
each. The exchange of a prisoner for a single shoe was even recorded.
Saladin, however, paid his soldiers fifty dinars for every one of the 240
Templars or Hospitallers who had been captured.§ They were all offered
conversion to Islam, but only a few accepted; the rest were handed over
to decidedly amateur executioners. Imad al-Din tells us that Saladin:

> Ordered that they should be beheaded, choosing to have them dead rather
> than in prison. With him was a whole band of scholars and sufis and a
> certain number of devout men and ascetics; each begged to be allowed to

---

* Richard, J., 'An Account of the Battle of Hattin Referring to the Frankish Mercenaries
in Oriental Moslem States', *Speculum*, April 1952, pp. 168–77.
† In Scanlon, p. 113.
‡ The monument was only rediscovered in the 1990s and was even allowed to fall into
a state of disrepair shortly after Saladin's death. See Leisten, T., 'Mashhad Al-Nasr:
Monuments of War and Victory in Medieval Islamic Art', *Muqarnas*, vol. 13, 1996,
pp. 7–26.
§ Just as in European medieval warfare, prisoners of war in the Middle East were the
personal booty of the soldier who took their surrender and not of the commander.
Saladin therefore had to offer compensation to the 'owners' of the knights.

kill one of them and drew his sword and rolled back his sleeve. Saladin, his face joyful, was sitting on his dais; the unbelievers in black despair . . . there were some who slashed and cut cleanly, and were thanked for it; some who refused and failed to act, and others took their places. I saw a man who laughed scornfully and slaughtered . . . and how much praise he won, the eternal rewards he secured with the blood he had shed, the pious works added to his account with a neck severed by him!*

The bodies were denied burial and Saladin wrote in a letter that, 'not one of the Templars survived. It was a day of grace.'† This was not in fact true, the master was spared and entered captivity along with King Guy – the master was a valuable hostage, his men were not. The slaughter of the knights of the military orders was related to both a simple hatred for them and a fear of them, as they were the Muslims' most tenacious enemies. If they were released, they would not return to Europe: they would remain in Palestine to fight again. Their elimination also significantly reduced the manpower of the Crusader state.

The slaying of Reynald by the sultan's own hand was entirely related to the affront he had given by his attempts on Mecca and Medina, and by his slaughter of pilgrims. Reynald had watched as Guy was offered water by Saladin, which was an indication that he would be spared. However, when he took the goblet back from the king, the sultan made it very plain that he was not giving Reynald either water or mercy. He was offered conversion to save himself but refused, and after Saladin had decapitated him his head was sent to Damascus, where it was dragged through the streets.

The Crusader field army had ceased, to all intents and purposes, to exist, and there was little hope for any of the cities of the kingdom. Tiberias surrendered bloodlessly the next day. Saladin then moved on to Acre, arriving there on 8 July, and the city swiftly capitulated. Nablus, Nazareth and Toron followed suit, but Jaffa resisted and al-Adil sold the entire populace into slavery after storming the city. Saladin had dispersed his commanders to pick up these easy fruits of victory more quickly, but when he came to Tyre he found that his forces were not sufficient to the task of reducing the city. He therefore moved on to Sidon, which surrendered on 28 July, and then Beirut and Jebail, which

* In Gabrieli, p. 138.
† Melville, C. P., and Lyons, M. C., 'Saladin's Hattin Letter', in B. Z. Kedar (ed.), *The Horns of Hattin*, London: Variorum, 1992, p. 212.

both fell in early August. He subsequently turned back and once again passed by Tyre before accepting the surrender of Ascalon and Gaza at the beginning of September.

Tyre was then surrounded, but it was a strongly fortified town and its population grew as Frankish refugees flocked to it. A Christian fleet, carrying Conrad of Montferrat and a group of knights, unexpectedly arrived at Tyre, having dodged the Egyptian ships that had been providing flanking support for Saladin's campaign against the coastal cities. Conrad took command, and a few days later Saladin paraded his father, William of Montferrat, before the city walls, threatening to kill him if Conrad did not surrender. Conrad refused but Saladin did not kill the old man. Meanwile, the sultan had been besieging Jerusalem, as Tyre's ability to resist had been growing. Ibn al-Athir would later criticise the negligence of Saladin in this respect:

> The sole responsibility for Tyre's resistance lies with Saladin, who sent all the Frankish forces rushing off there and reinforced them there with men and money from Acre, Ascalon and Jerusalem. This fort was vital to the Franks and once it was gone the Franks abroad would no longer lust after this our land, and would surrender the territories they held without bloodshed.*

Modern historians have also criticised Saladin for conquering Jerusalem at the cost of leaving Tyre as a foothold for the Latins, but in truth he could not have predicted the ferocity of the West's response, in the form of the Third Crusade, to the fall of Jerusalem. He was also leading a jihad and would have found it impossible to divert his army from the Holy City. There have also been arguments that Jerusalem was not an important city to the Muslims in the Middle Ages and that its centrality to the jihad was merely a construction of the chroniclers of Saladin's life. This is indeed difficult to counter, but the presence of the Dome of the Rock in the city and the belief that Muhammad had stood on the Temple Mount, on which the Dome was constructed, made Jerusalem part of the Muslim heritage. The statement of the Fatimid missionary, Nasir-i Khusrau, that Jerusalem was an alternative centre of pilgrimage for those unable to go to Mecca, also indicates that its capture was of huge importance to the Muslims of Syria.†

---

* In Gabrieli, pp. 180–1.
† Nasir-i Khusrau was writing in 1046. See Hillenbrand, p. 48.

Balian of Ibelin conducted the defence of Jerusalem. He had received permission from Saladin to enter the city to escort his wife and children away to the safety of Tyre, but then wrote to the sultan to say that the populace were begging him to remain in the city. Saladin's chivalry extended not only to freeing Balian from his oath, but to providing Balian's family with safe conduct to Tyre. The siege commenced on 20 September. The attack began against the western sector of the wall, but there was fierce resistance and Saladin transferred his attack to the north. The citizens, threatened by the collapse of their walls, decided to surrender. On the 30th, negotiations commenced, whilst Saladin's mangonels continued a bombardment. The sultan's generous terms were quickly accepted. The city surrendered unconditionally and Latin Christians were allowed to buy their freedom at ten dinars for a man, five for a woman and one for a child. The poor were freed for a single payment of thirty thousand dinars. The bombardment stopped on 1 October and Saladin entered the city the next day. Saladin's brother, al-Adil, released a thousand captives that he had been awarded by the sultan and Saladin freed every elderly captive. Latin texts recount sacrileges in churches, but also that Syrian Christians were allowed to buy back the Holy Sepulchre. Tyre, Tripoli and Antioch all received Latin refugees from Jerusalem.

Saladin now turned to the castles that had frustrated the Muslims on so many occasions. Karak and Montreal were supposed to surrender upon the freeing of Reynald of Châtillon's stepson, but their garrisons then refused to do so and were subsequently invested. They took over a year to fall, but required relatively little of Saladin's resources to keep them besieged and to starve out their garrisons. Almost all of southern Palestine now belonged to Saladin, but Tyre remained a major irritation. He redoubled his efforts against it at the end of 1187 and ordered the fleet that was harboured at Acre to sail, despite it being winter, to complete a naval blockade. Saladin had realised, belatedly, that the conquest of Tyre would lock the Crusaders out of the Levant for good – Tripoli was still in Latin hands, but was too small a harbour for the armada of ships that would be required if Outremer was to be saved.

The portents for the city's fall were good. Saladin's troops' morale was high and they had plenty of siege equipment. Relief from the sea also seemed unlikely, as both the season and the Egyptian navy stood in its way. Unfortunately, the Egyptian fleet failed miserably, as their ships were boarded by Frankish raiding parties from the city on 30 December: five ships were captured with their crews. Five ships remained, but, having witnessed the ineptitude of his sailors, Saladin ordered them to lift the blockade and to sail to Beirut. They were, however, pursued by their own captured ships and, rather than make a fighting withdrawal, the Muslim sailors jumped overboard, abandoning their ships. The operation to terminate Latin ambitions in the Levant had turned into a debacle. Imad al-Din wrote that it 'showed that the naval administration of Egypt did not suffer from a superfluity of recruits and it could not muster suitable manpower. Instead it had to assemble ignorant men without skill or experience or any fighting tradition so that whenever these men were faced by danger they were terrified and whenever it was imperative to obey they disobeyed.'* The maritime fiasco profoundly demoralised Saladin's land forces, and they exerted pressure on the sultan to raise the siege over the winter. The siege engines were abandoned during their hurried retreat to winter quarters at Acre.

The army mobilised again in the spring of 1188. The armies of Hama and Aleppo neutralised Antioch's threat, whilst Saladin moved up the coast. He had no fleet cover, as he was concerned over Egypt's defence, and the unhindered entrance of sixty Sicilian-Norman ships into Tyre in the autumn must have been a galling sight. News then came of a new and vast invasion of the Levant being planned in the West. Saladin's senior commanders insisted that all the Syrian ports that they held should be destroyed to prevent their use by the Crusaders. Saladin rejected their demands and instead refortified the ports. This was a grave strategic error, but an understandable one. Saladin knew that possession of the Syrian coast was vital to the defence of Egypt and still held a sizeable fleet that had generally been able to match the Western navies. He could not have known just how vast the Western armada soon to be unleashed upon Syria was.

On land the successes kept coming. Safad surrendered in December and Belvoir in January 1189. Lattakieh surrendered in July and smaller castles and towns fell almost weekly. Only Antioch, Tripoli and Tyre, as well as the fortresses of Marqab, Crak des Chevaliers and the castle at Tortosa, remained in Crusader hands.

Saladin had released King Guy following entreaties from Queen Sibylla in July 1188. Guy had promised to leave the Holy Land immediately and never return, but reneged on his pledge and was in Tyre by early 1189.

---

* Ehrenkreutz, A. S., 'The Place of Saladin in the Naval History of the Mediterranean Sea in the Middle Ages', *Journal of the American Oriental Society*, April–June 1955, pp. 100–16.

Then, in April, a Pisan fleet of fifty-two ships arrived. Tensions between Guy, now a king without a kingdom, and Conrad, now the popular saviour of Tyre, caused Guy to align himself with the Pisans, and he and a few troops marched out to besiege Acre in August, with the Pisans sailing in support.

Saladin, now resting his forces in Damascus, would have been unworried. A Crusader attempt on Sidon had already failed and Acre's garrison was twice as large as Guy's 'army'. Acre also had an impressive double curtain wall and an easily defendable port. Guy was fortunate, however, that the Egyptian fleet once again failed the sultan and both Danish and Frisian fleets were able to deliver troops to Tyre. These contingents were followed to Acre by further forces of French and Germans. Saladin set out to meet this growing threat in September 1189, but could only muster a small force. He had hoped to attack Guy on the march, but his emirs refused to take the difficult route this required, and he now faced the Franks in prepared positions, with their fleet lying near at hand offshore. He made an attack on the 16th; his right wing under Taqi al-Din forced its way into Acre, but then retired as the mounted warriors did not feel capable of tackling the *Franj* infantry at close quarters. Saladin's attack also spurred Conrad to bring further reinforcements from Tyre to Acre. Another attack was made on 19 September, during which supplies were delivered to Acre's garrison. The Crusaders then attacked and were repulsed on 22 September; they were also pushed from a small hillock that rose above the road to Tyre.

There was a vicious battle on 4 October. Templar knights came out at the charge to attack the left flank of Saladin's army. Taqi al-Din then feigned retreat, hoping to draw the Templars away from the main Crusader body and then surround them. Unfortunately, Saladin misread this move and sent reinforcements to his nephew, which then caused confusion in the centre. Guy saw this and made a charge. The Muslim centre caved and there was panic in the rear of the army as Crusaders penetrated the camp after chasing Taqi al-Din's forces from the field. However, they were so elated at the booty they found there that none of them thought to cut down Saladin's tent, which would have completely destroyed the Muslims' will to fight. A riderless Frank horse then caused panic in the Crusader infantry, as they thought that the knights who were plundering had been slaughtered.

Saladin saw this collapse in the Crusader centre and quickly organised a charge. There was now pandemonium in the Crusader lines, as the

Muslim cavalry came on – in the rout, the master of the Temple was killed and Conrad had to be rescued by Guy. Three Frankish women, wearing armour and fighting in the front line, were also killed, according to the Muslim chroniclers. Then Saladin's emirs abruptly stopped their advance and surrounded him. They demanded that he send a contingent to bring back their servants, who had fled with their treasure when the Crusaders had plundered the camp. This dark comedy of errors ended as a bloody draw. The position was unchanged: Acre was besieged and so were its besiegers.

The Egyptian fleet, using Haifa as a base, attempted to maintain the supply of Acre. On 25 December, fifty galleys broke through the Pisan blockade, entered the city's harbour and captured two Christian vessels. The Pisans' resupplying of Guy's army required no such heroics, and they were unchallenged by the Muslim ships that lay at anchor in Acre. The Crusader army completed a trench around their positions and constructed three siege towers over the winter. Saladin had been given no choice but to grant a respite to the Crusaders: he was ill and disease was spreading through his camps. He withdrew to winter camp on 16 December. Disturbing news had come in October of the presence of a vast Crusader army under the German emperor Barbarossa in Constantinople; news now came that it had reached Konya. Apparently no other prince in the Islamic world was worried, though – Saladin received emissaries from the sultan of far-away Khurasan requesting Saladin's aid in reclaiming his throne. Saladin dismissed all his emirs from the siege; only he and his *askari* stayed on through the grim winter months.

At the end of April 1190, the Crusaders made an attempt on the city. Acre's garrison sent a swimmer to Saladin to warn him of the attack and he brought his army to the Crusader rear. Despite this distraction, the Crusaders continued their attack, and their towers resisted all the Muslims' efforts to burn them down with Greek fire. Then, from the populace, came a 'man of Damascus who was a passionate collector of pyrotechnic devices and ingredients for reinforcing the effects of fire. His friends reproached and rebuked him for his passion, but he replied that it was an occupation that did no harm to anyone and which interested him as a hobby.' It was about to harm a great many people. Greek fire was once more launched at the towers and the Franks manning them laughed and danced about when they saw that the containers could not make their structure burn. Unfortunately for them, the man from Damascus was just getting his range. His tailor-made naphtha was then loaded up and shot at the towers, exploding on impact. Each of the towers was burnt to the ground and the Franks were given a 'foretaste of Hellfire'.*

Saladin at last started receiving reinforcements from the Jazira and Mosul, and he attacked the Crusaders over an eight-day period in May, though without success. He knew he had to break the siege before the arrival of Emperor Barbarossa's army in Syria. In June, upon hearing that the army had reached the gates of Cilicia, the sultan ordered the destruction of the defences of Tiberias, Jaffa, Arsuf, Caesarea, Sidon and Jubail. On 13 July, Saladin dispatched every Turcoman he could muster, along with his Syrian contingents, to the north. However, Barbarossa had died crossing the River Saleph in early June and his army had broken up; only five thousand Germans continued on to Tyre.

A second convoy of Egyptian galleys fought their way through the Pisan fleet to Acre in June 1190. It was a brave act, but was also counter-productive as this fleet consisted of almost all the remaining galleys in the sultan's navy, and once it had entered Acre it remained there, only making a few isolated sorties against the Pisans. This effectively ended any chance of maintaining the supply of Acre's garrison in the long term. The crews of the ships joining the garrison only increased the number of mouths to feed.

The Crusaders, who had also got word of the death of Barbarossa, made a mass infantry attack on 25 July, but were slaughtered in their thousands. By now the siege was becoming an apocalyptic scene. The besieged garrison of Acre and the Crusaders were starving, pestilence struck at all the camps and Saladin had to retire to new positions, as the simple volume of death that had taken place between his lines and those of the Crusaders made the passage of further contagion through his troops inevitable. Despite all this, the 'fourth horseman' – war – continued on his way. Henry of Champagne had now arrived at the siege with a large contingent of French troops and he applied them to bringing a battering ram to the gates of the city. However, it was destroyed by fire, perhaps by the ingenious hobbyist of Damascus.

More Muslim ingenuity was displayed in August 1190 to resupply Acre:

> The besieged were in dire need of food and provisions. A group of Muslims
> embarked in Beirut with a cargo of four hundred sacks of grain, onions,

* The description of the Damscene hobbyist and his attacks on the Franks are from Ibn al-Athir in Gabrieli, pp. 198–200.

mutton and other provisions. They dressed in Frankish clothes, shaved their beards, put some pigs on the upper deck where they could be seen from a distance, set up crosses, weighed anchor and made for the city. When they came into contact with enemy ships the Franks accosted them in small boats and galleys saying, 'we see that you are making for the city,' thinking that they too were Franks. The Muslims replied, 'but haven't you taken it yet?' 'Not yet'. 'Then we will make for the Frankish army but there is another ship travelling with us on the same wind; warn it not to enter the city'. There was in fact a Frankish ship behind them on the same route making for the army. The patrol-boat saw it and made off to warn it. Thus the Muslim ship was able to follow its own course and entered a port on a favourable wind safe and sound by God's grace. They brought great joy, for the inhabitants were now suffering severe hardships.*

Frankish inventiveness was also displayed in September, when a siege tower, supported by two galleys, was launched to attack the Tower of Flies, one of the city's main defensive towers on the seaward wall, and fireships were set adrift to try to burn the Muslim ships. The tower was burnt, but the fireships failed to ignite the Egyptian galleys.

The winter saw Saladin running out of money and suffering from repeated fevers. His emirs were complaining about the length of the siege and the impact it was having on *their* wealth and he was receiving paltry support from the caliph. The armies of Mosul and of the Jazira had also effectively deserted him. He completely lost control of the coast: large ships with deep draughts and two or three decks were deployed by the Pisans; these could carry cargo and arms in their lower holds and still have space for troops on the upper decks.†

Despite being surrounded, the Crusader army still maintained their logistics. Tyre, Tripoli and later Cyprus sat at the head of their supply chain, which was maintained by five hundred Scandinavian ships, along with fifty-two Pisan vessels and two Genoese and one Venetian squadron. Baha al-Din wrote that 'the ships transformed the coast into a forest of masts.'‡ This force was many, many times stronger than Saladin's navy and, in a desperate attempt to redress this situation, Saladin sent to the North African Almohad sultan. However, the mission had been doomed to failure many years before by Tapi al-Din's raids on the sultan's lands.

---

* Baha al-Din in Gabrieli, pp. 200–1.
† Lane, F., 'Tonnages, Medieval and Modern', *Economic History Review, New Series*, vol. 17, no. 2, 1964, pp. 213–33.
‡ In Ehrenkreutz, 'The Place of Saladin', pp. 110–16.

The fourteenth-century historian Ibn Khaldun describes the fate of the mission and gives an accurate description of the naval balance of power during the Crusades period:

> When Salah al-Din Yusuf Ibn Ayyub, the ruler of Egypt and Syria at this time, set out to recover the ports of Syria from the Christian nations and to cleanse Jerusalem of the abomination of unbelief and to rebuild it, one fleet of unbelievers after another came to the relief of the ports. The fleet of Alexandria could not stand up against them. The Christians had had the upper hand in the eastern Mediterranean for so long, and they had numerous fleets there. The Muslims on the other hand, had for a long time been too weak to offer them any resistance there. In this situation Salah al-Din sent Abd al-Karim Ibn Munqidh, a member of the Banu-Munqidh, the rulers of Shayzar, as his ambassador to Yaqub al-Mansur, the Almohad ruler of the Maghrib at that time, asking for the support of his fleets, to prevent the unbelievers from achieving their desire of bringing relief to the Christians in the Syrian ports. Al-Mansur sent him back to Salah al-Din, and did not comply with his request.*

In fact Sultan al-Mansur also permitted Genoese ships to enter North African ports on their way to Syria.†

All communications between Saladin and the garrison were now reduced to the courageous men swimming with messages, pigeon post and swift, light vessels crewed by Christian deserters. Letters from this time between the sultan and his chancellor in Egypt have the tone of a despondent and exhausted man, but he still managed to conduct an operation – admittedly confused and disorganised – to bring relief to Acre's garrison in February 1191. Unusually, the Crusaders' fleets had withdrawn for the winter and Muslim transports were able to sail unopposed into the harbour. Saladin had hoped to bring out as many of the exhausted garrison as possible, but Acre's desperate civilians rushed to the little fleet and the transports were soon too full to accommodate any but a few of the weary troops. An exchange of garrison troops for fresh troops failed because no one would volunteer for such a disagreeable duty; the garrison was now down to one-third of its former strength.

---

* From *The Muqaddimah: An Introduction to History*, translated from the Arabic by F. Rosenthal, edited by N. J. Dawood, London: Routledge and Kegan Paul, 1958, vol. I, pp. 211–12.
† Labib, S., 'The Era of Suleyman the Magnificent: Crisis of Orientation', *International Journal of Middle Eastern Studies*, November 1979, pp. 425–51.

Gales then caused losses of some of the ships, and the return of the Franks' fleets ended the operation.

Taqi al-Din was allowed to leave the siege in March 1191, as Saladin had granted him the governorship of Harran and Edessa. He took with him seven hundred Mamluks and strict instructions not to attempt to expand the borders of his new territories. Taqi al-Din blatantly ignored Saladin's orders and attacked cities beyond the sultan's lands and defeated an army of Anatolian Turks near Lake Van. He also invaded Armenia before dying there in October. All this brought an angry reaction from the caliph and Saladin had to write to Baghdad to repudiate his nephew's conduct. His family had failed him once more: he was so short of money that even the caliph's stingy contributions were vital, and Taqi al-Din had put these small payments in jeopardy. Furthermore, the fallout from his nephew's adventuring later required the frequent dispatch of both al-Zahir and al-Adil and their *askaris* to the north during the desperate campaign against Richard Lionheart in the autumn of 1191. The loss of Taqi al-Din's regiment also required Saladin to pull his army back from the immediate combat zone and to straighten his lines on 4 June.

French and English contingents of the Third Crusade had begun to arrive in April with Philip II of France. Richard Lionheart arrived from Cyprus, which he had taken from the Byzantines, on 12 June 1191 and surprisingly requested a parley with Saladin. This was refused on the grounds that commanders only meet after terms are agreed, but al-Adil was dispatched to meet with the king. Three days of discussion produced nothing. King Philip of France then led an attack on Acre, but Saladin made a diversionary attack on the eastern end of the Crusader line and the Kurdish garrison, under their valiant officer, al-Mashtub, sallied out of Acre to send Phillip's men back beyond their own lines and to burn his siege engines.

King Richard then brought up his own siege engines, which included a gigantic mangonel named 'God's own catapult'; he began a systematic destruction of Acre's towers. The Maledicta tower came close to collapse on 2 July 1191 and this stirred Saladin to dispatch a force of cavalry to attempt a breakthrough to the garrison on 3 July, but they were held by the Crusader infantry. Saladin then instructed the garrison to attempt a breakout on the night of the 4th. However, this also failed despite a diversionary attack by the whole army; deserters were blamed for informing the Franks about the sultan's intentions. Whatever the case, it was obvious that the situation was hopeless. On 5 July, Richard's sappers brought the Maledicta tower down. Fortunately, the rubble of the tower prevented ingress into the walls and two Crusader attacks were beaten back over the next few days, but time was running out for the desperate garrison. On 12 July, al-Mashtub sought terms with Richard.

Saladin was not party to the surrender negotiations, but when the conditions for release of the garrison were set, he gallantly attempted to meet the obligations set by Richard – the return of the True Cross, sixteen hundred Crusader prisoners and a payment of two hundred thousand dinars. The sultan was given one month to comply. Just before the deadline, Saladin asked for and was granted an extension to 20 August. He requested a further parley with Richard on the 15th, but then did not attend the meeting. The deadline passed and, rather than enslaving the prisoners, as was expected, Richard began a massacre. As many as three thousand men were butchered. Baha al-Din describes the effect the slaughter had on Saladin's army:

> As soon as the Muslims realised what had happened they attacked the enemy and battle raged, with dead and wounded on both sides, continuing with increasing vigour until night fell and separated them. The next morning the Muslims wanted to see who had fallen and found their martyred companions lying where they had fallen, and some they recognised. Great grief seized them and from then on they did not spare enemy prisoners, except well known persons and strong men who could be put to work.
>
> Many reasons were given to explain the slaughter. One was that they had killed them as a reprisal for their own prisoners killed before then by the Muslims. Another was that the King of England had decided to march on Ascalon and take it and he did not want to leave behind him in the city a large number of the enemy soldiers. God knows best.*

Another more deleterious effect of the massacre on the sultan's army was that, when he called for fresh troops for the campaign, none came from the cities of Syria and Mosul and those that he had, already exhausted and demoralised by the long and unrewarding campaign, refused to garrison any fortified place, in case they should suffer the same fate as the men of Acre. Given that his funds were exhausted and that his forces virtually refused to engage Richard's troops, it is simply astounding that Saladin was able to counter Richard at all. Perhaps the knowledge that the Crusaders had lost so many men at Acre through disease, famine and battle buoyed the sultan at this darkest moment.

---

* Baha al-Din in Gabrieli, p. 224.

Perhaps he hoped simply to thwart Richard until the king was forced to return home, or to erode the Crusaders' desire for Jerusalem through the tenacity of his defence. Estimates of the Franks' losses at Acre are upwards of fifty thousand men, but there must also have been a deeper belief within Saladin's soul that the work he was undertaking was both sacred and vital. His response was that of a human spirit facing adversity and is the reason why the sultan has accrued so many admirers in both the East and the West down through the centuries. His speech to his troops before they rode out to meet Richard's march on Ascalon shows both courage and faith: 'Only our army is facing the army of infidelity. There is none among the Muslims who will come to our succour and there is none in the lands of Islam who will help us.'*

Richard's route of advance caused Saladin a great deal of anxiety. He headed down the coast towards Jaffa. From Jaffa, it was possible for the English king to strike inland for Jerusalem, and to threaten Ascalon and thereby Egypt. He was also able to transport a great deal of his supplies by ship, and the sea secured his right flank. There was no way that Saladin could counter this, as the last of his Syrian fleet had been lost to the Crusaders with the capitulation of Acre. Saladin therefore sent troops ahead of Richard's column to burn crops and to destroy the fortifications and ports at Caesarea, Arsuf and Jaffa – no men willing to defend them could be found among the army.

The pattern of the campaign was set early. Richard's column left Acre on 22 August and attempted to maintain an unbroken and disciplined march. The knights rode in five companies, with a screen of heavy infantry covering their left flank, which was relieved by reserves marching with the baggage train on the army's right. Saladin's troopers continually tried to break the column up and to detach groups of infantry, who could then be surrounded and killed or captured. Meanwhile, Saladin rode with the bulk of his army, shadowing the Crusaders and hoping for an opportunity to launch an attack in force. Crusader prisoners were brought to the sultan, questioned, and then killed.

Scouts were also sent out to look for terrain favouring a general engagement, but no opportunity for a large-scale attack presented itself – until 1 September, by which time the Crusaders had passed Athlit, had been resupplied by their fleet and had disembarked large numbers of

---

* Cameron Lyons, M., and Jackson, D. E. P., *Saladin: The Politics of the Holy War*, Cambridge: Cambridge University Press, 1982, p. 320.

reinforcements. At the Nahr Zerka, or 'River of Crocodiles', Saladin tried to taunt knights out of the column to meet him on open ground, using charges against the column and archery assaults. Baha al-Din recorded how the Crusaders 'kept steadfastly in perfect formation, undismayed and undisturbed'.* In truth, such discipline had been the key to all the Franks' successes in the Levant.

On 3 September, the Crusaders were forced to turn inland as the coastal route was impassable. Saladin's troopers took advantage of the open country through which the column was now passing and killed virtually all the Templars' horses in attacks on the rearguard. Richard was also wounded whilst taking part in a desperate defence of the column. His troops were also short of food, a downside to having so vast an army, and he sent emissaries to Saladin to propose a parley. The discussions between al-Adil and Richard, however, ended quickly and Richard's army was afforded the protection of forests as they continued towards Arsuf. Saladin waited on the other side of the woodlands and prepared to offer battle.

The battle was fought on 7 September on a plateau that ends abruptly in a cliff on the seaward side and runs away to scrubland on the other. Richard's aim was to reach the town of Arsuf by the day's end, which would put him only nine miles short of Jaffa. Saladin's aim was to destroy the Crusader army before it reached its objective, as at Hattin. The Frankish knights were arrayed in three parallel columns and their extreme left flank was defended by infantry armed with crossbows and spears. Saladin's troopers had failed to punch through this curtain of heavily armoured foot soldiers before at Acre and he knew that he needed to provoke the knights into a charge, in order to be able to break the column up. To this end, he concentrated on the Hospitallers at the column's rear, utilising archery and a number of charges, with heavily armed Mamluks of the *askari* coming to close quarters. The battle commenced in this manner at nine in the morning and Saladin's tactics had still not achieved anything by one o'clock, as the Crusaders closed on Arsuf. Saladin therefore increased the pressure on the Hospitallers, and concentrated his fire on their infantry. This final provocation caused the Hospitaller master to break ranks and charge along with a number of his knights. At this the sultan might have rejoiced, but the Crusader infantry was still exhibiting magnificent discipline – whilst they opened their ranks to allow more knights to join the

---

* Gabrieli, p. 228.

charge, they also maintained their stoical defence of the column and took a heavy toll on the Muslim troopers with their crossbows.

The Muslims were by now heavily committed to the attack, with some of the troops even dismounted and firing into the Crusaders' ranks; Richard realised that that the time for a charge was now perfect. He therefore formed up his household troops and his counter-attack was enough to break Saladin's assault and to send the sultan's troops reeling from the field. Some Muslim troops saved themselves by jumping into the sea from the cliff. Saladin managed to make a rapid reorganisation in the midst of this chaos and, when the Crusader attack had begun to lose momentum, he sent his *askari* forward. They pushed the Franks back, but Richard still had an uncommitted reserve: as this came forward, Saladin's troops were sent, once more, on to the defensive. Saladin hurriedly organised a further counter-attack, but Richard responded with a further charge that decided the day. The numbers of troops lost by Saladin in the battle have been wildly exaggerated by Western chroniclers, and the sultan was ready to engage the Crusaders again only two days later. However, the fact remains that Saladin had failed in his aim: the Crusaders reached Arsuf. On 10 September, they marched into the ruins of Jaffa.

Saladin took a force down to Ascalon to demolish its walls, as he still feared that Richard might march for Egypt. He returned to Jaffa on 24 September and then rode to Jerusalem to see to the strengthening of its defences. He dismantled all the castles surrounding the Holy City and on 1 October he rejoined his main forces, which had withdrawn to Ramla. He also dispatched al-Adil to Ibelin, from where he could harass the Crusader base. From here, al-Adil opened negotiations at Richard's request on 3 October.

Saladin knew that Richard was under pressure in Europe, as Phillip of France had left the Crusade and was now threatening Angevin lands. He also knew that friction between Conrad of Montferrat and Richard over the throne of Jerusalem was ongoing and worsening. He must have felt, therefore, that, although Richard could not be defeated by the forces at his disposal, he could be 'waited out'. In order to strengthen his negotiating position, he also began talks with Conrad and sent Arab irregulars on night raids to steal from the Crusaders and to kill sentries.

The negotiations with Richard went nowhere. He insisted on the return of the True Cross, Jerusalem and all the lands from the coast to the Jordan, though he did offer his sister in marriage to al-Adil, so that Saladin's brother might rule Palestine in coalition with his Angevin queen. The offer was dismissed out of hand by the sultan, despite being enthusiastically received by his weary troops. Conrad's proposal for a coalition against Richard was entertained, but it was still obvious to the sultan that Richard was the man who had to be stopped on the battlefield, and who had to be bargained with.

At the end of October the Crusaders began moving from Jaffa to positions on the Jerusalem road. Atrocious weather aided Saladin, as it slowed the advance down and gave the Muslims time to withdraw and destroy fortified positions as they did so. By early January 1192, morale in the Crusader camp was collapsing, despite the fact that they were only twelve miles short of Jerusalem. Saladin's tactics at this point were to avoid large-scale engagements with the Franks and to strike at Richard's lines of communication with Jaffa. This forced the Franks back towards Ascalon on 21 January. Saladin continued to refortify Jerusalem and rotated his troops, releasing the men of Sinjar from duty and replacing them with Egyptian levies. However, his *askari* Mamluks remained with him in the field, as they had for the last four years; he also received some Anatolian Turcomen into his forces.

Saladin harried the Crusader withdrawal to the coast; this, combined with snow and hail, caused many desertions from Richard's forces. More desertions followed once the Crusaders found that Ascalon had been so thoroughly destroyed under the sultan's watchful eye that no food could be landed there until the harbour was repaired. Seven hundred of Richard's knights left for service under Conrad of Montferrat. Reports of the Crusaders' poor condition, and that Richard was preparing to leave the Levant due to the machinations of his brother, Prince John, against him, allowed Saladin to release many of his men on leave until May 1192. Meanwhile, raids and sorties continued, with the capture of men, women, children, cattle and booty by both sides. A low-level war of attrition was fought during the spring and almost managed to hide the fact that a stalemate had ensued.

As part of his exit plan, Richard tried to reinstall Guy of Lusignan on the throne of Outremer, but the majority of the barons opted instead for Conrad of Montferrat. Meanwhile, negotiations continued between Saladin and Richard, though they consistently foundered on the sultan's determination not to allow Ascalon to remain in the Franks' hands, and because Richard could not leave the Holy Land without having secured something solid for Outremer and, perhaps more importantly, for himself. With a view to expediting Richard's passage home, Saladin may very well have helped Richard out with his 'monarch problem'. Conrad fell to the daggers of two Ismaili Assassins in Tyre in April 1192 – Saladin's *modus vivendi*, dating from the 1170s with Sinan, may have secured the marquis's murder for Richard. In his protracted and friendly talks with al-Adil, Richard must have discussed his difficulties with Conrad. After the murder, Richard's nephew, Henry of Champagne, was rapidly put forward as an alternative candidate for the throne and married Conrad's widow, Isabella. She was of Jerusalem's royal line and thereby made Henry's kingship legitimate. Baha al-Din puts the blame for the murder of Conrad on Richard. Ibn al-Athir, however, wrote that Saladin contracted with Sinan for the deaths of the marquis and of Richard, but that the Assassins missed their second mark.*

Despite Conrad's convenient death and increasingly bad news from England, Richard still obstinately refused to quit the Levant. The draw of Jerusalem was perhaps too strong. He struck south towards the fortress of Darum and Egypt on 17 May 1192. The speed with which Richard took Darum gave Saladin no time to respond, but it is also doubtful whether he could have brought an army into the field with any rapidity at this juncture. Morale was collapsing and the treasury was exhausted. Saladin had never been a prudent guardian of the state's coffers; as early as 1171 he had devalued Egypt's currency to meet the costs of its defence. This was reckoned as 'a calamity in Egypt, because gold and silver left Egypt, not to return again' and 'to say the name of a pure gold dinar was like mentioning the name of a wife to a jealous husband, while to get such a coin in one's hand was like crossing the doors of paradise.'†

However, he was not entirely to blame for the lack of trust placed by merchants and citizens in Egypt's currency. Gold coins struck by the Crusaders throughout the eleventh and twelfth centuries copied Arabic dinars, and their introduction into the monetary system of the eastern Mediterranean was one of the earliest, albeit accidental, instances of economic warfare. The Arabic dinar was so untrusted by the fourteenth century that an alternative for international trade was looked for by merchants and found in the 'new' gold ducats of the Italian maritime

---

* For a full account of the political fault lines running through Outremer at this time and the murder itself, see Waterson, *Ismaili Assassins*, pp. 168–73.

† Al-Maqrizi in Ehrenkreutz, A. S., 'The Crisis of Dinar in the Egypt of Saladin', *Journal of the American Oriental Society*, July–September 1956, pp. 178–84.

republics.* An important element of the control of trade therefore moved from the East to the West during this period.

Saladin's apparent recklessness is excused by the simple fact that his spending saved Egypt and Syria from the Franks; none of it went on luxuries for the sultan. His only other expenditures were on the building and rebuilding of religious institutions – when he died, his personal fortune was so depleted by his long contest with the Crusaders that he possessed only one gold, and forty-seven silver, coins.

Richard forced the sultan into the field at the head of a near-mutinous army with a second attempt on Jerusalem on 7 June. Small parties were sent out to attack the Crusaders' supply line, but one that was led by Saladin's standard bearer was decimated by Richard at the head of a squadron of cavalry, and the Crusaders advanced in fairly good order up to within sight of Jerusalem's walls, at Bait-Nuba, on 12 June. Richard's arrival in Jerusalem's environs caused near-panic in its garrison, but a successful raid on the Crusader camp and another on their supply lines buoyed the army's spirits a little. However, when Richard plundered an Egyptian caravan of nearly five thousand camels and mules carrying gold, silver, weapons and medicines for Saladin's *askari*, there was a blunt refusal to continue the campaign from his most loyal troops. It was only when al-Mashtub, one of the heroes of Acre, stepped forward to reiterate his loyalty to the sultan that the immediate risk of mutiny died away. Saladin was therefore unable to respond to Richard's attack until fresh contingents arrived. He poisoned the water sources around Jerusalem and could only hope that the Crusaders were weakened enough by the heat, his raiding parties and by internal dissent to prevent them from attacking the city.

Fortunately his judgement was correct and Richard returned to negotiations on 5 July, as word came of troops arriving in Damascus from Mosul, Sinjar and Diyarbakir. Negotiations broke down again over Ascalon, but the Crusaders were now retreating, their forward position at Jaffa was being held by sick and injured troops and the bulk of the army had fallen back to Acre. Saladin tried to take advantage of Richard's deteriorating position with an attack on Jaffa. His force of Kurds, Turcomen and Turkish *askari* broke down the city's outer walls by mang-onel fire and poured into Jaffa on 31 July. The Kurds and the Turcomen

---

* Ehrenkreutz, A. S., 'Arabic Dinars Struck by the Crusaders: A Case of Ignorance or of Economic Subversion?', *Journal of the Economic and Social History of the Orient*, July 1964, pp. 167–82.

were the first into the city, but refused to be led on to the capture of the citadel and instead set about plundering. They had endured so much over the last few years with so little reward that they doubtless felt that this was their time. However, as they exited the city – no doubt looking forward to enjoying their loot and their captives – they were assaulted by the sultan's *askari* Mamluks and their riches were seized.

The citadel remained untaken, while chaos reigned in the Muslim army. Then, on 1 August, as Saladin's Mamluks were in the act of extorting money for safe passage from civilians trapped in the citadel and then beheading them, galleys carrying Richard and a body of knights sailed into the harbour. Saladin ordered an immediate assault on the citadel and an archery assault on the king's galley, which was fast approaching the shore. Richard waded ashore despite this fusillade and the Crusaders very rapidly built a palisade on the shore. Richard then led an attack into the city, and a general rout then ensued with the whole Muslim army being chased out to the small village of Yazur, where Saladin and his emirs managed to restore some semblance of order. However, the sultan's army was still not fully under his control, and to gain time he offered to parley with Richard. He knew that the king had been in the process of loading his horses and men onto transports bound for Europe before the call for help had come from Jaffa, and that he needed to bring his Levantine adventure to a close. Furthermore, unloading his warhorses and making them ready for combat would take time. Again, the negotiations went nowhere: the Crusaders used the time to reinforce their position, and Saladin spent it planning a riposte.

On the night of 4 August, Saladin led a party of troops out to the city walls to begin a diversionary attack to cover a second group that was sent to raid Richard's camp and to capture or kill the king if possible. The operation soon unravelled, as none of the troopers in the second party wanted to fight on foot in the Crusader camp, and violent arguments between Turks and Kurds continued until dawn broke and they were discovered. As the Crusaders rushed to their defences, Saladin repeatedly ordered his men to attack the camp but no one moved. Exasperated, the sultan ordered al-Mashtub's brother to lead his Kurds forward, but his only response was, 'give your orders to those Mamluks of yours who beat up the troops at Jaffa.'* The attack was called off, and Saladin was fortunate that his diversionary attack

---

* In Gibb, p. 89.

had actually succeeded in penetrating the city. Another loss of face for the sultan at this juncture might just have tipped the army into a full-scale mutiny. Richard was able to form a counter-attack that threw the Muslims back, but their initial success had emboldened Saladin's men and they prepared for a further attack on the city. Saladin had overwhelming numerical superiority over his foe, but could not make it count because his troops lacked trust in their commander, and simply because no emir or trooper wanted to tackle Richard.

Richard organised his defence as a 'hedgehog' of infantry spearmen backed by crossbowmen, with a very limited force of cavalry in his rear. He placed his line just outside the city walls. Muslim detachments did attempt to ride the Crusaders down, but none penetrated the line. Surprisingly, given the morale of the army and the fact that their dead were piling up, the Turks and Kurds kept coming on; in order to relieve the pressure, Richard had to launch a cavalry charge, but the Muslims stubbornly refused to yield the field and came close to victory in the ensuing cavalry battle. Detachments of the Crusader infantry fled to the harbour, but they were stopped and rallied by Richard. The Crusader resistance continued until dusk, and, strictly speaking, Richard won the day. Strategically, however, they had gained nothing by the defence of Jaffa, except a bargaining chip for yet another round of negotiations. The city, filled as it was with corpses, however, was not a healthy place to be negotiating from. Richard fell sick and subsequently rushed into a treaty, so that he could leave for Acre as soon as possible. By the terms of the accord, a truce of three years and eight months was agreed; the Crusaders were given open access to Jerusalem for pilgrims, along with possession of the coast from Acre to Jaffa, but Ascalon returned to Saladin's possession. The armistice was signed on 2 September 1192. Within a fortnight the armies were dispersed and Richard was on his way back to Europe.

Saladin was not a great battlefield general. He failed at Mont Gisard, Arsuf and Jaffa, and he lost Acre. On the other hand, he was a great war leader. His political acumen and intelligence gathering was the key to his victory at Hattin, and his personal attributes and selfless commitment to the jihad were what maintained his army in the field throughout the long, unrewarding contest against the Third Crusade. The last years of his life were spent on the battlefield in an exhausting defence of Islam and yet he still upheld the highest standards of civil governance. Following Nur al-Din's example, he maintained the rule of law and gave an example of moral leadership that was the antithesis of almost every other government of the time. At times his actions were those of a man tilting at windmills, but his naive attachment to an ideal meant that he achieved epic feats that mere generalship could not have accomplished. When discussing the terms of the final treaty with Richard, Saladin had said to his emirs:

> We have become accustomed to fighting the Holy War and indeed we have achieved our aim. Now it is difficult to break off what has become customary . . . we have no other occupation other than that of making war . . . If we give up this work what shall we do? If we destroy our hope of defeating them, what shall we hope for? I am afraid that with nothing to do death will overcome me . . . my feeling is to reject the idea of a truce and in preferring war to prefer my honour and make it my leader . . . This duty has been placed upon me, it is my job, and with God's help I shall take the most determined and resolute course.

His emirs had replied:

> Divine grace assists you in all you give and take away, but you alone have looked to yourself as one accustomed to happiness, to the desire to serve God, to the acquisition of eternal virtue . . . In yourself you find a force and tenacity, and your indestructible faith marks you out as one to achieve the aims we strive for.
>
> But look too at the state of the country, ruined and trampled underfoot and your subjects beaten down, at your armies exhausted and sick, at your horses neglected and ruined . . . food is in short supply, and the necessities of life are dear . . . the rich are reduced to hunger, the poor to destitution. Straw is more precious than gold, barley unobtainable at any price.
>
> And if [the Franks] fail to get the truce they will devote all their energies to strengthening and consolidating their position. They will face death with high courage in the course of achieving their aims, and for love of their faith they will refuse to submit to humiliation. The best thing is for you to remember the verse revealed by God, 'and if they incline to peace you too should incline to it.'*

Saladin therefore left war to one side for the good of his people and of his soldiers, and went to Jerusalem and then on to Damascus. It was said that Damascus was his favourite city, as it had been the place of his boyhood. He died there, among his family, on 4 March 1193, of a fever. In simple terms, and without even throwing into the equation his conquest of the Holy City of Jerusalem, Saladin's personal talents and character confirm him as the greatest hero of the jihad.

---

* Imad al-Din in Gabrieli, pp. 235–7. The 'revealed verse' is Quran: Sura 8, v. 63.

~ 7 ~

Détente and Competition
The Descendants of Saladin

The Prophet said. 'The cases which will be decided first on the Day of
Resurrection will be the cases of blood shedding.'

Hadith, The Book of Tenderness

Saladin had seventeen sons and a host of other close male relatives. The
history of the period following his death is confused and complex, and
is dominated by internecine warfare between his Ayyubid successors.
During this time the unity achieved by Saladin between the major centres
of Islamic power, Damascus, Aleppo, Egypt and the Jazira, dissolved.
Egypt's hegemony slowly increased, since it was the only entity that
Saladin had had enough time to reconstruct as a sophisticated state,
with well-functioning ministries and bureaus. There was also a growing
reliance on Mamluks in the armies of the Ayyubids, along with an
increasingly large political role for the army in their states.

The reasons for the splintering of Saladin's empire are not difficult
to find. First, there was the 'patrimonial share' – by which all members
of the family were entitled to something. Second, Saladin's power had
been dispensed through an institutional apparatus that was weakly
constructed: whilst he had mobilised Islam through religious idealism
and moral authority, he had ruled through a 'tiny elite' made up of his
family.* The leap from regional governors to autonomous princes was a
very short one for Saladin's family to make.

---

* Humphreys, R. S., *From Saladin to the Mongols: The Ayyubids of Damascus, 1193–1260*,
New York: State University of New York Press, 1977, pp. 18–22.

The share-out gave the three main provinces to Saladin's sons and his son-in-law. Al-Afdal took Damascus, al-Zahir gained Aleppo and al-Aziz acquired Egypt. Saladin's brother, al-Adil, took the northern territories and Saladin's nephew, al-Muazzam, gained Transjordan. Homs went to the descendants of Shirkuh, and Hama to the descendants of Taqi al-Din Umar. However, the key to power lay with the old *askaris* of Saladin and Shirkuh, the Salahiyya and Asadiyya. Al-Adil had a long history with these soldiers and he used them to drive al-Afdal from Damascus in 1196. After al-Aziz's death in 1198, he then used his military muscle to usurp the throne of Egypt; in 1202, he forced al-Zahir to accept his suzerainty over Aleppo.

Al-Adil achieved all this with very little interference from the Crusaders. Both sides had been economically and militarily drained by the long contest of the Third Crusade and détente benefited everyone. The year 1197 saw the arrival of German Crusaders: much to the alarm of King Henry, they provoked al-Adil into bringing an army out against Acre. Having made a display of strength against the city, he subsequently turned on Jaffa. The city fell immediately, but the citadel held out. King Henry died in September and was succeeded by Amalric II, the King of Cyprus. Meanwhile, Jaffa fell bloodlessly to al-Adil. Using the resources of the German Crusade, Amalric II took Beirut and Sidon and hoped to use them as a bargaining chip for Jaffa's recovery. However, he then lost control of the German troops, who rushed on to besiege Toron. Al-Adil then compelled al-Aziz to bring the Egyptian army up to Toron. This broke the siege in February 1198; when the Germans returned home, Amalric II and al-Adil negotiated a peace to last for five years and eight months. Sidon was to be shared, Beirut went to the Franks and Jaffa went to al-Adil.

The new pope, Innocent III, was calling in Europe for another crusade, so al-Adil needed to secure peace with the Palestinian Franks. He knew that the Orientalised Franks were simply competitive neighbours who had an active interest in peace, as it allowed trade and revenue to flow. The low-level war fought between al-Adil and Amalric II – with raids down the coast by Muslim emirs and interception of Muslim convoys by Amalric II's naval forces – was an example of this competition and was as 'civilised' as a war could be. The Western Franks who would make up a crusade were, however, a totally different entity. A short description of his dealings with both kinds of *Franj* by Usama Ibn Munqidh illustrates the difference between Levantine Franks and the new arrivals:

One day I had gone in, said the *Allah Akhbar* and risen to begin my prayers, when a Frank threw himself upon me from behind, lifted me up and turned me so that I was facing the east. 'That is the way to pray!' he said. Some Templars at once intervened and seized the man and took him out of my way. I resumed my prayer but the moment they stopped watching him he seized me again and forced me to face the East repeating that this was the way to pray. Again the Templars intervened and took him away. They apologised to me and said, 'he is a foreigner who has just arrived today from his homeland in the North, and he has never seen anyone praying facing any other direction than East'. 'I have finished my prayers', I said, and I left stupefied by the fanatic who had been so perturbed and upset to see someone praying facing the *qibla*.*

The interdependency between Franks and Muslims in the region at the beginning of the thirteenth century is illustrated by petitions brought by Christians to the sultan. They also shed light on the Italian maritime republics' relationships with al-Adil. These relationships would become a central point in the diversion of the Fourth Crusade. A petition from Italian merchants to al-Adil describes their complex position within the war that was taking place between Egypt and Cyprus, but not with the Kingdom of Jerusalem:

In the name of God, the Merciful, the Compassionate. The slaves, the unjustly treated merchants, kiss the earth in the exalted presence of the Lord, the ruler, the Sultan al-Adil, may God prolong his days, unfurl in distant lands of the earth his banners, appoint the heavenly angels to assist his armies, and the kings of the earth to serve as his slaves; and report that they are people who have been unjustly treated. They are merchants who, sailing from Beirut, entered Alexandria, may it be protected. Dues have been collected from them, according to the custom followed with others before them, and they had the safety of God and the safety of this merciful empire. Having traded according to the custom of merchants before them, they intended to leave, but were prevented from this with the pretext that they were from Cyprus. In fact none of them is from Cyprus, they being Pisans and Venetians and one from Beirut . . . they had traded the greater part of their merchandise for buri fish, which has perished so that they had to throw it away, thus very little of their money remains and their ship is exposed to deterioration on the sea. They ask

---

* Gabrieli, p. 80. Usama was praying in the al-Asqa mosque, which perhaps shows that some degree of religious toleration existed during the time of Jerusalem's occupation by the Crusaders. The *qibla*, in every mosque, is the wall facing Mecca. Medieval Christians commonly faced east to pray.

from the mercy of the sultan to look into their affair and graciously allow them to go, since they are poor . . .*

The Fourth Crusade was launched in 1202 and initially its target had been Egypt. King Richard had twice, during the Third Crusade, tried to persuade his army to march on Egypt. He knew that without Egypt, Outremer had little hope of a future. Egypt had also been weakened at this point by the failure of the Nile flood for the previous five years. Al-Adil received letters from the Crusaders, titling him the 'the impious invader and occupier of the Holy Land' and informing him that they would soon attack his realm. However, budget considerations soon cast a pall over the enterprise. This is not entirely surprising. The Venetians, who would supply the naval support and transport for the Crusade, were still out of pocket from the Third Crusade. Furthermore, given that a ship's life-expectancy in this period was only ten years, this precluded the use of vessels from the Third Crusade for the Fourth Crusade. Venice had also conscripted one-half of its manpower to arm and man the galleys and the transports for the venture.† Al-Adil's mutually beneficial trade relationship with the Venetians, with the risks of damaging both their own immediate interests and of becoming involved in a long war in Egypt, were weighed against the potentially more lucrative and easier conquest of Constantinople. The Crusade was diverted and Egypt was spared. Al-Adil concluded a further treaty with Amalric II, in which he ceded Jaffa and Ramla in return for six years of peace and the chance to further his trade relations with the Venetians and Pisans. Amalric II died in 1210 and was succeeded by John of Brienne.

Al-Adil kept the peace, but could do nothing to prevent the Fifth Crusade landing on Egypt's shores in May 1218. The Crusaders dug in on the banks of the Nile and then assaulted Damietta's citadel on 25 August, using towers mounted on ships. Al-Adil's son, al-Kamil, moved a force up close to Damietta, from where he was able to supply the garrison. Every Frankish attack over the next fourteen months was thrown back, but during this time al-Adil died and further political turmoil erupted when Anatolian Turks marched on Aleppo. Al-Kamil

---

* Stern, M. S., 'Petitions from the Ayyubid Period', *Bulletin of the School of Oriental and African Studies*, vol. 27, no. 1, 1964, pp. 1–32. The petition is preserved in the Archivio di Stato, Pisa.

† Queller, D. E., and Day, G. W., 'Some Arguments in Defense of the Venetians on the Fourth Crusade', *American Historical Review*, October 1976, pp. 717–37.

initially managed to contain the fallout linked to the death of the sultan
and also managed to send forces to Aleppo to deter the Turks. However,
more and more Franks were arriving at Damietta. The chain securing the
waterway and access to the city was broken and Damietta was assaulted
by ground troops. Al-Kamil did everything in his power to prevent the
Franks making any progress up the river. He built a pontoon bridge to
station troops across the river, but the Franks cleared it after a hard battle.
He sank cargo vessels to block the river, but the Franks dredged an old
canal to bypass the obstruction. He offered the Crusaders the restoration
of all former Crusader lands west of the Jordan for the evacuation of
Egypt and a thirty-year truce. It was refused, despite the fact that winter
was setting in, because more English and French troops had arrived in
October. Al-Kamil's troops fought the Crusaders from a camp upstream
of Damietta, but in February he had to leave these positions and the
Crusaders were able to encircle Damietta.

Al-Kamil was forced to leave the siege, as his Egyptian Kurdish
emirs were plotting in Cairo to replace him with his brother al-Faiz.
Al-Kamil's other brother, al-Muazzam, brought his *askari* down from
Damascus and this was enough to make the conspirators flee, but not
enough to save Damietta. The city fell on 8 November 1219, after
months of desperate resistance. Its garrison was simply too sick to carry
on the fight. Al-Muazzam returned to Syria to destroy the fortifications
of Jerusalem, and it was now added to the cities being offered to the
Franks in exchange for retiring from Damietta. Whether the Ayyubids
were really prepared to hand over al-Quds we shall never know, because
the Franks once again refused the offer. Al-Kamil knew that Jerusalem
was worthless strategically, as it would be impossible to hold against the
combined forces of Damascus and Egypt. In domestic terms, however,
its loss, at a time when al-Kamil's rule was very fragile, might have
been his undoing. The *ulama* and populace of Damascus were certainly
enraged when he later signed the city over to Frederick II:

> So I ascended the *minbar* of the great mosque of Damascus in the
> presence of al-Nasir . . . it was a memorable day for not one of the people
> of Damascus remained outside in the course of my oration. I said, 'the
> road to Jerusalem is closed to the companies of pious visitors! O desolation
> of those pious men who live there; how many times have they prostrated
> themselves there in prayer, how many tears have they shed there! By Allah,
> if their eyes were living springs they could not pay the whole of their debt of
> grief; if their hearts burst with grief they could not diminish their anguish!

May God burnish the honour of the believers! O shame upon the Muslim rulers! At such an event tears fall, hearts break with sighs, grief rises up on high . . .'*

In March 1220, al-Muazzam attacked Caesarea to divert Frankish attention from Damietta, and the Crusade's leadership fell out over what to do next. King John left Damietta for Acre, from where he hoped to make a claim on the vacant throne of Armenia. However, the siege continued and al-Kamil attempted to break the deadlock by sending a fleet to attack Cyprus. It surprised a large number of Frankish vessels off Limassol and sank or captured all of them. Crusaders then began to desert from Damietta. Despite these marginal successes, al-Kamil was also desperate to end the war, as famine was spreading across Egypt. In early spring the Franks refused his offer of the return of virtually all the lands taken by Saladin, as well as the True Cross. They insisted on an additional indemnity of three hundred thousand dinars for the destruction of Jerusalem's walls.

This was a mistake as a recent rebellion of emirs in the Jazira had finally been put down, which released the forces of Damascus and Mosul for service in Egypt, and the flood season was beginning. On 12 July 1221, following King John's return, and confident that the Holy Roman Emperor, Frederick, was about to set out on Crusade and would reach them soon, the Crusaders attempted an advance up the Nile. The army was composed of five thousand knights and over forty thousand infantry, and was supported by over six hundred ships. There was panic in Cairo and its garrison had to use force to prevent its inhabitants from fleeing. The Franks tried to force al-Kamil back from the Nile tributary of the Bahr-Ashmun, but, with the help of the Mosul regiments, his forces resisted the attack. Then al-Kamil sent ships down a lower tributary and the army of Damascus got itself between the Frankish army and Damietta. By mid-August the Franks were surrounded and running out of supplies. Al-Kamil launched an attack down the Nile with galleys sailing down the river alongside the army. Three Frankish vessels were taken and the Franks were pushed into the unwelcoming arms of the army of Damascus. Al-Kamil then ordered that the Nile flood-gates be opened and the Crusaders suddenly found themselves with only a narrow causeway above water to take them back to Damietta. Al-Kamil's lightly armed Nubian auxiliaries hunted stragglers through the boggy

---

* Sibt Ibn al-Jawzi in Gabrieli, pp. 273–4.

flood plains, as the Crusaders attempted to retreat. A few Crusader ships made it past the Egyptian blockade and back to Damietta, but thousands of troops were surrounded and many ships were captured.

The Crusaders still held Damietta, but al-Kamil now had the fate of a trapped army to negotiate with when the Crusaders came to him seeking terms. He offered the return of the True Cross and safe passage from Egypt, in exchange for Damietta's return, eight years of peace and a prisoner exchange. As a curious epilogue to the whole affair, the Franks made one more demand:

> At the time of the peace the Franks found that they had at Damietta some enormous masts for their ships and they wanted to take these away with them to their own land. The governor refused permission for this, so they sent messages to al-Kamil complaining about it and saying that these masts were their own property, and that according to the terms of the treaty they should be free to take them. Al-Kamil wrote to the governor commanding him to hand over the masts but he persisted in his refusal: 'The Franks took the *minbar* from the great mosque of Damietta', he said, 'and cut it up and sent a piece to each of their kings. Let the sultan command them to return the *minbar* and the masts will be theirs.' The sultan did write to the Franks about this referring them to what the governor had said and the Franks, unable to return the *minbar*, gave up their claim to the masts.*

The sons of al-Adil, relieved of the attentions of western Europe, fell into internal wrangling. Al-Kamil and al-Ashraf, the emir of the Jazira, began intriguing against al-Muazzam, who had fought with them at Damietta. Upon his death, they did the same to his son, and by 1229 they had divided all of al-Muazzam's former lands between them, with al-Kamil adding Transjordan and Palestine to Egypt and al-Ashraf taking Damascus. This arrangement lasted until al-Ashraf's death in 1237.

Jerusalem's throne passed to the German emperor, Frederick, through marriage to King John's daughter. In 1227 he sent a thousand men to bolster Outremer's forces, but did not travel to the Holy Land himself until September 1228. In 1226 al-Kamil had sent an embassy to Frederick, offering the return of all the territories taken by Saladin. This was a bizarre thing for the Sultan of Egypt to be offering, but by this act al-Kamil hoped to prevent the launching of another Crusade that would be backed by Frederick's Sicilian fleet. Also, with this offer, he was not giving away anything *he* owned – these lands were al-Muazzam's,

---

* Ibn Wasil in Gabrieli, pp. 265–6.

with whom he was at loggerheads. Al-Muazzam died soon after al-Kamil commenced his intriguing with Frederick and al-Kamil's need for a Frankish buffer between Damascus and Egypt died with him.

Frederick was subsequently excommunicated by the pope and all danger of an armed Crusade passed. When Frederick arrived in the Levant in 1229 without an army, he was still courted by al-Kamil. Al-Kamil was now in control of Jerusalem and, with the treaty of Jaffa that had been signed in February, he gave it to Frederick, along with Bethlehem and a secure corridor from the coast. He retained the Dome of the Rock and the al-Aqsa mosque as a Muslim enclave, but Muslims were appalled by the treaty and Christians were equally disgusted. Al-Kamil's reasoning for making the accord seems to have been that he knew that Jerusalem was the draw for the Crusades – Crusades that had, and could continue to, assail his lands. Dispensing with it allowed him to look to other distant, but far larger concerns. The armies of the Mongol Khans were already marching west, and if they came to the Levant, peace with the Franks might just be the first step to an alliance against this new foe.

The real danger to Islam had always been from the East. The Crusaders had never been numerous enough to constitute a real threat to the entire *Dar al-Islam*. The first invasions of steppe peoples occurred with the Saljuqs and the later large-scale migrations of the Ghuzz Turcomen, which eventually caused the collapse of Saljuq power in eastern Iran. In 1194 a new Qipchaq Turkish dynasty, the Khwarazmians, emerged from the area east of the Aral Sea and took power in Iran. However, their nascent empire was very rapidly destroyed in a three-pronged assault by Chinggis Khan in 1219. By 1220 the Mongol conquest of the eastern territories of Islam was virtually complete and in 1230 there were further offensives into western Islam.

The year 1238 saw the failure of caliphal embassies to France and England that were seeking alliance against the Mongols, as well as the death of al-Kamil in March. His son, al-Adil II, ascended Egypt's throne and installed a minor prince named al-Jawwad in Damascus. Al-Jawwad proved not to be pliable enough, and when al-Adil II attempted to assert his control in the city al-Jawwad fled. Al-Jawwad then very smartly exchanged Damascus for territories in the Jazira with al-Adil II's older brother, al-Salih. In spring 1229, al-Salih took a large army down to Nablus to threaten the Palestinian territories of al-Adil II. Al-Salih's military muscle was provided by refugee troops of the

Khwarazmian armies that the Mongols had smashed in 1219 and 1220; despite these defeats, they were superb, if often disorderly and brutal, soldiers. Of the other Ayyubids, al-Nasir, the emir of Nablus, was in Cairo with al-Adil II in May and the emirs of Baalbek and Homs were conspiring to seize Damascus in al-Salih's absence. Al-Salih's only ally was al-Muzaffar of Hama.

Al-Salih occupied Gaza and extended his father's treaty with the Crusaders, but in late September he lost Damascus to the emir of Homs. The loss of his capital was a severe blow to al-Salih's esteem and most of his commanders deserted him. In October, he was then captured by al-Nasir. Al-Adil II was fleetingly dominant in the region and the Crusaders fortified Ascalon for fear of an invasion from Egypt; they also raided in Gaza in November 1239, but were easily defeated by the Egyptian army. In December 1239 al-Nasir retook Jerusalem and destroyed the Tower of David.

Al-Muzaffar made peace with al-Nasir in March 1240, but then al-Nasir and al-Adil II fell out over 'ownership' of al-Salih. On 21 April, al-Nasir released his prisoner and agreed to help him conquer Egypt in return for al-Salih's assistance in taking Damascus. The new Prince of Damascus, Ismail, quickly allied himself with the Franks – as al-Salih and al-Nasir walked into Cairo, virtually unopposed, in June.

In July 1240 the Franks attacked al-Nasir's lands along the Jordan, advanced to Gaza, and reoccupied Jerusalem. They were doing very well out of the Ayyubids' infighting and gained Sidon, Toron, Tiberias, Safad and the fortress of Beaufort from their new Damascene ally. Meanwhile, in the north, Homs was raided by Khwarazmian freebooters, who then went on to defeat the army of Aleppo on 2 November and threaten the city. Al-Mansur, the Prince of Homs, was therefore unable to campaign against Egypt with Ismail until he had defeated the Khwarazmians near Edessa in May 1241.

In the summer of 1241, Ismail, al-Mansur and the Franks attempted a joint invasion of Egypt; however, the venture failed and the Frankish–Damascene alliance then quickly fell apart. Ismail had lost confidence in the Franks – the Hospitallers had raided his lands – and he was subsequently offered a better deal by al-Nasir. Al-Salih had broken his word to al-Nasir on helping him to recover Damascus, and a new understanding with Ismail was therefore a logical move. The Franks were left out in the cold until they were courted by al-Salih, who now needed them as a counterweight to the newly united Muslim Syria, and an agreement was reached in early 1241. In the treaty, al-Salih only promised the Franks territories held by his Ayyubid opponents and the one 'Egyptian' parcel of land that he gave them, Gaza, was retaken by an Egyptian army in May 1241. This force then moved on Nablus, but al-Nasir's forces surprised it in the hills west of Jerusalem and, despite being severely outnumbered, routed it. A few weeks later al-Nasir made peace with al-Salih and abandoned the anti-Egyptian alliance. Ibn Shaddad recorded al-Nasir's disgust with Ismail over the fate of Muslim slaves being used by the Templars in Safad's reconstruction.* The slaves had planned a mutiny, but Ismail got word of the rebellion and informed the Templars' master: the slaves were slaughtered to a man.

Despite al-Nasir's defection, Ismail went on the offensive and attempted an invasion of Egypt in early summer. Ismail defeated al-Nasir at Nablus and was joined by a Frankish army at Gaza, which the Egyptian army had abandoned. Despite this promising start, the invasion failed dismally, as large numbers of Syrian troops deserted to al-Salih's army. The Egyptian army pursued the allies through al-Nasir's lands and routed them again at al-Fawwar on 22 August. The Templars then sent envoys to Cairo to sue for peace.

Then out of the woodwork came al-Jawwad. After a series of misfortunes and adventures, he had now returned to the political scene and he allied himself with Ismail. Al-Jawwad's mother was a Frank, so he was the natural candidate to send to the Templars in order to reattach them to the coalition. He succeeded in his diplomacy and joined the Franks in looting Gaza. Al-Salih turned al-Jawwad by guaranteeing Egyptian support for his claim on Damascus and sent three thousand cavalry into Syria in April 1242. In a complete volte-face, al-Salih then tried to arrest al-Jawwad, but he fled to Acre and al-Salih's troops returned to Egypt.

The Franks continued raiding al-Nasir's lands. He responded with a brutal sack of Bethlehem, carrying off its children into captivity and massacring a convoy of pilgrims returning from Jerusalem. On 30 October the Crusaders revenged themselves. They sacked Nablus, razed its Friday mosque and slaughtered its entire population, both Muslim and Christian, before retiring to Jaffa. Al-Salih sent a token force of cavalry to al-Nasir to invest Jaffa, but when the siege dragged on they were withdrawn. He then kept the Franks in limbo through six months

---

* In Jackson, P., 'The Crusades of 1239–41 and their Aftermath', *Bulletin of the School of Oriental and African Studies*, vol. 50, no. 1, 1987, pp. 32–60.

of fruitless negotiations and his navy achieved a small victory over a Frankish squadron off the Egyptian coast in May 1243.

Then al-Nasir, who had been let down once too often by al-Salih, joined Ismail, al-Mansur and the Franks in another attempt on Egypt. Ismail headed for Gaza; al-Nasir was then on the point of taking the Egyptian-held fortress of Shawbak when he was warned by messenger that Ismail's campaign had failed. In fact, Ismail's overt suspicion of al-Jawwad – who remained with the Frankish army and was still held in high regard by them – had destroyed Ismail's relationship with the Franks and the invasion had been abandoned. Ismail arrested al-Jawwad and imprisoned him in Damascus, where he died in 1244.

Then grim news came from the north. The Mongols had advanced through Iraq and into Anatolia. The Saljuq Sultan of Rum had allied with Aleppo and Mardin against them, but in June 1243 his army was crushed at the Battle of Kose Dagh. The fear of a Mongol invasion of Syria forced Ismail to abandon his attempts on Egypt, and he negotiated with al-Salih in September for a mutual recognition of each other's dominions. Al-Mansur of Homs also entered into agreement with al-Salih but this new union excluded al-Nasir. Al-Salih egged al-Mansur on to invade al-Nasir's lands, but was also urging the Khwarazmians, who had been expelled from the Jazira by the Mongols, to invade Syria. One of his letters fell into Ismail's hands and a new coalition against al-Salih was formed – this time al-Nasir was included, as were the Franks. By May 1244 Ismail's forces, along with a Frankish army, were drawn up outside Gaza and al-Nasir's army was mustering near Jerusalem. The alliance hoped to finish with al-Salih before the arrival of his new allies, but the Khwarazmians swept down through Syria in June 1244. They came through the Biqa valley and plundered Tripoli and then split into two armies, both headed for Damascus. Ismail intercepted the first group as it left Tripoli, but his units were surrounded and crushed, just south of Baalbek. Ismail's troops outside Gaza retreated to Damascus and al-Nasir took refuge in Karak. Then the Mongols made an incursion into Aleppo's environs, and Ismail and al-Mansur were forced to ride north. They were able to pay the Mongols off, but the distraction meant that they could not join with the Franks to confront the Khwarazmians before they could join al-Salih's Egyptian forces.

The Franks, devoid of allies and facing ten thousand Khwarazmian horsemen, quickly strengthened Jerusalem's garrison, but the patriarch and the masters of the Temple and Hospital then left the city. Perhaps they had

portended what would happen. On 11 July the Khwarazmians breached
the city's walls, massacred monks and nuns and killed the city governor
as he led a detachment against them. The citadel's garrison appealed to
Acre, but after receiving no reply they sent to al-Nasir, who had, after all,
been the last Muslim lord of the city. He sent troops to negotiate with the
Khwarazmians: safe passage from the city was given to the populace in
exchange for the citadel's surrender. Soon after two thousand Christians
returned to the city after seeing Crusader pennants flying from the citadel,
but it was a Khwarazmian ruse and they were massacred under the city
walls. Bedouins killed many more on the march and only three hundred
reached the safety of Jaffa. In Jerusalem, the Khwarazmians desecrated the
tombs of the Latin kings and set fire to the Church of the Holy Sepulchre.
They then marched to Egypt to join al-Salih's army.

Jihad may have been forgotten by the Ayyubids, but the destruction
of Jerusalem's holy places ignited a pious fervour among the Crusaders.
Troops came from every part of the kingdom to form the last great
army that Outremer would ever put into the field. Al-Salih disclaimed
any responsibility for the outrages in Jerusalem, but by now no one
was listening and he mobilised his Mamluk regiments to join the
Khwarazmians north of Gaza. All of Muslim Syria, with the exception
of Hama, allied with the Franks in the hope of ridding themselves of
al-Salih, and battle was joined at Harbiyya on 17 October 1244.*

The allied army attacked immediately upon sighting the Egyptians.
They had the advantage of numbers and they probably hoped to
outflank the Bahriyya Mamluk regiment† that made up al-Salih's left
wing and centre. The Franks formed the right flank of the army, the
armies of Damascus and Homs made up the centre and al-Nasir's troops
formed the left wing. The Mamluks broke the Franks' charge and then
the Khwarazmians, who had been mustered out to the extreme right of
the Mamluks, swung down upon al-Nasir's troops, crashing into their
flank and centre. The allies' entire left disintegrated and then the troops
of Damascus panicked and fled. Al-Mansur's troops attempted to hold
their ground, but the Crusaders then turned on their Ayyubid allies –
in disgust at their cowardice – and a battle within the battle ensued.

---

* Western sources call the battle 'La Forbie'.
† The regiment acquired its name because its barracks were on a large island in the
middle of the Nile in Cairo. The enormity of the Nile has meant that the Arabic word for
sea, *bahr*, has been applied to it. The Mamluks were garrisoned on the island because of
their known propensity for abusing and roughing up civilians.

A renewed Khwarazmian charge then pushed the Crusaders and the men of Homs into the Mamluks, who massacred them with maces and axes.

The Crusaders lost five thousand killed and eight hundred taken prisoner. Later the loss of this last field army became extremely significant when the Muslims began the reduction of fortified Crusader towns and castles. Without a relief force in the kingdom, these bastions would fall with ever increasing rapidity. The Ayyubids of Syria were also heavy losers; Ismail was ejected from Damascus in October 1245, when al-Nasir and al-Mansur recognised al-Salih as their suzerain. Only Aleppo's young prince, al-Nasir Yusuf, was able to exercise some degree of freedom.

Al-Salih repaid the Khwarazmians for their battlefield performance by arranging their liquidation using the armies of Homs and Aleppo in 1246. His Bahriyya regiment was replenished and strengthened through a continuing policy of Mamluk acquisition. He had started buying Turkish Qipchaq boys in the 1220s. The Mongol invasion of southern Russia had passed through the Qipchaq lands in the Caucasus: Cairo's slave markets were therefore overloaded with Qipchaq boys and prices had correspondingly collapsed. This made al-Salih's task of building a Mamluk army easier. He also advanced Mamluks through the army's ranks because he had no relatives to rely on as army leaders, having betrayed them all. Al-Salih showed an affection for his slave-soldiers that he had never shown to his family – after his death, and their usurpation of power in Egypt, the Mamluks made his mausoleum the centrepiece of much of their ceremony, including the manumission of novices.

Calls for a new Crusade following the disaster of Harbiyya were made, but only the pious King of France, Louis IX, responded. His army of twenty thousand men attacked Egypt in 1249. The Fifth Crusade had at least shown that the rulers of Egypt were prepared to sacrifice Jerusalem for their own safety, and the logic still prevailed that conquering Egypt was the key to holding Syria. Louis used shallow-draught boats to put a large force ashore near Damietta on 5 June, and the city fell the following day.

Ibn Wasil was scandalised by the poor resistance of the Muslim troops who rapidly abandoned the city, but in truth the sultan's health was failing and the entire state was virtually paralysed. From his sick bed Al-Salih ordered that every soldier from the garrison be hanged. The Mamluks who had been sent up to the city, but who had retired before the Franks, were, however, excused since they had at least destroyed the city's bazaar and all its supplies. The flood season came, but Louis had been prepared for it and his army was in good order when he commenced his march on Cairo on 20 November. Despite being gravely ill, al-Salih spent the flood season at al-Mansura with the Bahriyya:

> The army began to make such buildings that still stood inhabitable and set up markets. The wall facing the Nile was rebuilt and faced with a curtain wall. Galleys and fireships were brought up loaded with ammunition and troops and anchored under the wall and countless numbers of regular infantry and volunteers for the faith flocked to al-Mansura. A number of Bedouin Arabs also came and began to make raids and attacks on the Franks.

Al-Mansura was thus strengthened, but:

> Al-Malik al-Salih was weakening, his strength wasting away. The doctors, who were at his pillow day and night, now despaired of his life. His strength of mind and will remained as powerful as ever, but two diseases combined to overcome him; an ulcer in the groin and phthsis.*

Al-Salih died on 24 November. His heir, Turanshah, was far away in the Jazira. The sultan's Qipchaq widow, Shajar al-Durr, realised this was a recipe for political chaos and colluded with the senior Mamluk emir, al-Shuyukh, to conceal the sultan's death and she forged a decree naming him commander-in-chief of the army. Al-Shuyukh was an elderly but inspiring leader and he stopped the Crusader advance in its tracks on the bank of the Nile, opposite al-Mansura. He then moved his siege engines to the riverbank, ready to meet any Crusader attempt to cross it. The Crusaders endeavoured to bridge the river and the Mamluks unleashed a firestorm: darts coated in naphtha were used, and the Crusader, de Joinville, tells us that the ground around the Templar detachment could not be seen for the density of fire-darts covering it. Louis devised protective shelters for his workmen, but there was still no way to even begin building a crossing under such conditions.

On 7 February 1241, the Crusaders discovered a ford upstream. The Crusader plan was that no attack would take place until sufficient units had crossed and assembled on the other side of the river. This never happened, though, as the king's brother, ignoring orders, charged along the river after crossing, took the Muslim encampment on the river by

---

* Ibn Wasil in Gabrieli, p. 287. The sultan was probably dying from tuberculosis.

surprise and stormed into the city itself. The Mamluks were initially scattered through the streets by the Crusader cavalry, but then very rapidly barricaded the streets to prevent the Franks' withdrawal and killed virtually the entire force in hand-to-hand fighting.

The Bahriyya, under the junior emir Baybars, then moved out of al-Mansura to meet the rest of the king's forces, which had now crossed the river. The fighting lasted for the rest of the day. The Mamluks poured arrows and *naft*-darts into the Crusaders' ranks, and Louis organised charge after charge to try to relieve the pressure on his infantry. A late deployment of his crossbowmen won the day for Louis, as he held the riverbank and the Mamluks were forced to retire to the city. However, the campaign was, in fact, slipping away from him. Muslim reinforcements were arriving by the hour at al-Mansura. The Franks concentrated on constructing a pontoon bridge and digging trenches.

The Bahriyya launched an assault on 11 February and overwhelmed many of the Crusaders' positions, but they failed to burn the pontoon bridge, despite the use of glass grenades filled with *naft*. Muslim infantry cleared Crusaders from their trenches, supported by Mamluk mounted archers, firing darts through tubes mounted on their bows rather than arrows – two or three darts could be loaded into the tube and fired simultaneously to make a very effective harassing fire.

The Crusaders still held the riverbank and there was a standoff for eleven days. The elderly emir al-Shuyukh had recently died and the new sultan, Turanshah, did not arrive at al-Mansura until 28 February. A flotilla of small boats was then transported on the backs of camels downstream of the Crusaders: this little fleet very effectively cut the Crusader supply line from Damietta. The river and the Crusader lines were full of corpses: starvation and the filth surrounding them combined to cause contagion in the Frankish camp.

Louis made a desperate offer to exchange Damietta for Jerusalem; when it was rejected out of hand by Turanshah, he started a retreat on 5 April 1250. The Mamluks chased his army down the river and killed several thousand of his men. The rest of his troops, including a gravely ill Louis, surrendered. The Mamluks then massacred all the sick troops. There was an element of straightforward brutality to this action, but the Egyptians' resources were also incapable of dealing with the vast numbers of infected Franks, and Mamluks – as 'strangers' to the Middle East – always suffered disproportionately during epidemics in Egypt. They therefore had a morbid fear of disease.

Louis was ransomed in return for Damietta and four hundred thousand livres. The negotiations were begun by Turanshah, but they ended up being completed by a military junta of Bahriyya Mamluks – because on 2 May the young emir, Baybars, broke into Turanshah's tent during dinner, with a sword in his hand, and struck at the sultan's head. Turanshah warded off the blow and ran screaming for help to a wooden siege tower. Baybars's men, however, surrounded the tower and fired it. The sultan and his emirs fought their way out of the tower and ran for the river, but Baybars waded in after him and ran him through.

Turanshah had been appointing his own men to high office over Bahriyya officers, and may also have been a little mad, since he had been seen wandering around his palace at night slashing at candles with his sabre and muttering, 'so I shall deal with the Bahris!' The coup was therefore perhaps inevitable, especially given the fact that there was now a Qipchaq Turk hegemony within the state that was not balanced by any other ethnic group. Even the Kurds were a small minority in the upper echelons. This was one of the sequelae of al-Salih's Mamluk policy. Furthermore, the Bahriyya Mamluks' loyalty was also to al-Salih alone. When he had been imprisoned in 1240 by al-Nasir, Shajar al-Durr (then his maid-servant), Baybars and other Mamluks had been voluntarily imprisoned with him. Al-Salih had also given 'his men' the best *iqtas* in Egypt when he came to power, and had distributed lands captured during the long wars against his brothers to his Mamluks. He had also appointed a Mamluk governor to Damascus after its conquest in 1245, rather than bestowing it on one of his family. The Mamluks therefore had a lot to lose if Turanshah turned against them: as their loyalty was entirely to al-Salih, their *ustadh* or master, nothing was owed to his son, and he owed them nothing. Ibn al-Jawzi also suggested that al-Salih's treatment of his own kinsmen showed the Mamluks that putting royalty to death was of no import. His brother, al-Adil, had been imprisoned since 1240 and when al-Salih heard rumours of a coup in his name, 'al-Salih had said, "go to the prison to my brother al-Adil and take along some Mamluks to strangle him . . ." They went to him and strangled him. Then Allah put his son [Turanshah] at their mercy, so they killed him, molesting him as severely as he had his brother.'*

---

* In Levanoni, A., 'The Mamluks' Ascent to Power in Egypt', *Studia Islamica*, no. 72, 1990, pp. 121–44.

After the coup the Mamluks elected Shajar al-Durr to rule as queen of the Muslims. The role of women is fairly minimal in Islamic history, but Shajar al-Durr had often run the sultanate's affairs when al-Salih was absent, so she had her own seal for decrees and the Mamluks needed legitimacy for their new government. However, chaos immediately ensued because the coup leaders could not gain the full support of the army. Though they were essentially the core of the army and state, the Bahriyya only numbered about one thousand troops, within an army of some twelve thousand men. Furthermore, the sultan's close bodyguard, the Jamdariyya, were antagonistic to the coup leaders and there was even a faction within the Bahriyya that had attempted to kill Baybars for his regicide. The junta therefore selected the senior emir al-Muizz Aybeg as commander-in-chief, since he was both a Bahriyya Mamluk and had his own bodyguard of Mamluks, the Muizziyya. By this they hoped to widen their support base.

In July 1250 the junta also ordered the arrest of Kurdish emirs who were suspected of being pro-Ayyubid. This was a reaction to the loss of Damascus to al-Nasir Yusuf of Aleppo. Shajar al-Durr was also forced to abdicate in favour of Aybeg, who was then replaced only five days later by al-Ashraf Musa, a ten-year-old great nephew of al-Salih. The junta hoped that re-establishing the Ayyubid line in Egypt would placate al-Nasir Yusuf. Aybeg then made a political marriage with Shajar al-Durr, as the state split into factions – following either himself and the Muizziyya, or Baybars, the emir Aktay and the Bahriyya. Aybeg garnered enough support to become *atabeg* to the child sultan and through this managed to unite all the Mamluks under his command – just in time to deter al-Nasir Yusuf from a march on Cairo in February 1251.

Reports of a further vast Mongol army, primed to invade the lands of Islam again, began to reach Baghdad in 1253 and the caliph acted to try to bring peace in the Levant, as a prelude to creating a united front against the khan's army. An agreement was signed on 8 April that recognised Mamluk rule in Egypt, and an Ayyubid princess of Hama married Aktay, the commander of the Bahriyya. The war within Egypt rumbled on. Aybeg's right-hand man, Kutuz, murdered Aktay in September 1254 and Baybars and seven hundred Bahriyya troopers fled to Syria to become swords for hire. Aybeg then deposed the puppet sultan and sought a new political marriage. Shajar al-Durr responded to her husband's nuptial plans by having him slain in his bath in April 1257. She herself was killed within the same month and her body was found outside Cairo's citadel, the victim of a faction led by Kutuz that had put up her stepson as heir. Baybars and his exiled troopers made an abortive attempt on Cairo in 1258. Kutuz executed every one of them that he captured and Baybars vowed vengeance. His revenge would have to wait, however, for the Mongols had now unleashed their full fury on Islam.

~ 8 ~

Jihad and Nemesis
The Mamluk War Machine

Father of the poor and miserable,
Killer of the unbelievers and the polytheists,
Reviver of justice among all.
An engraving on Mamluk armour

In 1256 the great Mongol khan, Mongke, tasked his brother, Hulegu Khan, with exterminating the Ismaili Assassins of Persia – in revenge for an attempt on the great khan's life – and with bringing the caliph of Baghdad to submission. The first part of Hulegu's mission was fairly well completed by the beginning of 1258, and in February of that year he moved against Baghdad. The city was brutally sacked, the Tigris was choked with bodies and the caliph was rolled up in a carpet and kicked to death. A contemporary poet of Damascus, Ibn Abul-Yusr, wrote of the shock that the Muslim world felt:

The crown of the caliphate and the house whereby the rites of the Faith
    were exalted is laid waste by desolation.
There appear in the morning light traces of the assault of decay in its
    habitation, and tears have left their marks upon its ruins.
O, fire of my heart, for a fire of clamorous war that blazed out upon it,
    when a whirlwind smote the habitation!
High stands the Cross over the tops of its *minbars*, and he whom a girdle
    used to confine has become master . . .*

---

* In Somogyi, J. de, 'A Qasida on the Destruction of Baghdad by the Mongols', *Bulletin of the School of Oriental Studies*, vol. 7, no. 1, 1933, pp. 41–8.

The suggestion that the Mongols were pro-Christian would become significant later, when the armies of the khan reached the Holy Land. Hulegu moved on to accept the peaceful submission of Armenia and Georgia. Mosul made obeisance and the Saljuqs of Anatolia put their forces at Hulegu's disposal. Al-Nasir Yusuf sent his son to Hulegu's court to appeal for clemency, but Aleppo was taken – its fate was as bloody as Baghdad's and its great mosque was personally fired by the Armenian king. Al-Nasir Yusuf headed north to relieve Aleppo, but his army deserted him and he was captured by Hulegu. Damascus capitulated upon the Mongols' approach and Islam was disestablished as the official religion of the area. Bohemond VI of Antioch submitted to Hulegu and was swiftly excommunicated by Acre's papal legate for doing so. Hulegu then sent envoys to Cairo, demanding Kutuz's surrender. Kutuz had them cut in half in the horse market, and placed their heads on the city gates.

Kutuz had declared war on the superpower of the Middle Ages. He was a one-year sultan of an unstable dynasty and his act seemed like madness, but in truth he had no choice. The Mamluks were essentially a minority foreign dynasty ruling a large Arab country. Surrender meant exile, and that meant embracing the same fate as the Khwarazmians. Also, Kutuz felt he had a chance. Baybars and his exiles had returned in March 1260 under an oath of safety, they were the best soldiers in the Levant and every trooper counted now. There were probably only ten thousand regular cavalrymen in Egypt at this time, though Kutuz was joined by a number of troops from Syria and the Jazira who had fled the Mongol invasion.*

More importantly, Hulegu had taken a large part of his forces out of Syria in the summer of 1259. Mongke had died in August 1259 and his brothers Qubilai and Ariq Boke were very obviously prepared to make war on each other for the succession. Hulegu, the third brother, did not count himself as a candidate, but backed Qubilai, while the khan of the Golden Horde, Berke, backed Ariq Boke. Berke's powerful state lay directly north of Hulegu's new territories in Persia, and there had already been friction between them over Berke's conversion to Islam and Hulegu's persecutions of Muslims, as well as over territorial rights in Azerbaijan. Hulegu took his army to Maragha to meet any potential invasion of the Golden Horde. The Mamluks would therefore meet only

---

* Humphreys, R. S., 'The Emergence of the Mamluk Army', *Studia Islamica*, no. 45, 1977, pp. 67–99.

the remainder of his force, which was still admittedly considerable – led by Kit Buqa, one of his most experienced generals.

In the spring of 1260, the Mongols raided Ascalon and Jerusalem, and Kit Buqa sent detachments to Gaza and Nablus, thereby effectively surrounding the Frankish kingdoms on the coast. On 26 July 1260 Kutuz left Cairo: he had decided to meet the Mongols in Syria, rather than to wait for them in Egypt. He was worried that his Mamluk emirs might lose the will to fight and felt he had to act quickly. Fear was already spreading through the ranks and it was only when Kutuz made to ride out of the city, saying, 'I am going to fight the Mongols alone', that his troops followed him out of Cairo.

Kutuz sent an embassy to Acre, as the army had to march through Frankish lands to be able to intercept the Mongol advance through Syria. The Muslim writers of the time tend to gloss over this episode, but al-Zahir, who accompanied the sultan, suggests that the sultan asked the Franks for armed assistance, which they refused and granted only safe passage. Even this concession from the Franks may seem surprising, but the Mongols, despite their devastation of Muslim lands, had done little since to encourage the notion that they were potential allies, and their sack of Sidon had caused widespread panic in Acre. The Franks' policy had been to appease the Mongols, but even this had been difficult at times. As early as 1244, a Mongol division had demanded that Antioch's walls be razed and that three thousand maidens be provided to entertain the troops. In 1256 the patriarch of Jerusalem had written to the pope of his fears of a Mongol invasion, and in February 1260 Kit Buqa wrote to the Franks to inform them that the Mongols were destined for world domination and that they must level the walls of all their cities. The Mongol view of the Franks' capabilities is revealed by an entry in al-Qazvini's geographical encyclopedia, written for the Mongols in 1276:

> The land of the Franks (Ifranja): a great country and a vast realm in the territory of the Christians . . . They have a mighty king, and their numbers and armed forces are plentiful. Their king has two or three cities on the sea coast on this side, in the midst of Muslim territory, and he defends them from that direction. Every time the Muslims send someone there to conquer them, he sends someone to defend them from the other side. His armies are strong and powerful, and do not in any way feign flight in battle, but prefer death . . .*

---

* In Jackson, P., 'The Crisis in the Holy Land in 1260', *English Historical Review*, July 1980, pp. 481–513.

In 1260, therefore, the Mongols would have viewed the Franks of Syria as a weak opponent, but still one that had to be dealt with cautiously to avoid the risk of a crusade. For the Crusaders, a Mamluk defeat of the Mongols was then, on the whole, a desirable thing, if for no other reason than to preserve a balance of power, especially if it cost the Crusaders nothing in men.

Kutuz learnt that Kit Buqa was encamped at Ayn Jalut, the 'Spring of Goliath', at the foot of Mount Gilboa. The Mongol army probably numbered somewhere around twelve thousand men, but some of these troops were not Mongol: there were Georgian and Armenian auxiliaries and troopers from the Ayyubid armies of Syria. Battle was joined on 3 September and the Mongol right very quickly defeated the Mamluk left, but then the troopers of Kutuz's bodyguard counter-attacked and sent the Mongol right into disorder. Kit Buqa rapidly reorganised his forces and turned the battle again. Kutuz then threw off his helmet so that his troops could see him clearly and led a frontal charge. This caused disarray in the Mongol ranks and it seems that Kit Buqa was killed at this point. The Ayyubid forces then deserted the Mongols' left flank. The battle had started at dawn and by noon became a slaughter.

Following the battle, Damascus, Hama and Aleppo were all immediately abandoned by their Mongol garrisons. Baybars subsequently massacred a column of Mongol troopers, along with their women and children, at Homs.

Prior to the battle it had seemed that Islam was at an end. The Mamluks had, in one fell swoop, become the greatest warriors of the jihad, legitimised their dynasty and annexed Syria. Kutuz did not stay in the new province long, as he was increasingly nervous of Baybars's growing support among the emirs. Thus he was bringing the army back as fast as he could to Cairo, his political stronghold, when he was murdered by Baybars and his accomplices whilst hunting in the desert. Baybars claimed the sultanate and was granted it by Kutuz's very frightened chief-of-staff. He then rode into Cairo ahead of the main army to secure the treasury and to ensure that he was enthroned before the army could change its mind.

Mamluk resources had been stretched by the acquisition of Syria, so Kutuz had rewarded al-Ashraf Musa, the Ayyubid prince who had deserted the Mongols, by returning him to Homs. Al-Mansur Muhammad of Hama had been allied with the Mamluks from the outset and was also given back his city. Mosul returned to Muslim control and was given to a governor with strong Saljuq family links. A Mamluk governor, al-Halabi, was installed in Damascus and *iqtas* were distributed to leading families of the Bedouin of North Syria – at this juncture every ally was needed. These arrangements soon began to fall apart. Al-Halabi declared himself Sultan of Damascus, the governor of Aleppo was ousted by a group of Mamluks who looked dangerously independent, and the Mongols began raiding in the region. Secret payments from Baybars to Kurdish troops in Damascus's garrison cut short al-Halabi's rebellion – he fled the city, but was soon captured. The sultan briefly imprisoned the rebel but then restored him to favour. Al-Halabi was one of Baybars's *khushdash*, meaning that he had been a novice slave-soldier of the same *ustadh* and they would have billeted and trained together as young men. *Khushdashiyya* was a construct of relationships between slave-soldiers based on living and fighting together, and it both characterised and gave a structure to the Mamluk sultanate.

Six thousand Mongol troopers raided northern Syria in December 1260. The new Mamluk rulers of Aleppo shelved their plans for independence and went south to ally with al-Mansur of Hama and al-Ashraf of Homs. This still only gave a force of fourteen hundred men, but al-Ashraf decided to confront the Mongols just north of Homs. The day was foggy and the Mongols feared losing touch with their flanks, so they formed up in squadrons lined up on a short front, one after another. This robbed them of the advantage of their numbers. It also seems that sun glare on the fog reduced visibility and that the Mongol archers were unable to identify their targets in the Muslim force that was rapidly approaching. The Muslims released one flight of arrows during their charge and then struck the Mongols with their lances. The Mongols were then also attacked by Bedouin from the rear, and those that could fled the battlefield. They occupied Aleppo for four months, but deserted it when Baybars sent an army to threaten them: they had been warned about the Mamluk force by the Crusaders of Acre.

The Franks attempted to make more trouble for the new sultan with a raid into the Golan Highlands in February 1261, but their forces were badly mauled by Turcomen that Baybars had stationed in the region. Almost insignificant as these events were, they turned Baybars's attention to the Franks and to the thought that their elimination would preclude the Mamluks having to fight a war on two fronts. He began to build the army that would push the Franks into the sea.

The Mamluk army that Baybars produced was the only army capable
of defeating the Mongols on the battlefield. It was composed of mounted
archers – as the Mongol forces were – but a Mamluk trooper could surpass
the rate of fire of his adversary, and was entirely more disciplined. This
meant that once the Mongols were matched or defeated in the archery
duel, which was the first stage of any battle between these two steppe peoples, the Mamluks could then very rapidly move to a charge against their
now disordered opponents. Baybars's Mamluks did not need a screen of
infantry as the Crusaders did, behind which to marshal themselves before
sallying forth. Instead they were able to group their squadrons for the
manoeuvre in the heat of fluid, fast-moving cavalry battles, and to time
their charges to perfection, just as their enemy was breaking up or totally
committed to the battle and unable to disengage. This was a feat without
parallel in the medieval age. Mamluk battlefield communications were
impressive for the period and their commanders were second to none – but
their battles were chiefly won by what was instilled on the training ground
and their ability to know, almost instinctively, how to operate within units,
in a period where closely controlling more than just a handful of men was
near impossible. This was a natural offshoot of *khushdashiyya*. Mamluks
lived almost as brothers and the life of the barracks was everything.

Fighting heavily armoured Frankish knights and infantry at close
quarters, as we have seen, had always been a difficult proposition for
the Muslims. *Askari* troopers could undertake to challenge the Crusader
knight one-to-one, but there had been too few *askari* Mamluk troopers
up to this point. Baybars's Mamluks, however, were to be numerous.
The sultan's army was not a vessel of the state, the army *was* the state.
Revenue flowed into the purchase of Mamluk novices from the Caucasus
and Baybars concluded an accord with Berke Khan, both as a security
pact against Hulegu and to maintain the flow of boy-slaves. Baybars
invested in training facilities and lengthened the training times for his new
recruits. *Maydans*, or hippodromes, were built, as well as numerous *tibaq*
(barracks). There was also investment in horses: Mamluks rode stabled
horses that were fourteen hands high, as was the average European
warhorse of the time, and the Mamluks' steeds were armoured.

Each trooper was protected by a chain-mail shirt, which extended
from the knees upwards to the neck, and acted as a coif. The *hazagand*, a
jerkin of leather and mail, was also used, as it was suited to the hot Syrian
summer. Each trooper carried a sword, dagger, axe or mace, lance and
shield, as well as the ubiquitous composite bow and a wide-mouthed

quiver. The axe and mace tell us that the Mamluks, as at al-Mansura, would confidently undertake close-quarters fighting with the *Franj*.*

Overall, Baybars increased the size of the army during his reign to forty thousand horsemen, plus infantry and auxiliaries. The old Ayyubid elite forces, the *halqa*, were downgraded and the royal Mamluks became the core of the army. Each Mamluk novice was taught the Quran, how to pray and *sharia* law. Religious teaching was deliberately dogmatic and narrow, and the idea of religious toleration was shunned.

All training was conducted according to the precepts of the *Furusiyya*. *Furusiyya*, or war manuals, date from the first dynasties of Islam, but under the Mamluks they became almost sacred texts. They covered everything from the management, training and care of horses, cavalry tactics, riding techniques and the wearing of armour, to how to wield every type of weapon. Basic veterinary science and the art of polo playing were also addressed.

All training was carefully staged, with novices moving through training in simple tasks with little physical requirement, through to highly skilled tasks needing a great deal of strength and endurance. Qipchaq boys would all have handled bows and ridden ponies on the steppe before being 'harvested', but Mamluk training took them right back to basics again. Mounting and dismounting drills and point-blank-range archery practice was performed day after day. The novice would work through four bows of increasing strength. The final *qaws*, used for war, had a pull of about thirty kilograms. The Mamluk was, of course, a horse archer and the novice could not pass out of training without demonstrating accuracy with the bow at the gallop. Weapons are often paired in the *Furusiyya*. The *khanjar*, or dagger, for example, was paired with the lance for close-quarters fighting; the sword went with missile weapons, such as the javelin. Competency with the lance was shown through the *bunud* exercises. The recruit had to throw his lance, at the gallop, through a small ring at head-height and pick up small cones from the ground with the tip of his lance, once again at the gallop. The sword drills of the Mamluks required the novice, by the end of training, to be able to strike a bed of clay a thousand times without fatigue and also to be able to cut through reams of paper without cutting a soft cotton pillow placed below it. Passing out also required consummate swordplay as a cavalryman.

---

* For more on the training, structure and divisions within the Mamluk army, see Waterson, *Knights of Islam*, Chapter Five.

Measured lengths had to be cut from reeds at the gallop and the skilled simultaneous use of two swords was also expected.

In the *maydan*, the novices learnt movement as a unit and how to act in union – Baybars tried to ensure the same kind of unity in his state. The *ulama* had begun to impart their power over the people to successful generals of the jihad as early as the first quarter of the twelfth century, with the partnership between Il-Ghazi and al-Kashab in Aleppo. Baybars would now conclude that process by absorbing the *ulama* into the service of the army-state. There are four schools of Sunni jurisprudence, the Shafi'i, the Hanbali, the Hanafi and the Maliki, and Baybars gave equal power to each of them.* This was effectively a process of divide and conquer. There would never be a *qadi* powerful enough to speak out against the regime because the four schools were never on particularly good terms. Before making this skilful division, he used the Shafi'i school to approve the installation of his trump card: a caliph in Cairo. In fact, Baybars set up two caliphs. Both were refugees from Baghdad with Abbasid family connections. Al-Mustansir was enthroned on 19 June 1261, but six months later he was dispatched by the sultan on a one-way mission to reclaim Baghdad from the Mongols. Needless to say, he was not heard from again. Al-Hakim was then installed and 'reigned' until 1301, but of course had no power. He was wheeled out for legitimisation of Baybars's actions and to impress visiting dignitaries from the Golden Horde.† Baybars in fact, had very little need of caliphal legitimisation for his reign: the successful and destructive jihad he was about to launch on the *Franj* would do that for him.

The Holy War first struck Antioch in 1261. Bohemond VI's ties to both the Mongols and the Armenians made Antioch a threat to Baybars's northern cities. A series of raids continued unabated year after year, and the city would have fallen, but for Mongol support. In 1262, Saint Simeon was looted and Jaffa and Beirut were threatened; Baybars obtained al-Bira and Karak, two vital border fortresses, through trickery, and with his Mongol front secure he returned to the Franks. The death of Hulegu and continued infighting among the Mongols also freed Baybars from Mongol aggression during this period.

---

* Nielsen, J. S., 'Sultan al-Zahir Baybars and the Appointment of Four Chief Qadis, 663/1265', *Studia Islamica*, no. 60, 1984, pp. 167–76.

† Holt, P. M., 'Some Observations on the Abbasid Caliphate of Cairo', *Bulletin of the School of Oriental and African Studies*, vol. 47, no. 3, 1984, pp. 501–7.

Nazareth was sacked in February 1263 and the Church of the Virgin was levelled. In April, Baybars brought his troops to Acre, but the walls of the city stymied him. He thought he had secured enough assistance from the Genoese to take the city – they were his partners in the slave trade and also wished to move trade away from the Levant and up to the Black Sea ports. He did, however, plunder the city's environs. Baybars left Turcomen behind to raid Palestine throughout 1263. Many Frankish lords simply sold their possessions and left the Levant, such was the level of damage done by these depredations.

There was, of course, a danger of provoking a further crusade by these attacks on Outremer, but this had to be balanced against the risk of a Mongol–Crusader alliance. Baybars's espionage network had informed him that Hulegu had been in correspondence with the Franks of Syria and with King Louis IX of France. Baybars's solution to this problem was to avoid direct confrontation with Acre, but to aim at the other provinces of the Crusader kingdom. Bohemond VI of Antioch was beyond the pale in the eyes of most Franks, and was therefore an obvious target. The castles of the Hospitallers and Templars could also be attacked, as the political fault lines that ran though Outremer meant that their loss would be bound to please one faction or another.

In January 1265, Baybars was heading north to meet a Mongol threat to al-Bira, but it had been dealt with by the fortress's garrison before he arrived. He therefore turned the army that he had prepared for the Mongols on the Crusaders instead. The Hospitallers had been counter-raiding against the Turcomen that Baybars had settled in Palestine. The sultan's army therefore appeared before the great coastal Hospitaller castle of Arsuf in January 1265 to threaten the knights. Then it abruptly disappeared, only to reappear at the walls of Caesarea. The ability to re-deploy rapidly in this manner was a consistent feature of the Mamluk army, based as it was around a core of heavy cavalry. Its rapidity of movement constantly stretched the Crusaders, as their reinforcements and what was left of their field army never knew where the next blow would land. Caesarea fell quickly on 27 February after the Mamluks used makeshift rope ladders, constructed from their bridles, to haul themselves up the walls. The citadel surrendered on 5 March; Baybars razed the citadel and the lower town to the ground. Haifa suffered the same fate a few days later and there was a general massacre of the citizens, who were unable to get away by boat. Baybars then instigated his 'castle policy'. Ibn al-Furat tells us that, 'the Muslim army uproots Frankish fortresses and destroys their castles, while elsewhere we rebuild to withstand the Mongols.'* Baybars wanted to leave no viable landing place for further European invasions. Saladin's failure to eradicate Outremer had been due to the survival and loss of Tyre and Acre; since the destruction of Saladin's fleet in 1192, the Muslims had slipped even further behind Europe in the naval arms race.

Baybars moved onto Athlit, the grand Templar castle and town on the coast between Haifa and Caesarea. Its surrounding villages were burnt to the ground and its farmlands were plundered. Athlit itself, however, resisted the sultan's mangonels and he returned to Arsuf. Arsuf was garrisoned by 270 knights and was well provisioned. Baybars's Mamluks gained entry, though, on 26 April, after pounding the lower town's walls flat and filling the immense moat. The knights capitulated three days later on a promise of free passage to Acre; they knew no relief was coming, as Outremer had no field army after Harbiyya. Baybars reneged on his promise and sent the knights into captivity to ensure that they could not return to fight again. He then moved troops to Acre to guard the new border, which was now within sight of the city walls.

Baybars returned to Syria in June 1266. He made a feint at the castle of Montfort, but then moved suddenly to Safad in early July. Baybars's initial assault, involving a fourteen-day bombardment, failed to force the castle's defenders to surrender. This was despite a promise of one thousand dinars for every stone knocked out by his men and the fact that the Mamluks were hurling 450-kilogram rocks at the walls from their swing-beam counterweighted mangonels. The design may been French in origin, but al-Tarsusi described *Franj*, Arab and Turkish counterweighted mangonels as being quite distinct from each other.

After Baybars was almost killed by a well-aimed Frankish missile, he looked to a different method of bringing the castle down. He declared an amnesty for any native Syrians who wished to surrender to him. He knew that most of Safad's garrison were native Christians under the command of the Templars. There had certainly been no disloyalty whatsoever up to this point, but the sultan's guarantee created tension and suspicion between the two parties in the castle and the Syrians soon deserted wholesale. The Templars attempted to garrison the city's entire vast ring of walls, but it was hopeless. One of their few remaining native

---

* See Waterson, *Knights of Islam*, Chapter Five, for Ibn Furat's analysis and more on the Mamluk approach to their two-front war.

sergeants offered to parley with Baybars and returned from the sultan with a forged letter – allegedly from their master – calling on the knights to surrender. They came out under promise of safe passage to Crusader territory and were decapitated to a man. Safad was garrisoned and Baybars moved on. Toron fell to his first attack and Qara, a small Syrian-Christian village west of Damascus, had all its inhabitants slaughtered by a small detachment of his army, as they had been selling Muslims into slavery. The army returned to Egypt in autumn 1266 via the coast, and partook in what might conveniently be labelled as ethnic cleansing in the Christian villages and towns south of Acre.

Baybars had also sent one of his senior emirs, Kalavun, with an army to Armenia and to raid around Tripoli in the summer of 1266. Several forts and towns were taken in the region and the army then moved on to join up with the Ayyubid prince al-Mansur, before entering Armenia. Armenia's king had invaded Baybars's northern territories on several occasions between 1262 and 1264, but had failed each time to make any gains. The king had then negotiated with Baybars for neutrality and the payment of tribute to Egypt, but Baybars had demanded the ceding of frontier fortresses and the king could not comply for fear of the Mongols. Baybars wanted Armenia pacified in order to further isolate Antioch and Tripoli. The Armenian army waited for Kalavun's invasion at the Syrian Gates, but he avoided the pass, went straight over the mountains and began pillaging their lands. The Armenian army was then decisively beaten on the plain of Tarsus. Kalavun sacked the cities of Ayas, Adana, Tarsus and the capital Sis. Forty thousand captives were taken back to Aleppo.

The knights of the Orders and the French regiment of Acre, a gift from Louis IX, raided through newly Muslim-controlled lands in Galilee in October 1266. The Crusader army's camp was, however, raided by Bedouins and its vanguard was then ambushed by the new Mamluk garrison of Safad. Baybars had also sent an army to Antioch in autumn 1266. However, Bohemond VI was able to bribe the emirs heading it into withdrawing.

Baybars's army returned to Syria in May 1267. He used captured Hospitaller and Templar banners to get his forces close up to Acre's walls, but the ruse failed to get him into the city. His troops then ravaged the environs and the desperate Crusaders sent emissaries requesting a truce – it was granted, since Baybars had new information that Louis IX of France had again begun to plan a crusade in March 1267. The sultan feared that a coalition between Louis and Abagha, the new ilkhan of Persia, might be formed; he therefore decided in early 1268 to reduce Jaffa, the last Crusader city south of Acre. On 7 March he appeared before its walls. A Frankish mangonel once again nearly finished the sultan – in fact it killed three men standing close to him – but after only twelve hours his men took the city. The citadel's troops were allowed to leave for Acre, but the civilian population was either killed or enslaved. The city's fortifications were levelled; any marble or wood was sent back to Cairo to become part of the sultan's new Friday mosque.

If there was to be a joint Ilkhanid–European assault, then Bohemond VI would be a key player. Baybars therefore headed north for Antioch, but on the way an opportunity presented itself that was too good to miss. The Templars of the castle of Beaufort had been building a fort near the castle to enhance its defences. Unfortunately for them, only the fort's foundations were complete by the time Baybars's army arrived – these provided a perfect level base, in an otherwsie overwhelmingly hilly region, for the sultan's artillery. The walls crumbled after ten days and the captured Templars were sent to the slave markets. The castle was rebuilt, as it blocked a likely Mongol invasion route. Baybars then headed towards Tripoli, but decided that it was too strong to be taken quickly; he had not realised that Bohemond VI was in the city and could therefore have been either killed or captured. If this could have been achieved it would very likely have forced Antioch to negotiate a surrender. He also bypassed the Templars' strongholds of Tortosa and Safita after both pleaded for clemency.

The Mamluk army arrived before Antioch on 14 May. Baybars invested the walls with a third of his forces; Saint Simeon was encircled and the Syrian Gates were garrisoned to prevent any Mongol intervention. Bohemond VI's constable then made the incredibly foolish move of leading a sortie. He was captured and Baybars put him to work arranging the city's capitulation. The defenders refused to listen to him, however, and bombardments and assaults began in earnest. The thinly spread garrison could not cover every part of the city's walls – therefore, on 18 May, Baybars made a general attack on every sector. The inevitable break-in came on the Mount Silpius section, and it was followed by a whole day of murder and rapine. The city gates were sealed to ensure that no citizen could escape death or ransom. Baybars called a halt to the slaughter the next day; slaves and riches were distributed among the senior emirs. Baybars wrote to Bohemond of the sack:

Be glad that you have not seen your knights lying prostrate under the hooves of horses, your palaces plundered, your ladies sold in the quarters of the city, fetching a mere dinar a piece – a dinar taken, moreover, from your own hoard. If you had seen your churches destroyed, your crosses sawn asunder, the pages of the lying gospels exposed, if you had seen your enemy the Muslim trampling in the sanctuary, with the monk, the priest, the deacon sacrificed on the altar . . . the Churches of Saint Paul and Saint Peter pulled down and destroyed you would have said, 'Would to God that I was transformed to dust or would to God that I had not received the letter that tells me of this sad catastrophe.'*

Antioch's loss virtually finished the Crusaders in northern Syria. The Templars abandoned all their castles in the region and other small towns simply came over to the Muslims. Antioch was refortified because it protected the route from Mongol-controlled Anatolia, but it was never repopulated.

Baybars had by now secured his borders against Mongol attack; by his reduction of the ports he had reduced the risk of assault from Europe. He also worked on communications and early warning systems in Syria. The superb Mongol *yam* military postal system that covered the entirety of their lands was emulated, and the *barid*, or pony express service, came into existence. The *barid* effectively reduced twenty days' riding to three and covered the entire sultanate. A network of constantly manned pigeon towers was also established, as were border watchtowers that could warn of imminent attack with smoke signals and beacons. Militia stations guarded the roads of the sultanate, and a series of bridges over the Jordan allowed for the rapid deployment of the Egyptian army throughout Syria. Baybars made himself more secure at home with purges of emirs in 1263, 1265 and 1270; he also allied himself to Kalavun through marriage of the emir's daughter with the sultan's son.

Baybars's jihad had to fulfil the requirements for a just domestic regime, as well as the worthiness of its participants, in order to be legitimate. To this end, he had ordered his emirs to feed the poor at their own expense in 1263 when the Nile failed to rise and Cairo's populace was facing famine. He also tightened discipline in the army. Ibn al-Furat tells us that 'the army brought no wine in its train nor were there any lewd practices: there were only virtuous women, who brought the soldiers water to drink in the middle of the fighting'* and there was also legislation against

---

* In Hillenbrand, p. 320.

hashish consumption. Baybars increased his 'Islamic credentials' in 1269 when he brought the holy places of Islam under his guardianship. Like Saladin, Baybars was intolerant of 'heresy' within Islam and therefore started a long campaign against the Ismaili Assassins of Syria as well as other Shiite groups. The campaign against the Assassins' strongholds in northern Syria continued from 1265 to 1273. After this the sect members became little more than knives for hire and Baybars used them whenever he needed a political killing carried out.

Unlike Saladin, Baybars nurtured the economic base of his state. Trade relations were established with Aragon, and with Sicily's ruler, Charles of Anjou. Charles was particularly important to Baybars because of Charles's claim on the throne of Jerusalem, his territorial ambitions in Italy and plans for the reconquest of Constantinople. All this terrified the Italian maritime republics and drove them to make trade treaties with Baybars: Alexandria boomed as the Crusader ports' trade shrivelled away.

Louis IX's threatened crusade loomed large again in 1268 and Baybars therefore concluded treaties with Armenia, by which he gained border fortresses near Tripoli, and agreed a truce with Acre. He also arranged to have the Ismaili Assassins murder Philip of Montfort, who was effectively Acre's leader. Baybars then completed Ascalon's demolition and reviewed the fortifications of Alexandria and Damietta; the Nile was dredged to ensure that the deluge of 1218 – which had destroyed the Fifth Crusade – could be repeated and the sultan tried to import Indian war elephants to release on the Crusaders, though that proved to be logistically impossible.

Baybars's preparations were never tested. The Italians, who were to carry the Crusade to Egypt, were reluctant, as in 1204, to attack their trading partner, and the king's brother, Charles of Anjou, may very well have suggested the Crusade's rerouting to Tunisia on the specious assumption that its ruler wished to convert to Christianity. Pestilence then wreaked enormous damage on the Crusader army and King Louis died of dysentery, along with much of his army, on the shore near Tunis. Given the 'description' of Ibn al-Athir – that the First Crusaders had been dissuaded in 1097 from an invasion of Africa and had therefore invaded Syria – it seems almost ironic that this last great crusading venture was diverted from the Holy Land to Africa.

Baybars's last campaign against the Crusaders began in 1271 and, in order to forestall it, Bohemond VI paid Ismaili Assassins to try to kill the sultan. The attempt failed and in February the White Castle of the Templars fell easily to Baybars. He subsequently learnt that the same mistake had been made at the Crak des Chevaliers fortress as had been made at Beaufort, only this time the Franks had abandoned earthworks on a hill neighbouring the gigantic castle. The abandoned half-finished fort again made the perfect platform for Baybars's siege engines. The castle was encircled on 3 March, but heavy rain slowed down the transport of siege engines: the barrage therefore only began on 15 March. Sappers brought down one of the outer wall's towers and a successful assault was then launched along the one accessible spur of the mountain that the tower had protected. However, this only gave entry into the outer ring of defences and it was another two weeks before the inner enclosure fell. The knights that capitulated were given safe conduct to Tripoli.

The Hospitaller castle of Gibelcar was the next to fall. The sultan showed the way by helping to dig out the platforms for the siege engines and by steering carts carrying the disassembled mangonels through the thick forest surrounding the castle. It fell in only twelve days. On 12 June the Teutonic Knights lost their fortress at Montfort. Not one inland castle now remained to the Franks.

Baybars overreached himself in June 1271, when he sent a fleet disguised as Christian ships to raid Cyprus. He was concerned that after Prince Edward of England's arrival in Acre there might be a new union between Cyprus and Acre. Bad seamanship and inclement weather wrecked the fleet with the loss of eighteen hundred sailors and troops, and Baybars received an insulting letter from King Hugh of Cyprus telling of the debacle. The sultan replied:

> You have informed us that the wind has wrecked a certain number of our galleys, you call this a personal achievement and congratulate yourself on it. Now we in our turn send you the news of the fall of [fortresses] . . . In your case there is nothing remarkable for you to boast about in having taken possession of some iron and wood. To seize mighty castles is really remarkable! . . . You trusted in your God and we in ours. He who trusts in God and his sword is different from him who trusts in the wind. Victory brought about by the action of the elements is less noble than victory by the sword. In a single day we could send out more galleys whereas you could not rebuild a single bit of your castle. We can arm a hundred ships, but in one hundred years you could not arm a single fortress. Anyone who is given an oar can row but not everyone given the sword is capable of using it. If a few sailors are missing we have thousands more . . .*

---

* In Gabrieli, p. 321.

However, this was just bluster, and the fleet then also failed at Maraclea, a small fort off the coast near Tortosa. Baybars had expanded the navy by about forty more vessels, but it was still impossible to keep up with Western maritime power. It was fear that inspired the Mamluks' destruction of Syria's ports: in the long run, their policy would do enormous damage to the Muslim cause. By these acts, the Islamic world effectively turned in on itself, just as the Europeans were beginning to fully embrace venture and expansion. The advantage that the Europeans would later gain from their continued investment in navies and navigation of the oceans would lead to the dominance of the West. The Mamluk sultans were winning the Holy War, but in doing so they were effectively losing the future.

Prince Edward of England was in Acre in 1271, and his negotiations with Abagha Khan – discovered by the sultan's excellent spy network, which extended deep into both Acre and the Ilkhanate – were causing Baybars concern. A Mongol force of ten thousand troopers had entered Syria at the prince's behest and Baybars had had to bring heavy cavalry from Cairo to deter them from any further advances. The Mongols were probing at other points along the border and Baybars also had concerns over a Nubian incursion into Upper Egypt. He therefore chose to negotiate with Edward, and to use Charles of Anjou as a mediator. Charles was ideal for this role in the sultan's eyes, as he wanted to maintain the Crusader state's weakness so that it might look more readily to him to become its saviour and monarch. The *hudna* was agreed for ten years, ten months, ten days and ten hours on 22 May 1272. As an extra insurance, Baybars decided to have Edward assassinated. The prince was stabbed by a poisoned dagger as he lay sleeping in his chamber: the initial wound was not fatal and his assailant was killed, but the poison kept him near death for several months afterwards. He left for Europe as soon as he was able to travel and Abagha's failure to do more against the Mamluks during the prince's campaign did a great deal of harm to the Crusaders' confidence in the Mongols as allies.

Baybars returned to Nubian affairs, with a swift campaign and by replacing its king with a friendlier monarch. The remainder of his reign was concerned almost exclusively with the Mongol war. The war had become a low-level border war requiring the provisioning of fortresses, the sending of raiding and reconnaissance patrols, and negotiating with the Ilkhan's Mongol enemies. It was effectively stalemated. From the Mamluk point of view, this was perfect, as their war aims were limited to simply keeping the Mongols out of Syria and preventing any link-up between the Ilkhans and the Crusaders.

In 1274, Baybars got word of Pope Gregory X's plans for crusade in coalition with the unbaptised Mongols. The old pope, however, died soon after, but Baybars had been obliged to mobilise the sultanate's armies and in February 1275 he used these forces to raid Mongol-controlled areas of the Jazira and to invade Armenia again. He defeated a force of Crusaders and Armenians on the coast before raiding Tarsus. He then returned to Damascus in June 1275. To distract the Mongols further from their plotting with the Franks, Baybars entered into secret negotiations with the Mongols' Saljuq governor of Anatolia, to assist him in breaking away with the province's Saljuq princes from Mongol control. Baybars knew the venture would fail, but was prepared to back it just to foment trouble for the Ilkhan. In support of a purported Saljuq rebellion, the army of Egypt set out for Anatolia in February 1277. Baybars crushed a Mongol army near the garrison town of Abulustayn and took the capital, Qaysariyya. However, he could not secure the Saljuq puppet sultan and soon decided that the risk of trying to hold Anatolia was too great. By May 1277, the army was back in Syria.

Baybars died on 1 July 1277 in Damascus, at the age of about fifty. His achievement had been immense. The Mamluk sultanate had been created by his own hand and the army-state was powerful and well organised. He left it with secure borders, an efficient bureaucracy and a firm economic base. He was, without doubt, one of the greatest men of the period and, while he might have lacked the ideals of Saladin, his military and administrative skills were far superior. Though he had killed the last Ayyubid sultan of Egypt with his own hands, he had, even as sultan, continued to fight under the yellow banner of Saladin. Perhaps after the years of compromise and treachery that had personified the later Ayyubids, he had looked to complete the jihad of Saladin. Death robbed him of the opportunity of finishing the Holy War, but he had put everything in place for his successors to complete the task.

Baybars's son, Baraka, succeeded him, but failed to balance the powers in the state. His father's personal Zahiriyya Mamluks still held the higher positions of government and Baraka moved against them in clumsy purges, in order to make room for the promotion of men from his own bodyguard. He was removed from power in March 1279 by a clique of Bahriyya emirs, led by his father-in-law, Kalavun. Through generous concessions to his associates in the new junta, Kalavun succeeded in being elected sultan and, with a deft political touch, managed to bribe off or purge enough of the Zahriyya to make himself secure. He also formed a new powerbase within the state with the creation of his own personal regiment, the Mansuriyya.

Despite this careful statecraft, however, there was a rebellion in Damascus, which Hama, Aleppo and Safad soon joined. Kalavun's lieutenants met the rebel forces in battle at Gaza in May 1280, and again at Damascus on 21 June, and defeated them both times. Northern Syria was still barely under control, though, when word came of an imminent and large-scale Mongol invasion mustering on the border.

Kalavun quickly renewed a peace treaty that Baybars had originally made with Bohemond VII of Tripoli, as well as making a fresh agreement with the Franks of Acre. He also negotiated with Bedouin tribes for their support in the coming conflict. On the eve of battle there were reports from spies in Tripoli that Mongols had been seen in boats arriving at the city and that Abagha Khan was attempting to open a second front. Further intelligence, however, confirmed that these were *Franj* wearing Mongol headgear to confuse Kalavun's strategy. The Mongols came onto the battlefield near Homs with forty-four thousand Mongols, five thousand Georgians and three thousand Anatolian Turks and Armenians. Hospitaller knights from Margat had also joined the army and its front extended some twenty-four kilometres from Hama to Salamiyya. Kalavun had about thirty thousand men to meet this force.

Battle was joined in the early morning of 29 October and the Mamluk left wing soon broke. The Mongol right chased down the local infantry of Homs and then, convinced of total Mongol victory, they stopped at the side of Lake Homs to rest. Their comrades were, however, being soundly beaten on the rest of the field. The Mongols of the centre and left had become one confused mass, crushed between a Mamluk centre that had held firm and a rapidly advancing Mamluk right wing. It broke and fled and was pursued by the entire Mamluk army. Kalavun then found himself virtually deserted, apart from his close bodyguard, when the Mongols who had been resting on the lakeside suddenly returned to the field. The sultan hushed his drummers as he watched from the cover of some low hills as the returning Mongols slowly realised that the rest of their army was in full retreat. They then set off, hoping, no doubt, not to be left behind. The retreat turned into a debacle and the loss of life among the Mongols and their allies was immense.

It would not have taken much for Kalavun to have lost the battle. Abagha Khan had tried hard to encourage the European monarchs to join him, sending envoys to Italy in 1276 and to England in 1277 – the presence of even a small Frankish enemy force in the Mamluk rear might have been enough to tip the balance. These overtures would continue through to the end of Outremer, as a letter of 1289 from the Ilkhan Arghun to Philip the Fair of France shows:

> We agree to your proposition which you conveyed to Us last year . . . 'If the armies of the Ilkhan go to war against Egypt, We too shall set out from here and go to war and to attack . . . in a common operation.'
>
> And We decided . . . after reporting to heaven, to mount our horses in the last month of winter [1290] . . . and to dismount outside Damascus on the fifteenth of the first month in spring [1291] . . . if by the authority of heaven, We conquer those people, We shall give you Jerusalem.*

It was not to be. Mistrust and distance were enough to kill any such accord. The Franks of Outremer then seem to have decided that there was no hope of rescue either from the East or the West and they looked to survive simply through goodwill treaties with the sultan. Their new absentee king, Charles of Anjou, had been killed in 1285 in the war that followed the conspiracy known as the 'Sicilian Vespers', and the whole of Europe was at loggerheads over the succession to his kingdom. Another *hudna* was granted to Acre in 1283, primarily because defeating the Mongols had severely stretched the Mamluk army and it needed to be rebuilt. Of course, truces and treaties could also be weapons, because they could exploit the political fissures that ran through Outremer. In 1267 Baybars made an accord with the Hospitallers, and then made war on the Templars and Antioch. His treaty with Beirut in 1269 made the city virtually a protectorate of the Mamluk sultan, and effectively detached it from the Crusader kingdom.†

Survival was therefore guaranteed for the Latins of Acre for a little while longer. However, the weakness of Armenia invited attack and the Mamluks campaigned there in both 1283 and 1284, chiefly to obtain wood and iron for Mamluk siege engines. Armenia was granted a humiliating peace treaty with payment of tribute in 1285.

A truly appalling succession of Ilkhans came to the throne of Mongol Persia between 1282 and 1295. They left their state near collapse and Kalavun had little to worry about on his eastern border, giving him a free hand against the Franks. In 1285 he brought his army up to the walls

---

* In Morgan, D., *The Mongols*, Oxford: Blackwell, 1990, p. 184.
† See Holt, P. M., *Early Mamluk Diplomacy 1260–1290: Treaties of Baybars and Kalavun with Christian Rulers*, Leiden: Brill, 1995.

of Margat. The Hospitallers, like the Armenians, had to pay for their presence at the Battle of Homs. At first the siege went badly: the castle was positioned high on a mountain and its mangonels could therefore outrange the Mamluks' siege engines. It also took a month for Kalavun's engineers to sap and then fire a mine they had dug under one of the main towers and beneath the castle's inner walls. When the walls came down, however, there was no resistance and the Hospitallers were allowed to retire to Tripoli; the castle was rebuilt and garrisoned.

The little fort of Maraclea, which had defied Baybars, still remained a problem in the absence of an effective fleet, but when Kalavun threatened Tripoli he made its destruction his price for withdrawing his army. Then, in 1287, an earthquake levelled the walls of Lattakieh, which had reverted once more to Crusader control, and it surrendered to the sultan. In October 1287 Bohemond VII of Tripoli died and factions began to tear the city's unity apart. Kalavun had been intriguing with the Embracio family – whose antecedent we first met under the walls of Jerusalem, back in 1099 – against Bohemond VII since 1279. Now his plotting extended to the Venetians who finally appealed to the sultan for assistance against the Genoese in the city. Kalavun immediately revoked the treaty of 1283.

The death of Kalavun's favourite son had stopped plans for Tripoli's reduction in 1288, but in March 1289 the Egyptian army began the siege. This was enough briefly to unify the Christians within the city's walls: galleys under Venetian, Genoese and Pisan colours filled the harbour and supplied the city; King Louis IX's regiment from Acre and Cypriot knights joined the garrison. Tripoli was surrounded by the sea and could only be attacked via a narrow causeway. Kalavun lined up his catapults opposite the city to give covering fire, but it was hard-going for his men – the thin neck of land made it difficult to make their superior numbers tell, and the defenders could use all their forces on one small section of wall. Kalavun therefore opted to rely on concentrating his artillery on the south-east corner of the land walls. After a month, two towers disintegrated and the Venetian and Genoese ships in the harbour promptly upped anchors and sailed away from the doomed city. This desertion caused chaos inside Tripoli – seeing this, Kalavun ordered a general attack on 26 April. High-ranking Franks took ship for Cyprus and abandoned the citizens. Every Christian man was killed and every woman or child was enslaved; the mayor, Embracio, was among the slain. Mamluks even rode their horses as far as they could into the sea and then swam, whilst pulling their mounts along by the reins, to an island off Tripoli where many Christians had taken refuge. The Ayyubid prince Abu'l Fida, who was present at the massacre, visited the island after the carnage and stated that he could not stay there for the stench of corpses.

Bohemond VII's bones were exhumed and strewn around the city by the Muslim citizens and by the *ghazis* that had joined Kalavun's jihad. The small fortresses of Botron and Nephin were also easily taken after Tripoli's capture. Tripoli's walls were levelled, while Kalavun continued Baybars's 'scorched-earth' policy along Syria's coastline, and another Embracio, Peter, offered the submission of Jebail.

Kalavun's emirs now called for the liquidation of Acre, but he knew that its reduction would require a massive investment in siege engines. He therefore renewed the truce with the city, but used the new *hudna* to build, among other things, the largest mangonel ever seen in the Middle East: al-Mansura, 'the Victorious'. He knew that Acre would use this time to try to gather support from the West, but that the ongoing fallout from the Sicilian Vespers would ensure that little help would come. In fact, the only 'Crusaders' to respond to the call were disturbingly similar to those who had joined the People's Crusade in 1095. Gangs of unemployed city folk from Lombardy and Tuscany took the Cross. They were transported to Acre by the Venetians, who, because of their commercial contest with Genoa, cared enough about Acre to commit twenty galleys to its defence.

Most of 1290 was peaceful, but in August a riot ensued in Acre after the seduction of a Christian wife by an Eastern merchant. Every bearded man that the Italian mob could find was killed and, although the city authorities soon restored order, Kalavun had his *casus belli* and his army was ready. He sent out misleading messages that he was leading an army into Nubia and left Cairo on 4 November 1290. However, he died only five miles into the march. The task of finally removing the *Franj* from Syria would therefore fall to his young son, Khalil al-Ashraf, whom the sultan had never trusted and about whom he had once stated: 'I will not set Khalil over the Muslims.'

Despite his father's doubts, it only required a few judicial murders for Khalil to establish himself. In truth, Kalavun had been just as efficient as Baybars, if perhaps more subtle, at extinguishing all resistance to his reign. This fact and the continued enthusiasm for the jihad against Acre was enough to ensure the security of Khalil's throne and for him to reject

Acre's pleas for clemency in January 1291. He used his father's funeral to inflame further the Egyptians' fervour for Holy War, before taking the army to Syria in March. The call to the Syrians for jihad was made in the great mosque of Damascus and the *ghazis* recruited there actually outnumbered regular army troopers. Men of the *ulama* helped to push the new mangonels to Damascus's outskirts. Snow delayed the army of Hama and the deployment of the vast mangonel, al-Mansura, to Acre. A journey that normally took only eight days actually took a month, as oxen pulling the one hundred carts – carrying the disassembled parts – died of exposure.

Acre's garrison was bolstered by the arrival of troops from Cyprus, and the Hospitallers and Templars garrisoned in the city had strengthened the city's walls. Frankish ship-artillery in the harbour fired upon the right flank of the besieging army, until a storm wrecked many of them. The Crusaders also had the courage of desperation and refused to close the city's gates: they left them open and fought at the foot of the walls. Christian knights also rode out daily to offer battle and single combat. The Muslim sources record successes for Mamluk champions in every one of these duels.

The bombardment of the city lasted six weeks and involved ninety mangonels, the largest number ever assembled in the Middle East. The Franks padded the walls with straw to dampen the missiles' impact, but the Mamluks fired these with incendiary arrows. The advance into the city was halting and difficult. The siege engines would punch a hole through a wall and then groups of infantry would move through these and attempt to hold a position. Other troops would work at filling in the ditches between broken walls with rubble whilst under fire from the towers above. The knights of the military orders often counter-attacked during these operations and the equipment they stripped from the Mamluk dead was displayed on Acre's inner walls. The sultan was furious at the lack of progress and had a number of his emirs arrested on suspicion of collusion with the enemy. The King of Cyprus arrived in Acre, but he was sick and soon realised that the city's position was hopeless; he left the city three days later. The bombardment was redoubled and sappers dug at every one of the city's towers. The Crusaders burnt the Tower of King Hugh on 8 May as it was crumbling away due to the mines dug beneath it. The Tower of the English then fell, along with Countess Blois's Tower. A section of wall above Saint Anthony's Gate then came down and with it the Tower of Henry II. The Mamluks charged through what was now a gaping hole in the outer walls, but were held at Saint Anthony's Gate, and denied entry to the city proper by a desperate stand from the Templars and Hospitallers.

On 17 May the *Franj* pleaded for a truce with tribute. This was refused, but Khalil offered safe passage upon abandonment of the city. The negotiations ended abruptly when the Crusaders attempted to kill the sultan with a well-aimed rock from a mangonel. Khalil ordered a general offensive. The attack began at dawn on 18 May with the continuous beating of three hundred drums. The defenders' heads were kept down by endless volleys of arrows and every part of the walls was assaulted. The Mamluks forced the Accursed Tower and then fought their way along the walls to secure Saint Anthony's Gate. The gate was opened and the troops flooded in. Within three hours *ghazi* banners were flying on every battlement.

Four tall towers remained untaken and many of the city's knights had fled to them. Safe passage was offered for surrender, but as Mamluks entered the first tower to clear it they began to grab at women also taking shelter there. The knights swiftly closed the tower's gate and killed every Mamluk inside it. The other towers gave up under renewed pledges of safety, but the first tower's knights lasted another three days before accepting honourable surrender. Even then, as they were leaving the tower, there were killings as Mamluks sought revenge for the murder of an emir who had been killed during negotiations. The knights still in the tower then threw five Muslim captives from its windows and a bloody fight ensued. The exasperated sultan ordered the tower mined. The Muslim troops evacuated the tower and it collapsed, killing everyone inside. Meanwhile a brutal sack was being carried out in the city by the *ghazi* irregulars. Male inhabitants of the city were killed regardless of their faith, whilst women and children were taken for enslavement. Richer inhabitants could not escape as they had at Tripoli: they were tortured until they revealed where their gold and silver was hidden.

Khalil ordered the destruction of Acre's walls and then accepted the surrender of the last few cities held by the Franks. Saida, Beirut and Tyre were all evacuated and dismantled. The Holy War was over. Its wounds would, however, linger on.

Epilogue

A Haunted Coast
The Aftermath of the Jihad

It is preferable to hear the flatulence of camels, than the prayers of fishes.
Medieval Arab proverb

During the sack of Tripoli Mamluks had ridden and swum with their horses out into the sea in order to reach one of the city's island outposts. In the sixteenth century, the Portuguese openly professed a plan for taking Mecca through an amphibious operation and then forcing an exchange of the holiest city in Islam for Jerusalem,* whilst Columbus's journals contained a master plan for recovering the Levant for Christendom via an alliance with the grand khan and creating a stranglehold on Egypt's Indian trade. From as early as 1321, with the establishment of the Order of Christ in Portugal, such 'alternative' crusading schemes abounded. None of them ever achieved its aims, but they were as significant as the Mamluks' refusal to abandon their steeds when faced by the obstacle of the sea.

The Muslims won the Holy War for the Levant in the thirteenth century, but the sequelae to this victory were extremely damaging to the civilisation that achieved it. The Muslims desolated Syria's coastline – and with it much of the country's economy for centuries to come – for fear of a return of the *Franj*, but there was more of consequence to this destruction than just finances. The reason that the *Franj* had been able both to survive in their isolated outpost and to strike at Islam with repeated crusades was that they took control of the sea. The Ayyubids

---

* Hamdani, A., 'The Ottoman Response to the Discovery of America and the New Route to India', *Journal of the American Oriental Society*, July–September 1981, pp. 323–30.

and Mamluks both came from peoples of mountains and steppes, and both were harnessed to the land. The destruction of the Syrian coastline was a bold statement that this was a border that was not to be crossed by either side. The Muslims, excepting the piratical activity of the North African emirates and a brief flurry of shipbuilding and naval attacks on Cyprus under the Mamluk sultan Barsbay in the 1420s,* largely abandoned naval warfare and strategy. Meanwhile the Europeans were using the compass and portolan charts to venture further and further from the Mediterranean, and they were doing so in fully rigged carracks. Viewing the sea as a border did more than just surrender the eastern Mediterranean to the Europeans: it restricted the Muslim world's horizons at the very moment that Europe was looking to the waters of the oceans. When Europe truly 'went global' in its commercial, and perhaps more importantly, in its strategic outlook, the Muslim world was poorly placed to catch up, despite the Ottomans' best efforts and intentions.

Admittedly, some of the reasons for the 'rise of the West' lie well outside of the Middle East, and it has been suggested that the devastating impact of the Black Death, the collapse of the Mongol regime in China and the reorientation of the new Ming dynasty to China's north had much to do with this. The Chinese abandonment of the South China Sea and giving up of active sea trade allowed the Portuguese, Dutch and English to create a new world trade and geopolitical system. In this theory there was a 'fall of the East' that paved the way for the West's new hegemony,† but the fact remains that the Muslims surrendered control of the Mediterranean, a long-contested sea that separated them from their European rivals, at a crucial juncture and eased the West's nascence.

In 1291 Islam had destroyed the *Franj*, and the Mongols' Persian state would collapse in 1335, so a forthcoming great 'fall' would have been the furthest thing from the minds of the Mamluks, but the seeds of decline had been sown. Medieval Islam had never, in truth, paid much attention to Christian Europe – if it had, it might have seen the Reconquista of Spain as something that threatened rather more of the Muslim world than just al-Andalus, and as a precursor to the later European invasions of the Levant. This attitude was strengthened by victory over the Crusaders. The Muslim world became even more complacent

---

* The sultan's vessels were often in fact crewed by Venetian renegades.
† Abu-Lughod, J. L., *Before European Hegemony: The World System, A.D. 1250–1350*, Oxford: Oxford University Press, 1989.

about, and contemptuous of, their crude European adversaries. Latin Christianity was banned and Western merchants were restricted both in the places they could land and in where they could travel. There was interest only in the military technology of the West and nothing of the culture that had produced it, but the militarisation of Muslim society that the Crusades had enforced on the Muslim world perhaps made this inevitable. Stifling of creation and expansion of horizons was inevitable given that the Mamluks were a military clique and a minority in the state that they ruled; change was potentially dangerous and could lead to a challenge to the dynasty. Intellectual challenges were also unlikely from within the state, because the jihad had been a Sunni enterprise, and its champions, from Nur al-Din down to the Mamluk sultans, were intolerant of heterodoxy and free-thinking concepts, and remained narrow and dogmatic in their faith.

At the outset of the Muslim–Crusader conflict a fierce Christian unity overpowered the independent Muslim polities arrayed before them. There was also a shortage of well-trained regular Muslim troops in the Syrian arena, a lack of political will to oppose the Franks and no identification between the populace of Syria and the Turkish military men. The jihad that crystallised among the princes of the Jazira – and made faltering progress through them to Zangi, the conqueror of Edessa – would lead to the unification of Syria under Nur al-Din. From this point on, the eventual fall of Outremer became inevitable, but it took the tenacity, morals and bravery of Saladin to hasten the end of the Frankish kingdom and the ideal of jihad to maintain an army in the field for long enough to defeat the ambitions of the Third and Fifth Crusades. With the evolution of the Mamluk army of the Ayyubids and of the Mamluk sultanate, a Muslim army essentially became the state and produced the best soldiers of the medieval world. The unity of the Franks had also deserted them by this time, while the Mamluks held both the caliphate and *ulama* captive, and would remain the most important polity in the Middle East until the early sixteenth century. The end of the jihad saw Syria and Egypt become the most important states in all of Islam, as Iraq and Persia had been desolated by the Mongol invasions, but it also planted the seeds of these states' decline. The legacy of the jihad against the Crusaders would also feed into the founding legends of a new dynasty just beginning its rise to power. At the end of the thirteenth century, the Ottoman dynasty grew up out of the wreckage of post-Mongol Anatolia. The Ottoman Empire would one day call *ghazis* to its banner and carry a very different kind of Holy War all the way to the gates of Vienna.

One final trend is also unhappily detectable in this period: the growing brutality of war and increase in the incidence of slaughter of prisoners and civilians. The way of war in the Middle East before the Crusades was one of limited war with specific objectives. By the end of the period we can see what von Clausewitz called 'total war', a situation where destruction had become an end in itself. The First Crusade's bloody sack of Jerusalem was perhaps conventional by European standards of the age, but it was alien to the Levant's culture and mores. However, by the mid-thirteenth century the Middle East had entered an age of blood. Reprisal and extermination of opponents were characteristics of the Mongol invasion of the Middle East, but also became increasingly common in both Muslim and Christian treatment of defeated opponents. Abu'l Mahasin sums up the mind-set in his description of the treatment of the defenders of Acre:

> It is marvellous to observe that Almighty God permitted the Muslims to conquer Acre on the same day and at the same hour as that on which the Franks had taken it. They gained control of Acre in 1191, after the famous siege, on Friday 17 Jumada, and at the third hour of the day. They promised to spare the lives of the Muslims and then treacherously killed them. God permitted the Muslims to re-conquer them at the third hour of 17 Jumada. The sultan gave his word to the Franks and then had them slaughtered as the Franks had done to the Muslims. Thus Almighty God was revenged on their descendants.*

The path back from such a place of violence is a long journey. We have not returned from it yet.

---

* In Gabrieli, p. 349.

Bibliography

Abu-Lughod, J. L., *Before European Hegemony: The World System, A.D. 1250–1350*, Oxford: Oxford University Press, 1989.

Al-Sarraf. S., 'Mamluk Furusiyah Literature', *Mamluk Studies Review*, vol. 8, no. 1, 2004, pp. 141–200.

Amitai-Preiss, R., 'Mamluk Espionage Among the Mongols and Franks', *Asian and African Studies*, 1988, pp. 173–81.

—— *Mongols and Mamluks: The Mamluk–Ilkhanid War, 1260–1281*, Cambridge: Cambridge University Press, 1995.

Angold, M., *The Byzantine Empire 1025–1204: A Political History*, second edition, London: Longman, 1997.

Asbridge, T., 'The Significance and Causes of the Battle of the Field of Blood', *Journal of Medieval History*, vol. 23, no. 4, 1997, pp. 301–16.

—— *The First Crusade: A New History*, London: The Free Press, 2005.

Ayalon, D., 'Studies on the Structure of the Mamluk Army-III', *Bulletin of the School of Oriental and African Studies*, 1954, pp. 57–90.

Bacharach, J. L., 'African Military Slaves in the Medieval Middle East: The Cases of Iraq (869–955) and Egypt (868–1171)', *International Journal of Middle East Studies*, November 1981, pp. 471–95.

Barber, M., 'Frontier Warfare in the Latin Kingdom of Jerusalem: The Campaign of Jacob's Ford, 1178–79', in J. France and W. G. Zajac (eds), *The Crusades and their Sources: Essays Presented to Bernard Hamilton*, London: Ashgate, 1998.

Bent, S., *Justice Oliver Wendell Holmes*, New York: Vanguard Press, 1932.

Blair, S., *Islamic Inscriptions*, Edinburgh University Press, Edinburgh, 1988.

Bosworth, C., 'The Political and Dynastic History of the Persian World 1000–1217', in J. Boyle (ed.), *The Cambridge History of Persia. Volume Five: The Saljuq and Mongol Periods*, Cambridge: Cambridge University Press, 1968.

—— 'Abu 'Amr 'Uthman al-Tarsusi's Siyar al Thughur and the Last Years of Arab Rule in Tarsus', *Graeco Arabica*, 5, 1993, pp. 183–95.

Brett. M., 'The Battles of Ramla (1099–1105)', in *Orientalia Lovaniensia Analecta: Egypt and Syria in the Fatimid, Ayyubid and Mamluk Eras*, edited by U. Vermeulen and D. Louvain de Smet, Leiden: Brill, 1995.

Brundage, J., *The Crusades: A Documentary History*, Milwaukee: Marquette University Press, 1962.

Byrne, E. H., 'Genoese Trade with Syria in the Twelfth Century', *American Historical Review*, January 1920, pp. 191–219.

Cahen, C., 'The Turkish Invasion: The Selchukids', in K. Setton (ed.), *A History of the Crusades, Volume One*, London: University of Wisconsin Press, 1969.

Cameron Lyons, M., and Jackson, D. E. P. , *Saladin: The Politics of the Holy War*, Cambridge: Cambridge University Press, 1982.

Creasy, E. S., *Fifteen Decisive Battles of the World: From Marathon to Waterloo*, London: Bentley, 1851.

Croce, B., *La Storia Come Pensiero e Come Azione*, Naples: Bibliopolis, 1938/2002.

Crone, P., *Slaves on Horses: The Evolution of the Islamic Polity*, Cambridge: Cambridge University Press, 1980.

Darke, H., *The Book of Government or Rules for Kings: The Siyar al-Muluk or Siyasat-nama of Nizam al-Mulk*, London: Routledge, 1960.

De Rachewiltz, I., *Papal Envoys to the Great Khans*, London: Faber and Faber, 1971.

Dekmejian, R., and Thabit, A., 'Machiavelli's Arab Precursor: Ibn Zafar al-Siqilli', *British Journal of Middle Eastern Studies*, November 2000, pp. 125–37.

Edbury, P., and Rowe, J., *William of Tyre, Historian of the Latin East*, Cambridge: Cambridge University Press, 1988.

Ehrenkreutz, A. S., 'The Place of Saladin in the Naval History of the Mediterranean Sea in the Middle Ages', *Journal of the American Oriental Society*, April–June 1955, pp. 100–16.

—— 'The Crisis of Dinar in the Egypt of Saladin', *Journal of the American Oriental Society*, July–September 1956, pp. 178–84.

—— 'Arabic Dinars Struck by the Crusaders: A Case of Ignorance or of Economic Subversion?', *Journal of the Economic and Social History of the Orient*, July 1964, pp. 167–82.

—— *Saladin*, New York: State University of New York Press, 1972.

El-Azhari, T., *The Seljuqs of Syria during the Crusades: 1070–1154*, translated by Winkelhane, Berlin: Schwartz-Verlag, 1997.

Fink, H., *Fulcher of Chartres: A History of the Expedition to Jerusalem 1095–1127*, translated by F. Ryan, Tennessee: University of Tennessee Press, 1969.

France, J., 'Technology and Success of the First Crusade', in V. Parry and M. Yapp (eds), *War, Technology and Society in the Middle East*, London: Oxford University Press, 1975.

—— *Victory in the East: A Military History of the First Crusade*, London: Cambridge University Press, 1994

Gabrieli, F., *Arab Historians of the Crusades*, translated by E. Costello, Berkeley: University of California Press, 1969.

Gibb, H., 'The First and Second Crusades from an Anonymous Syriac Chronicle', *The Journal of the Royal Asiatic Society*, 1933, pp. 69–101.

—— 'Notes on the Arabic Materials for the History of the Early Crusades', *The Bulletin of the School of Oriental and African Studies*, 1935, pp. 740–54.

—— *The Achievement of Saladin*, London: Routledge, 1962.

—— 'The Caliphate and the Arab States', in K. Setton (ed.), *A History of the Crusades, Volume One*, London: University of Wisconsin Press, 1969.

—— 'The Rise of Saladin', in K. Setton (ed.), *A History of the Crusades, Volume One*, London: University of Wisconsin Press, 1969.

—— *The Life of Saladin*, Oxford: Oxford University Press, 1973.

Gillingham, J., 'Richard I and the Science of War in the Middle Ages', in J. Gillingham and J. C. Holt (eds), *War and Government in the Middle Ages: Essays in Honour of J. O. Prestwich*, Woodbridge: Boydell & Brewer, 1984.

Grousset, R., *Histoire des Croisades et du Royaume Franc de Jerusalem: L'anarchie Musulmane et la Monarchie Franque*, Paris: Plon, 1934.

—— *Histoire des Croisades et du Royaume Franc de Jerusalem: Monarchie Franque et Monarchie Musulman l'equilibre*, Plon, Paris, 1935.

Haarmann, U. W., 'Ideology and History, Identity and Alterity: The Arab Image of the Turk from the Abbasids to Modern Egypt', *International Journal of Middle East Studies*, May 1988, pp. 175–96.

Hamdani, A., 'The Ottoman Response to the Discovery of America and the New Route to India', *Journal of the American Oriental Society*, July–September 1981, pp. 323–30.

Hammad. M., *Latin and Muslim Historiography of the Crusades: A Comparative Study of William of Tyre and Ibn al–Athir*, PhD thesis. UMI Dissertation Services, Michigan, 1987.

Hillenbrand, C., *The Crusades: Islamic Perspectives*, Edinburgh: Edinburgh University Press, 1999.

Hitti, P. K., *An Arab-Syrian Gentleman and Warrior in the Period of the Crusades: Memoirs of Usama Ibn Munqidh*, Columbia, NY: Columbia University Press, 1929.

Holt, P., *The Memoirs of a Syrian Prince*, Wiesbaden: Steiner, 1983.

—— 'Saladin and His Admirers: A Biographical Reassessment', *The Bulletin of the School of Oriental and African Studies*, vol. 46, 1983, pp. 235–9.

—— 'Some Observations on the Abbasid Caliphate of Cairo', *Bulletin of the School of Oriental and African Studies*, vol. 47, no. 3, 1984, pp. 501–7.

—— *The Age of the Crusades: The Near East from the Eleventh Century to 1517*, London: Longman, 1986.

—— *Early Mamluk Diplomacy 1260–1290: Treaties of Baybars and Kalavun with Christian Rulers*, Leiden: Brill, 1995.

Hourani, A., *A History of the Arab Peoples*, London: Faber and Faber, 1991.

Humphreys, R. S., 'The Emergence of the Mamluk Army', *Studia Islamica*, no. 45, 1977, pp. 67–99.

—— *From Saladin to the Mongols: The Ayyubids of Damascus, 1193–1260*, New York: State University of New York Press, 1977.

Ibn al-Qalanasi, *Dhayl Tarikh Dimashq (Damascus Chronicle of the Crusades)*, translated by H. A. R. Gibb, London: Luzac and Company, 1932.

Ibn Khaldun, *The Muqaddimah: An Introduction to History: Volume 1*, translated from the Arabic by F. Rosenthal, edited by N. J. Dawood, London: Routledge and Kegan Paul, 1958.

Irwin, R., *The Middle East in the Middle Ages: The Early Mamluk Sultanate*, London: Croom Helm, 1986.

—— 'Church of Garbage', *London Review of Books*, 3 February 2000, pp. 38–9.

Jackson, P., 'The Crisis in the Holy Land in 1260', *English Historical Review*, July 1980, pp. 481–513.

—— 'The Crusades of 1239–41 and their Aftermath', *Bulletin of the School of Oriental and African Studies*, vol. 50, no. 1, 1987, pp. 32–60.

—— *The Mongols and the West, 1221–1410*, Harlow and New York: Pearson and Longman, 2005.

Kennedy, H., *The Prophet and the Age of the Caliphates: The Islamic Near East from the Sixth to the Eleventh Century*, London: Longman, 1986.

Krey, A. C., *The First Crusade: The Accounts of Eyewitnesses and Participants*, Princeton: Princeton University Press, 1921.

Labib, S., 'The Era of Suleyman the Magnificent: Crisis of Orientation', *International Journal of Middle Eastern Studies*, November 1979, pp. 425–51.

Lambton, A. K. S., 'The Theory of Kingship in the Nasihut al-Muluk of Ghazali', in *Theory and Practice in Medieval Persian Government*, London: Variorum Reprints, 1954.

Lane, F., 'Tonnages, Medieval and Modern', *Economic History Review, New Series*, vol. 17, no. 2, 1964, pp. 213–33.

Leisten, T., 'Mashhad Al-Nasr: Monuments of War and Victory in Medieval Islamic Art', *Muqarnas*, vol. 13, 1996, pp. 7–26.

Lev, Y., 'Army, Regime, and Society in Fatimid Egypt, 358–487/968–1094', *International Journal of Middle East Studies*, August 1987, pp. 33–65.

—— *State and Society in Fatimid Egypt*, Leiden: Brill, 1991.

Levanoni, A., 'The Mamluks' Ascent to Power in Egypt', *Studia Islamica*, no. 72, 1990, pp. 121–44.

Lewis, B., 'Kamal al-Din's Biography of Rashid al-Din Sinan', *Arabica. Revue D'Etudes Arabes*, vol. XIII, fasc. 3, 1966, pp. 231–2.

Lilie, R., *Byzantium and the Crusader States: 1096–1204*, translated by J. Morris and J. Ridings, Oxford: Clarendon Press, 1988.

Little, D., 'The Fall of Akka in 690 / 1291: The Muslim Version', in M. Sharon (ed.), *Studies in Islamic History in Honour of Professor D. Ayalon*, Leiden: Brill, 1986.

Maalouf, A., *The Crusades through Arab Eyes*, translated by J. Rothschild, London: Al-Saqi Books, 1983

Melville, C. P., and Lyons, M. C., 'Saladin's Hattin Letter', in B. Z. Kedar (ed.), *The Horns of Hattin*, London: Variorum, 1992.

Morgan, D., 'The Mongols in Syria 1260–1300', in P. Edbury (ed.), *Crusade and Settlement*, Cardiff: University College Cardiff Press, 1985.

—— *Medieval Persia*, London: Longman, 1988.

—— *The Mongols*, Oxford: Blackwell, 1990.

Nicolle, D., 'Medieval Warfare: The Unfriendly Interface', *Journal of Military History*, vol. 63, no. 3, July 1999, pp. 579–99.

Nielsen, J. S., 'Sultan al-Zahir Baybars and the Appointment of Four Chief Qadis, 663/1265', *Studia Islamica*, no. 60, 1984, pp. 167–76.

Paine, L., *Saladin: A Man for All Ages*, London: Hale and Co., 1974.

Peters, E., *The First Crusade: The Chronicle of Fulcher of Chartres and Other Source Materials*, second edition, Philadelphia: University of Pennsylvania Press, 1998.

Peters, P., *Jihad in Medieval and Modern Islam*, London: Nisaba–Brill, 1977.

Pryor, J. H., *Geography, Technology and War: Studies in the Maritime History of the Mediterranean 649–1571*, Cambridge: Cambridge University Press, 1988.

Queller, D. E., and Day, G. W., 'Some Arguments in Defense of the Venetians on the Fourth Crusade', *American Historical Review*, October 1976, pp. 717–37.

Raymond d'Aguilers, *Historia Francorum Qui Ceperunt Iherusalem*, translated by J. Hill and L. Hill, Paris: Bibliothèque National de France, 1969.

Richard, J., 'An Account of the Battle of Hattin Referring to the Frankish Mercenaries in Oriental Moslem States', *Speculum*, April 1952, pp. 168–77.

Richards, D., 'Ibn al-Athir and the Later Parts of the Kamil: A Study of Aims and Methods', in D. Morgan (ed.), *An Introduction to Medieval History Writing in the Christian and Islamic Worlds*, London: SOAS Publications, 1982.

Riley-Smith, J., *The Crusades: A Short History*, London: Athlone Press, 1990.

Runciman, S., *A History of the Crusades. Volume One: The First Crusade and the Foundation of the Kingdom of Jerusalem*, Cambridge: Cambridge University Press, 1951.

Sachedina, A., 'The development of Jihad in Islamic Revelation and History', in J. Turner–Johnson and J. Kelsay (eds), *Cross, Crescent and Sword: the Justification and Limitation of War in Western and Islamic Tradition*, New York: Greenwood Press, 1990.

Scanlon, G., *A Muslim Manual of War*, Cairo: American University at Cairo, 1961.

Sivan, E., *L'Islam et la Crosaide: Ideologie et Propagande dans le Reactions Musulmanes aux Croisades*, Paris: Librairie d'Amerique et d'Orient, 1968.

Smail, R. C., *Crusading Warfare 1097–1193*, second edition, Cambridge: Cambridge University Press, 1995.

Somogyi, J. de, 'A Qasida on the Destruction of Baghdad by the Mongols', *Bulletin of the School of Oriental Studies*, vol. 7, no. 1, 1933, pp. 41–8.

Stern, M. S., 'Petitions from the Ayyubid Period', *Bulletin of the School of Oriental and African Studies*, vol. 27, no. 1, 1964, pp. 1–32.

Tritton, A. S., 'The Tribes of Syria in the Fourteenth and Fifteenth Centuries', *Bulletin of the School of Oriental and African Studies*, vol. 12, 1948, pp. 567–73.

Tyerman, C., 'Were there any Crusades in the Twelfth Century?', *English Historical Review*, June 1995, pp. 553–77.

Waterson, J., *The Knights of Islam: The Wars of the Mamluks*, London: Greenhill Books, 2007.

—— *The Ismaili Assassins: A History of Medieval Murder*, London: Frontline Books, 2008.

White, L. Jr., 'The Crusades and the Technological Thrust of the West', in V. J. Parry and M. E. Yapp (eds), *War, Technology and Society in the Middle East*, Oxford: Oxford University Press, 1975.

Index